ILLEGAL **HARMONIES**

MUSIC IN THE 20TH CENTURY

ILLEGAL **HARMONIES**

MUSIC IN THE **20TH CENTURY**

ANDREW FORD

ABC
BOOKS

Published by ABC Books for the
AUSTRALIAN BROADCASTING CORPORATION
GPO Box 9994 Sydney NSW 2001

This edition first published July 2002

National Library of Australia
Cataloguing-in-Publication entry
Ford, Andrew, 1957–.
 Illegal harmonies: music of the 20th century.
 Includes index.
 ISBN 0 7333 1130 X.
 1. Music—20th century—History and criticism. I.
 Australian Broadcasting Corporation. II. Title.
780.904

Text designed by Kerry Klinner
Set in 11.5/14.5 pt Berkeley by Midland Typesetters Maryborough, Victoria
Colour separations by Colorwize, Adelaide
Printed and bound in Australia by Griffin Press, Adelaide

5 4 3 2 1

CONTENTS

for
Cathy Strickland
and
Tim Pye

By the same author

Books
Composer to Composer: Conversations About Contemporary Music
Undue Noise: Words About Music.

Music on CD

Whispers (Tall Poppies TO053)
Harbour (TP128)
Icarus (TP150)

PREFACE

A ustralia is not a bad place to write a history of 20th-century music. The continent's indigenous peoples remain repositories of some of the longest continuous musical traditions on the planet; but in terms of composed (at least, notated) music, there are no traditions to speak of. Australia's most famous composer of this — or any other — century, Percy Grainger, had already gone to Europe before the century began; apart from a couple of years in Melbourne during the early 1930s, he remained an expatriate, finally taking US citizenship. It wasn't until the 1960s that Australia had composers who could be properly considered a part of the modernist movement to which most 20th-century music somehow relates, whether by belonging to it or rejecting it. But this is one of the reasons Australia is an appropriate vantage point from which to survey the musical developments of the last hundred years: for the most part, they happened somewhere else, and a little distance from them — geographically speaking, quite a lot of distance — is potentially an advantage.

One of the most striking characteristics of music in the 20th century is its migration from the heart of Europe. To think about composers in the early years of the century is to think, first and foremost, of Vienna and Paris. But this is demonstrably no longer the case. Music may have been composed in the United States, Africa, Asia and Australasia before the 20th century, but it was only during it that it came to be taken seriously in Europe — seriously enough to have challenged and, to a degree, revivified composition on that continent. Now, at the end of this hundred years — this arbitrary slab of time — new musical developments can happen anywhere and, thanks to another 20th-century phenomenon, the sound recording, they can be heard everywhere.

Today, musical composition in Australia is as flourishing and multi-faceted as it is anywhere else in the world. Moreover, it offers a microcosm of stylistic plurality. It also represents a further important development in 20th-century composition. Clearly, there were female composers a hundred years ago, but they were seldom encouraged and their achievements were marginalised. Lili Boulanger (sister of the influential pedagogue Nadia) might have become the great talent who could not be ignored, but she died in 1918 at the age of 24. There is still some way to go, but in the last hundred years more and more women have made their musical voices heard. For some reason, Australia has always been rather ahead of most other countries in this regard. Of course they have had to fight the usual fights, but women have long been a significant presence in this country's music. Today, three of the most interesting Australian composers under 40 — probably the three most interesting — are women.

Illegal Harmonies began as a series of ten 90-minute radio programs, first broadcast on ABC Classic FM in 1997. In writing and presenting the scripts, I felt I was talking to a broad cross-section of listeners, all of them intelligent and curious about the music of their own time, but most of them not musicians. It seemed to me likely that, at some point in their childhoods, these listeners might have blown down a recorder or played a C major scale on a piano, but I didn't want to assume much more than that. The musicologist Wilfrid Mellers once said that if you were not talking technically about music, then you were not talking about music at all, and I think he was quite right. But I also believe that, a lot of the time, you can talk technically without employing the jargon of which music has such an alarming amount. It's not always possible, however, and there will, perhaps, be two or three pages in this book where it would help if the reader had a tiny amount of music theory behind them. If not, these short passages can be skipped, I hope, with no real damage to the general thrust of the discussion.

I have attempted to preserve the tone of the original broadcasts in the following pages. Virtually everything that was in those programs is also in the book, except for the sound of the music itself. There is also a lot of material that will be new to those who heard the radio series. Every script was pruned twice before going to air: the printed script itself was shortened, then recorded, then edited again as the music was mixed in. Ninety minutes, it seemed, was never long enough. I am very pleased to have had the opportunity to restore many of these missing passages; some chapters contain 2000 to 3000 words that were not used in the programs.

There are many people to acknowledge for their help in making the series and now the book. The most important of them is Maureen Cooney, because it was she who came up with the original idea, asked me to write and present the series, sold it to ABC Classic FM, and then produced the ten programs with care, patience, humour and a keen ear for my linguistic absurdities and pretensions. I can't thank her enough. Similarly, I must thank Peter James of ABC Classic FM for committing himself and the resources of his network to the project, and for remaining interested in its progress while never once interfering with its content.

Some long-suffering friends were generous enough to read drafts of the scripts. Among them, I particularly wish to thank Cathy Strickland, whose apparent enthusiasm and regular demands for the next chapter were as helpful as her practical suggestions. Ingrid Rahlén went through drafts with a fine-tooth comb, her intelligence and friendly scepticism forcing me to question virtually every opinion I had ever held (at least, that's how it felt). Roger Smalley read the book when it was nearly completed, his suggested changes always resulting in improvements to my original. Martin Buzacott, Gerald English, Brooke Green, Penny Lomax, Margaret Morgan, Tim Pye and Belinda Webster all read chapters or parts of chapters and their comments, too, were unfailingly constructive.

In the twelve years I was on the Faculty of Creative Arts at the University of Wollongong, my students taught me a great deal. I would particularly like to acknowledge Brian Daly for his observations about Jimi Hendrix, Michael Dunn for his about Gershwin, and Phil Slater who pointed out the family resemblance between the works of Conlon Nancarrow and Cecil Taylor. I am indebted to various others for specific insights that appear in the book. Some came from chance remarks (twenty years ago, for example, Sir Michael Tippett mentioned to me that he had heard broadcasts of Schoenberg's *Verklärte Nacht* and Vaughan Williams's *Fantasia on a Theme by Thomas Tallis* one day apart and had noticed how old-fashioned the former sounded in comparison to the latter); others have come as the result of exposure to a set of ideas over a period of time (Richard Langham Smith's lectures and writings about Debussy were my starting point for thinking about that composer's music). Vincent Plush introduced me to Thoreau's remark about 'home cosmology' and pointed out its significance for Ives. Larry Sitsky discussed the Russian modernists with me. Richard Meale and Peter Sculthorpe allowed themselves, at various times, to be sounding boards for some of the ideas in the book.

There are so many omissions in *Illegal Harmonies* that it hurts to think about them. Dozens of important figures are not even mentioned, many of them among my favourite composers: Busoni, Fauré, Szymanowski, Scelsi, Kurtág, Andriessen (at least their names have made it into the preface!); others are mentioned only in passing. The reason for this is that, up to a point, I have been more concerned with musical examples than with their creators. For Kurt Schwitters, say, to receive more detailed attention than Ravel is, at one level, patently absurd. There isn't a note of Ravel's that I don't love, and his music is so obviously greater than that of Schwitters (who wasn't even really a composer) that it seems silly to point it out. But Schwitters wrote the *Ursonate*, and in a curious way that unique piece has been more important — or, at least, influential — for music in the later part of the century than the far richer and more sophisticated works of Ravel.

I trust any intelligent reader will find plenty here with which to disagree. *Illegal Harmonies* isn't an even-handed survey of musical trends, just a record of some of my own views (and doubtless, prejudices) about music in the 20th century. And by the time you read the following words, those views may already have begun to change a bit.

Andrew Ford

WHAT'S **MODERN**?

isten. What do you hear?

Well, unless you are in an anechoic chamber, stripped of your wrist-watch, you can probably hear lots of things. Even in the chamber you would hear your breathing and, perhaps, your heart-beat; and you'd hear them to a degree that the mildest hypochon-driac might find disturbing, because you wouldn't normally notice these sounds at all. We are surrounded by sounds all the time, but we tend not to hear them; our brains are very good at editing what our ears pick up. If we stop, for a moment, to listen, there they are: the ticking clock, traffic noise, fragments of conversation, birdsong, a distant barking dog, a passing plane. They are examples of what the American composer John Cage called 'illegal harmony'.

Harmony is created by bringing sounds together. At school, we learn how to do this in a formal, musically conventional fashion: we learn about chords and keys and modulation, and we are given rules for using them. This is the textbook way; this is *legal* harmony. Everything else, including the simultaneous sounding of clocks, dogs and aeroplanes, is *illegal* harmony. John Cage said we should begin to listen to these sounds and to appreciate them, rather than block them out.

Cage stands in a paradoxical relationship to the Western 20th century. Many of his ideas regarding the inclusive nature of music have their roots in Eastern philosophy. The notion that by listening to sounds, by learning to enjoy illegal harmonies, we might be experiencing music owes a lot to Zen Buddhism; equally, the attitude of calm acceptance that this demands is found in Hindu teaching. The West's growing interest in such matters is itself, of course, largely a 20th-century phenomenon, but it could also be argued that the century needed John Cage in order to help it cope with the din of modern life. The 20th century was the noisiest in history. It is hard for us to imagine a time before cars and planes, pneumatic drills and computer games, radios and televisions. How we listen — or don't listen — is, perhaps, the key issue when considering the music of the 20th century.

In the last hundred years, musical styles have changed at an unprecedented rate, keeping pace, it seems, with technological developments. A lot of these changes have been considered 'illegal' at the time, though not necessarily in Cage's sense of the word. Composers have flown in the face of existing orthodoxies, deliberately flouting established rules, some of them only newly established. These developments have consistently challenged the way we listen.

In 1899, the man who would one day become John Cage's teacher wrote a string sextet called *Verklärte Nacht* ('Transfigured Night'). It was one of Arnold Schoenberg's first major works, and it went on to become his most popular; but to the Viennese jury who considered it for performance, *Verklärte Nacht* proved unacceptable. Schoenberg, the jury members pointed out, had written a chord that didn't exist; it was not to be found in any textbook; it was, if you like, illegal.

In 1917, Schoenberg arranged the piece for string orchestra, revising it again in 1943. It is in this comparatively lush scoring that *Verklärte Nacht* is most often played today. Since World War II, the work has enjoyed regular performances in the concert hall, and been recorded many times. It is often discussed in terms of Schoenberg's pivotal role in early modernism. But just how modern is *Verklärte Nacht*? The original sextet borrowed its instrumentation from

Brahms, its harmony was broadly Wagnerian, and it owed its free-wheeling form and extra-musical program to the example of Richard Strauss's symphonic poems. The musical development follows a scenario by the poet Richard Dehmel, in which two lovers walk through a moonlit forest. The woman tells the man she is pregnant, but not by him. The turbulent music evokes the lovers' conflicting emotions, but in the end the man tells the woman he'll accept the child as his own, and as they walk on, hand in hand, their love transfigures the night. Both the programmatic nature of Schoenberg's *Verklärte Nacht* and the sound of the music mark it out as one of the great works of late Romanticism — and of course it's none the worse for that — but even at the time of its composition it wasn't really modern, in spite of that illegal chord.

There is an instructive comparison to be made between Schoenberg's work and another string-orchestra piece, composed a decade after *Verklärte Nacht*. Ralph Vaughan Williams is not usually considered an especially progressive composer, and he certainly wouldn't have thought of himself as one. But with the opening bars of his *Fantasia on a Theme by Thomas Tallis*, a cool breeze freshens the hot-house atmosphere of late Romanticism. In a very real sense, what Vaughan Williams was doing in this piece was more modern than Schoenberg's torrid tone poem, because it came out of the blue. Vaughan Williams's music owed nothing to late Romanticism; his style was in no sense current. Harmonies like these hadn't been heard for 300 years — since the age of Tallis, in fact — and, as any text-book will tell you, the composer's shifting block chords with their parallel fifths were quite illegal. We tend to think of Schoenberg's music as more modern than Vaughan Williams's because his harmonic language is more convoluted, and also because with the benefit of hindsight, we know where his music was headed: ten years after *Verklärte Nacht*, Schoenberg would stretch tonality until it snapped. But there's more to being modern than the ability to write a good strong dissonance. It all comes down to tradition.

Schoenberg was a traditionalist. At the time of *Verklärte Nacht*, his musical language was very much a product of his environment, and essentially it remained that way. Like a child learning to speak, Schoenberg was influenced by those around him. To the names of Brahms, Wagner and Strauss, we might add Liszt and Mahler, and

Schoenberg's teacher and brother-in-law, Alexander Zemlinsky. For a composer at the turn of the 19th century, before the invention of radio and with sound recording in its infancy, live music was all there was. And live music meant new music, to an extent unthinkable a century later. Composition was taught via an apprentice system, as it often still is. This meant that student composers tended to inherit their teachers' musical styles, and then, if the students were any good, they built on them. Today, because of the availability of recordings, a young composer can augment a teacher's input with the music of a thousand years and a thousand different cultures, but at the beginning of the 19th century, what was current, and in large degree what was local, provided the staple diet of musical experience.

In German and Austrian music, the composers' apprentice scheme had been in operation for centuries, giving rise to an unbroken chain of great composers: Haydn had taught Beethoven; Beethoven overlapped with Schubert, who overlapped with Schumann, who knew Brahms. Schoenberg was simply the latest runner in a musical relay race. The continuity of this tradition accounted for the dominance of the Germanic style at the end of the 19th century. By contrast, the history of French music was full of holes, and it was the same story in the British Isles, which was why Vaughan Williams turned to the 300-year-old Tallis for his model. But that is also why Vaughan Williams sounds so fresh: as a composer, he had to invent his own voice. By the beginning of the 20th century, in France and Britain and many countries besides, the urge to rebel against Teutonic domination and develop independent styles of composition had become irresistible. This impulse to be different would inspire the greatest musical works of the century, the landmarks by which we measure musical history; but eventually it would also destroy the traditional view of history as progress. For when all the traditions have gone, what is there left to rebel against? When all musical styles are permissible and equally valid, how can there be illegal harmonies?

In terms of the rate of change in musical style, the first decade of the century was perhaps the most remarkable. It is surely no exaggeration to suggest that by 1910 — at any rate, by 1914 and the outbreak of the Great War — all of the major 20th-century developments in Western classical music had been set in motion. The chief centres of this activity were Vienna and Paris, with their diametrically contrasting attitudes to tradition and their radically different views of the future.

The Austrian capital was beginning to experience the onset of a severe hangover during the dying stages of the 350-year party that had been the Habsburg Empire. This mood of national introspection, not to say shame, could scarcely have been a more appropriate environment for the publication, in 1900, of Sigmund Freud's *The Interpretation of Dreams*. If public dreaming were no longer entirely viable, private dreaming certainly was, and Freud's books showed how the murkier depths of the subconscious could be understood and tapped as an artistic wellspring. In 1910, the year before his death, Gustav Mahler himself had a four-hour consultation with Freud, and the composer's frankly autobiographical symphonies epitomise the self-conscious late Romantic artist. Mahler's younger colleague Schoenberg was fascinated by Freud's theories, too, and they would soon fuel his greatest works. But in one sense, Schoenberg never gave up on dreams of empire; Habsburgs or no Habsburgs, he continued to believe in his musical heritage. Faith in this tradition, however, came with certain responsibilities: this was a mantle that not only had to be worn, it had to be maintained. With all due deference to what had gone before — Bach, Beethoven, Wagner and Brahms — Schoenberg knew that the language of music must continue to develop, because tradition demanded it. History demanded it. 'I am obeying an inner compulsion stronger than any upbringing,' was how Schoenberg described his sense of duty to the art of music. One simply can't imagine a French composer saying this.

The Parisian landscape at the turn of the century was newly dominated by the Eiffel Tower (and we may guess what Freud made of that). Eiffel's iron erection was simultaneously a glorification of the technology that made its construction possible and of Parisian modernity in general. It had been completed in 1889, for the Paris World Fair, so it also symbolised the city's gregarious nature. French composers like Satie, Debussy and Ravel may have had no obvious national tradition behind them, but this was potentially an advantage, because it freed them from the responsibilities that such traditions bring. When French composers looked at the German tradition it wasn't with envy; on the contrary, they saw a target at which to take aim. They did this in various ways, one of which consisted of lampooning the self-aggrandising nature of late 19th-century Germanic art. In *Children's Corner* (1908) for example, Debussy's Golliwogg pauses in mid cake walk, for a brief, *Tristan*-esque reverie. He seems to hear the opening strains of Wagner's music-drama as if from a distance, he mulls them over, gives a bit of a shrug, and then gets on with his cake walk — a very up-to-the-minute, very un-Germanic bit of ragtime.

A further attempt at establishing Gallic autonomy involved the wholesale excavation of the last great period of French music. Just as Vaughan Williams had consulted the ghost of Tallis, so his colleagues across the English Channel turned to France's Golden Age, which extended from Lully to Rameau and Couperin. This archeological dig through the manuscripts of the early 18th century was not particularly scholarly, but then that was never its motivation. In dusting off dance forms such as sarabands, pavans and minuets, Satie, Debussy and Ravel discovered genuinely French models, and their early works are full of these references and appropriations. The simple form of Maurice Ravel's *Menuet antique* (1895) for instance, not only celebrates Frenchness, it cocks a calculated snook, once again, at the grandiloquence of Wagner.

Leading the French charge against Wagner was Erik Satie. Everything about Satie was at odds with the architect of Bayreuth. From time to time, he eked out a living as a cabaret pianist, and he was a regular denizen of Parisian cafe society. We can no more picture Wagner tickling the ivories at Le Chat Noir, than we can imagine the score of *Parsifal* being sketched in the cafes of Montparnasse. It is hard to know exactly how seriously Satie took himself. His titles include such apparent spoofs as *Bureaucratic Sonatina*, *Things seen to the right and left (without spectacles)*, *Dried-up embryos*, and *Flabby preludes . . . for a dog*. The scores themselves are littered with exhortations to the performer to play 'affectedly', 'very shiny', 'like a nightingale with toothache', and to the two performers of *Aperçus désagréables* ('Unpleasant ideas'), Satie warns: 'Don't talk!' Obviously there's humour in Satie's music, and it's a disarming, debunking brand of humour. But many of his instructions to performers, though quirky, are oddly specific.

Satie's pieces, at any rate in the last years of the 19th century and the first years of the 20th, are characterised by simplicity on almost every level. In terms of form, his preferred models were slow, stately dances; it has been suggested that they are this way because they were composed in his head on his long daily walks from cafe to cafe. Texturally, the music leans towards a single line of melody performing elegant arabesques above a repetitious chordal accompaniment. As for harmony, there is an avoidance of modulation; Satie's harmonic language is predominantly static, serving to anchor the free-floating melodic line, much as a kite-flier controls a kite. And the pieces are frequently short. All of this is in stark contrast to the through-composed music–dramas of Wagner which avoid existing forms, exalt counterpoint and chromatic harmony, and are both overwhelming in effect and epic in scale.

Satie's own notorious excursion into epic length came around 1893 in his aptly-named *Vexations*. One vexing aspect of this piano piece is that it lasts somewhere between 12 and 24 hours, depending upon the pianist's interpretation of the instruction 'very slow'. The notation is vexing, too. The harmony is very chromatic by Satie's standards — almost non-tonal — and the chords are notated with bizarre enharmonic changes, so they don't read the way they sound. But the principal vexation concerns the 840 repetitions of just two lines of music. It is possible to view *Vexations* as both reaction and discovery. Undoubtedly the length of the piece is a comment of sorts on the scale of late German Romanticism, and perhaps this also accounts for the chromatic nature of the music. But where Wagner's chromaticism always led, after some hours of harmonic procrastination, to the home key, Satie's does not. Instead, it leads, every few minutes, back to the start of the piece. Such dogged purposelessness can be heard as a form of protest, but it can also be taken as the forerunner of a good deal of 20th-century music. Most obviously, in its sheer lack of an aim, it anticipates the music of John Cage, and in its use of repetition, it provides a model for 1960s minimalism.

One immediate consequence of Satie's rejection of conventional 19th-century development was its effect on the music of Claude Debussy. From the standpoint of our own time, Debussy's radicalism is often overlooked; so much else has happened in the intervening years — developments that seem both bolder and more daring — that the originality of Debussy's music can easily elude us.

Undoubtedly, part of the problem stems from the conventional view of Debussy as an 'impressionist', a painter in sound of some vague, veiled images: windy plains, sultry Spanish nights, sunken cathedrals, gardens in the rain. But I don't think Debussy was an impressionist.

The term 'impressionism' was first applied to painters like Claude Monet. It was, in truth, a critic's label and a derogatory one at that, but Monet and his followers brazenly appropriated it. Far from being the vague art it is often taken for, impressionism in painting is precise and realistic. Monet's multiple views of water lilies and haystacks and the cathedral façade at Rouen may be greatly removed from the photographic clarity we normally associate with representational art, but Monet was never seeking to offer that kind of experience. On the contrary, he painted only what he saw, which is why it's realistic. The human eye sees light and interprets the patterns it creates as a water lily or a haystack or the front of Rouen Cathedral. When we look at a representational painting, the artist has performed for us the job our brains normally do: the light is interpreted. Monet's art refuses to make this translation. He presents, in paint, the light itself; any interpretation remains our responsibility, and this is precisely why there are so many versions of the lilies, the haystacks and the cathedral: the light changes from painting to painting, and because Monet's subject was light itself, each painting is, by definition, of a different subject.

We know that Debussy disliked impressionist painting, and so for that reason alone it seems odd to attach the label to his music. But if Debussy had been an impressionist composer, what might his music have sounded like? What would be the sonic equivalent of Monet's technique?

Strictly speaking, musical impressionism would need to take Monet's principles regarding light, and apply them to sound. It would present these sounds without comment, without interpretation. Impressionistic music would leave its listeners in the same position as Monet's onlookers, giving them the task of making sense of these sounds. All of this describes rather well, say, the music of John Cage, but it is hardly appropriate to Debussy. The French composer's reputation as an impressionist derives largely from his use of titles that sound like those of impressionist paintings, but these titles can be misleading. We have to bear in mind that impressionism was not the only artistic movement in turn-of-the-century Paris. More influential were the symbolists.

Symbolism was a movement that crossed art forms. It is tricky to talk about, because a lot of it is intentionally obscure, but there are certain symbols that had a common currency in French art of this period. The circus was one of the chief forms of popular entertainment, and artists made use of the circus ring as a symbol of sterility, of things going round and round and getting nowhere. Perhaps this was at the back of Satie's mind when he wrote *Vexations*. Another recurrent symbol in painting and writing, as well as music, was the child: the innocent child, the sick child, the poor child, the naughty child, the wise child, the bored child. These children are everywhere from the poetry of Jules Laforgue and Paul Verlaine, to the early paintings of Picasso. Ravel's opera *L'enfant et les sortilèges* ('The Child and the Magic Spells') has for its protagonist a naughty boy who learns wisdom. Most notably, Alain-Fournier's classic novel, *Le Grand Meaulnes*, has examples of all these sorts of children.

Children crop up regularly in Debussy's music, from the tortured boy Yniold in *Pelléas et Mélisande* to the somewhat more fortunate children of *La boîte à joujoux* ('The Toy Box'). The first piece of his piano suite, *Children's Corner*, is called 'Doctor Gradus ad Parnassum', and these titles alone should alert us to the symbolic content of the music. *Children's Corner* is not so much for children as about children. Parnassus was the Muses' sacred mountain in central Greece, and *Gradus ad Parnassum* ('The Steps to Parnassus') was a collection of a hundred graduated piano studies by the late 18th-century composer, music publisher and piano manufacturer Muzio Clementi. The idea was that by following the steps the student would eventually join the Muses at the mountain top. But anyone who has ever worked their way through Sig. Clementi's exercises will enjoy the joke in Debussy's title. 'Doctor Gradus ad Parnassum' is more than a witty parody of one of these interminably dull teaching pieces: we actually find ourselves eavesdropping on the hapless student's practice session. We are in the presence of a bored child — that archetypal symbol of frustrated dreams — forced to sit at the keyboard and practise, when playing outdoors is the enticing alternative. It is the same with the fourth piece of the set, 'The Snow is Dancing', and with other pieces such as 'Gardens in the Rain' from *Estampes* and 'The Wind on the Plain' from the first book of *Préludes*. These pieces are not about inclement weather, so much as its consequences. Wind, rain and snow mean enforced piano practice, and all of these pieces are characterised by figures that relate to such tedium: scales, arpeggios, and other repeated figures typical of studies and exercises.

The arch-symbolist was the poet Stéphane Mallarmé, at whose Tuesday gatherings Debussy was a frequent visitor, but there were many other figures in all branches of the arts who embraced the symbolist aesthetic. What constitutes that aesthetic is hard to sum up. I suppose it amounts to the refusal to call a spade a spade, but not every symbol in symbolist art stands for something specific. In Maurice Maeterlinck's play *Pelléas et Mélisande*, for example, there is a scene in which servants wash bloodstains from the castle steps. The source of the bloodstains is never explained, so we must assume that, like so much else in the play, it is a symbol. But of what? It's impossible to know: perhaps no more than a general sense of foreboding. In Debussy's opera based on Maeterlinck's play, the scene is omitted.

Symbolist art tends to function at more than one level. Most of the recurrent symbols — like the circus ring and the child — share commonplace origins. Symbolism lends the everyday object or event a sort of magic universality, but on the surface the object remains commonplace, and that is part of symbolism's power. In making his operatic setting of Maeterlinck's *Pelléas et Mélisande* (first performed in 1901) Debussy continually underlined the humanity of the characters. Even if most of what they have to say to each other is riddled with mystery, the way they say it is remarkably normal. These fairytale people employ a singing style that is closer to real speech than anything in the previous two hundred years of opera (with the possible exception of Mussorgsky's *Boris Godunov* which was a model of sorts for Debussy): *Pelléas* is practically an aria-free zone. There are only two real examples of song. The first occurs as Mélisande sings to herself while she combs her absurdly long hair; the second more genuine attempt at an aria comes immediately after the lovers admit to their mutual feelings, and Pelléas begins singing about how Mélisande's voice sounds as though it had come to him from over the sea in spring. But he has no sooner begun than he interrupts himself, musing incredulously on what has occurred.

It is interesting to compare the love scene in *Pelléas* with the corresponding duet in Wagner's *Tristan und Isolde*. Both these liaisons are illicit, and each will end in musical *coitus interruptus*. In Act 2 of *Tristan und Isolde*, time stands still for the lovers as they extol the pleasures of eternal night, longing to be inseparable in death; in Act 4 of *Pelléas et Mélisande*, the darkness in which the lovers hide has the simple and immediate advantage of keeping them from being spotted by Mélisande's husband, Golaud, who is getting closer by the second. Where Wagner's lovers sing their hearts and lungs out for well over half an hour, their melodic lines becoming ever more ecstatic and suggestively entangled, Debussy's pair are struck momentarily dumb by their admissions of love. Pelléas blurts out his true feelings, the orchestra falls silent, and Mélisande quietly confesses that she feels the same. Then, Pelléas, astonished by her confession, whispers to Mélisande to repeat herself because he cannot believe he has heard her correctly. It is such an arresting moment because it is so close to reality and this is not what we expect of opera, any more than is the frantic groping that now ensues in the moments before Golaud arrives with his sword to put an end to the scene and, indeed, to Pelléas.

The most immediately striking aspect of Debussy's opera is its mixture of mythical setting with a dark undercurrent, occasionally erupting into brutality as when Golaud, fired by a masochistic relish in the details of his young wife's infidelity, forces his small son Yniold to spy on the lovers and to provide a running commentary on what he sees (which turns out to be very little); or when he pushes Mélisande to the ground, seizes her hair and pulls her around, forwards, backwards, to the left and to the right, turning the sign of the cross into domestic violence. These frankly ugly scenes have often been overlooked by commentators, but they are fundamental to the opera. The early 19th-century American poet and novelist Edgar Allan Poe was a great favourite of the French symbolists — both Mallarmé and Baudelaire made translations of his writings — and his spirit hovers over *Pelléas et Mélisande*.

The other notable characteristic of Debussy's opera is the moments of repose, even stasis, that punctuate the action. There is a lot of waiting in *Pelléas*; extended scenes in which nothing much happens. The most extreme example of this is the single scene that makes up the fifth and final act, set at Mélisande's bedside. She has given birth — whether to Pelléas's or Golaud's child we are never really sure — and now the royal household is waiting for her to die. The music is almost entirely tranquil, the only stage 'action' coming after more than twenty minutes, when the serving women in the room fall to their knees, signifying the moment of Mélisande's death.

In *Pelléas et Mélisande*, Debussy was at his most original, formally and stylistically, when he was also at his most naturalistic. Our lives are not like the linear narratives of 19th-century opera, and the events in our lives lack the neat and certain conclusions that 19th-century opera provides. When people declare their love they become tongue-tied: they blurt and whisper and stammer, as Pelléas and Mélisande do. When we are awaiting a death, we lapse into paralysed inactivity, like the courtiers in Debussy's opera. *Pelléas et Mélisande* is a fairytale, and sometimes an infuriatingly oblique one, but it also deals in reality. It is not a work of musical impressionism, and yet in one regard, at least, it is close to impressionism. For in observing the human behaviour and speech patterns of everyday life, in hearing them as they really are and in allowing them to colour and structure his music, Debussy's ear resembles Monet's eye.

By the same token, early 20th-century writers such as Henry James, James Joyce and Virginia Woolf abandoned the serial story-telling of novelists like Austen, Dickens, Balzac and Zola, for something altogether more three-dimensional. Perhaps I ought to say 'four-dimensional', since the principal characteristic that unites modernist novels is a consideration of time and the ways in which we perceive it. Not many of us live perpetually in the present; our daily lives are invaded by memories of the past — nostalgic and regretful; often, perhaps, faulty — and by hopes and fears for the future. Sometimes these moments are conscious, but equally they can occur spontaneously, in dreams and daydreams, or suddenly be triggered by a familiar sound or smell. The richness and complexity of our inner lives are what early modernist writers most frequently explored, and they tended to do so in ways that mirror the convoluted, time-distorting realities of our own experience. In Henry James's *The Ambassadors*, for example, a boat comes round a bend in the river, and it takes 60 pages to do so, because the real events of those pages are happening somewhere else: in the mind of the observer; in the mind of the reader. The boat on the river is the visual backdrop to the real business of the imagination. Similarly, in Virginia Woolf's *To the Lighthouse*, the novel is spent in anticipation of the journey: the trip is in the future tense; the present is occupied by our imagination.

Probably the most significant of all the early 20th-century writers to be concerned with time — certainly the one most closely linked to Debussy — was Marcel Proust. In *A la recherche du temps perdu* ('Remembrance of Times Past'), Proust deals with memory on a grand, multi-volume scale. More pertinently, Proust was aware of the ambiguous relationship between music and time; he recognised that while music exists in time, it's also capable of distorting it when it cuts its listeners off from the ticking clock. Admittedly Proust's musical references tend to be to 19th-century composers, and especially to Wagner, but there are also perceptive comments on Debussy himself. Proust's writing as a whole seems to reflect the musical preoccupations of the composer, the narrator's pathological introspection persistently recalling those moments of rapt stillness in Debussy's music.

The American composer Carl Ruggles, commenting approvingly on Debussy, added that there was nothing wrong with him that a couple of weeks of fresh air couldn't cure, and his remark points to a danger in Debussy's art and in modernism in general. The more introspective the art, the more tied to symbols and understatement, the less worldly it becomes. It may be realistic enough, but in delving into the inner life of humanity, modernist art risks losing sight of the events and actions that make up life on the surface. Of course, a composer like Satie never lost this contact with the world of cafes, circuses and music halls, just as Ravel and Stravinsky would soon be drawn to the language of jazz (however poorly they understood it), but for another group of composers at the start of the 20th century there was a different aspect of everyday life that could be tapped for musical inspiration. And it had to be tapped quickly, because it was disappearing.

In 1905, when the Australian composer Percy Grainger met Joseph Taylor of Lincolnshire and heard him sing 'Brigg Fair', he was part of a salvage operation to recover the remnants of a dying oral tradition. With the enclosure of agricultural production and the industrial revolution, a collective amnesia had begun to overtake people who had once been the repository of a rich and varied folk culture. Frank Kidson, in the introduction to his 1891 volume *Traditional Tunes: a collection of ballad airs*, comments that the folk song 'is fast disappearing before the modern productions, and any young ploughboy who should sing the songs his father or grand-father sung, would be laughed to scorn'. We can't know how many songs were lost before the collectors began their work, but the efforts of folklorists across Europe succeeded in the preservation of a vast number of this endangered species. Some of these folklorists were academics, some were enthusiastic antiquarians, and some, significantly, were composers. Among the best known were Vaughan Williams and Gustav Holst in Britain, Percy Grainger in Britain and Scandinavia, and Béla Bartók and Zoltán Kodály in eastern Europe. The last pair published their findings on Hungarian folk music in the same year that Grainger met Mr Taylor.

It must have been an arduous business, lugging cumbersome early recording equipment across miles of countryside in search of inevitably elderly people, and then persuading them to sing their songs into the unlikely looking mechanical contraption. So, it is hard to escape the conclusion that the zeal with which these composers approached the task is further evidence of the desire to discover fresh musical impulses and be rid of the influence of Austro-German music. By 1906, when Grainger came to record Mr Taylor, the singer had forgotten all but the first two verses of his song. Consequently, Grainger had to add verses from two other songs in order to pad out his choral arrangement. To hear Grainger's 'Brigg Fair' is not only to appreciate the composer's fidelity to every vocal nuance of Joseph Taylor's original performance, but also to perceive the opening up of melodic possibilities which that performance and its permanent record allowed. It is perhaps the first concrete instance — certainly not the last — of the influence of recording technology in shaping the music of the 20th century.

Since composers began writing music to fulfil their own wishes, there have always been those who searched for new ways of express-ing themselves. If for no other reason, it is easy to appreciate the wish on the part of composers throughout Europe to find alternatives to the dominant Germanic style of the 19th century. Even such a distinctive composer as the Bohemian Dvořák had been heavily indebted to Brahms. However, in the music of Dvořák particularly, as with his compatriot Smetana before him, there had also been an eagerness to employ tunes that had local associations. Composers had made use of folk melodies at least since late medieval times, but in Dvořák's case there is a specific political dimension to the use, because it wasn't only Austro-German *music* that dominated late 19th-century Europe.

Talk of nationalism in music is potentially as misleading as talk of impressionism. It is simplistic to identify nationalist tendencies whenever something like a folk melody comes within earshot; it is too neat, too catch-all. Still, it cannot be denied that in the first decade of the 20th century, the music being composed in Europe and beyond was more stylistically varied than it had ever been before, and much of this variety came from an intensification of national accents linked to the discovery of folk song. Besides those composers already named was a host of others, forever associated with their countries of origin: Edvard Grieg in Norway, Jean Sibelius in Finland, Leoš Janáček in Czechoslovakia, Hugo Alfvén in Sweden, and Enrique Granados and Manuel de Falla in Spain. Some were at the ends of their careers, some at the beginning, and frankly some were rather better composers than others, but all had distinctive national voices.

Arguably, the most distinctive national voice of them all was America's Charles Ives. Although we still tend to think of him as a backwoods man, an eccentric experimenter, oblivious to the developments in European music, in fact Ives was musically well educated, and in one sense he was hardly an experimentalist at all: his first symphony could easily be mistaken for the work of Dvořák. Ives, indeed, was a traditionalist in his continued faith in the Beethovenian grand gesture, and he frequently employed the traditional moulds of European music. Yet if he was not an untutored innocent, he was certainly an original, and the material he poured into those European moulds was uniquely American.

Ives's father was an accomplished musician with a military training; at the age of seventeen, George E. Ives had led the Brigade Band of the First Connecticut Heavy Artillery during the siege of

Richmond in the Civil War. George Ives believed in a strictly conventional musical training, but he had a questing imagination,
fuelled by his belief that human beings had a duty to use their
divinely-given gifts to the fullest. He also had a passion for illegal
harmonies. He would have the members of his family sing 'Swanee
River' in E flat, while he accompanied them on the piano in C, in
order to stretch their ears; and he cultivated in his son a genuine
love of the complex sounds thrown up by the simultaneity of unrelated keys, rhythms and musical types. The casual juxtaposition of
found objects in Charles Ives's own music had its origins here, and
these objects consisted of all the musical paraphernalia of post-Civil
War America. Revivalist hymns, college songs and marching tunes
populate his musical landscapes, and he was well versed in the
ragtime rhythms of early jazz emerging from the former Confederate
states to the south. But, at heart, he was a New Englander, resembling nothing so much as a musical version of the writer and
philosopher Henry David Thoreau, both in his love of what was
around him (Thoreau called it becoming expert in 'home cosmology') and in his unconventional attitudes towards the independence
of existence of these musical objects: Thoreau's famous essay 'On the
Duty of Civil Disobedience' might have served as the blueprint for
much of Ives's music. The central movement of *Three Places in New
England* (1908–14) is entitled 'Putnam's Camp, Redding, Connecticut', and it is a prime example of Ives's collage technique, up to a
dozen marching bands colliding with each other in unbridled,
joyous pandemonium.

As a prophet of trends in the music of the century, Ives has few
rivals. He experimented with quarter-tones (another enthusiasm that
came from his father), he composed works employing several simultaneous tempos, his complex orchestral textures were often the
result of multiple ensembles working independently of each other,
and he quoted extensively. After World War II, composers would
exploit all these techniques, and yet Ives completed the bulk of his
composing before World War I. Needless to say, he heard very little
of it performed. Although he died as late as 1954, it was not until
the mid-1960s that performances of his music occurred with any
regularity and recordings began to become generally available.

Ives even foresaw the possible coexistence of tonal and

non-tonal music, and the tension thus created, in his small master-piece, *The Unanswered Question* (1906). A group of strings plays off-stage. It presents slow, consonant music, always extremely quiet. A solo trumpet poses a musical question; an on-stage quartet of flutes, playing independently of the off-stage strings attempts an answer. The trumpet asks its question again — and again — and each time the flute quartet's answer grows more frenetic and disso-nant, until the question, asked one last time, remains unanswered. The title and the nature of *The Unanswered Question* suggest some sort of an extra-musical agenda, and Ives provided a rather inscrutable description of the piece to back the theory. The strings represent the silence of the druids who see all, but say nothing; the trumpet is asking the perennial question of existence; the flutes are 'the fighting answerers'. It is certainly possible to conclude that Ives was asserting the ascendancy of consonance over dissonance, and, if that were the case, *The Unanswered Question* would be a provocative statement indeed. But we know this can't be true, because Ives was so obviously thrilled by cacophony. Like his father, Ives believed 'You won't get a heroic ride to Heaven on pretty little sounds', he described Haydn as 'easy music for the sissies', and (perhaps apoc-ryphally) he challenged an audience member who booed a piece by his friend Carl Ruggles to stand up and take his dissonance 'like a man'.

I suppose we should resist the rather obvious conclusions to be drawn here: Ives the American pioneer; Ives the frontiersman; Ives the 'rugged individualist'. It is all too stereotypical to be of use. And yet it is difficult to imagine Arnold Schoenberg relishing his own creation of dissonance in quite the same red-blooded, macho way, and impossible to think of him sullying his art by welcoming march-ing bands into his works. If Ives's creative palette was the world around him — indeed, as he entitled his unfinished magnum opus, the *Universe* — Schoenberg, to whom we must now return, drew inspiration from his tradition and from the world within, now avail-able to the Viennese as never before, thanks to Sigmund Freud.

In one sense, Schoenberg's music was deeply pure; it had a purity born of the duty he felt to the tradition of which he found himself a part. Schoenberg recognised a pattern in 19th-century music; a growing tendency to push harder and further at the limits of tonality which, in one way or another, had provided the harmonic framework of European music at least since the Renaissance. By the late 18th century, that harmonic framework had achieved its simplest and boldest manifestation, and the music of the Classical composers celebrated this boldness in a form whose structure depended upon the clearly defined boundaries it offered: sonata form. In a Classical sonata, the tonic — or home key — provides a gravitational pull over the music. The first theme or subject of a sonata movement strongly asserts the tonic, and we know that whatever else may happen in between, the music will return to this key at the end. A second, contrasting subject usually follows in the dominant key, a fifth higher than the tonic and its closest relative. These keys act as twin poles; the music gravitates towards them and in so doing establishes a firm hierarchy, a pecking order, for all the other notes.

There is nothing arbitrary about this hierarchy; it comes from the harmonic series, a naturally occurring sequence of overtones found in any vibrating object, but most clearly apparent when the object has the simple formal properties of a violin or piano string or a length of brass tubing like a French horn. Classical music emphasised the relationships between the first few notes of the series. Mathematically, these relationships are the simplest, and it was in keeping with the ideals of the 18th-century Enlightenment that the music of the day should have been ordered according to perceivable scientific ratios; the composer Pierre Boulez once linked the diatonic language of Classical music to the physics of Newton, given the sense of tonal gravity on which sonata form depends. It is equally fitting that in the Romantic age of the 19th century, when artists were heroes, composers should have attempted to assert their will over these laws of nature, manhandling the hierarchy, pushing it to its limits. By the beginning of the 20th century, the hierarchy was in jeopardy. In the hands of Wagner, Liszt, Bruckner, Mahler and Scriabin, and in Schoenberg's *Verklärte Nacht*, harmony had reached a level of complication — we call it chromaticism — that made the next step as apparent as it was logical: abandon the hierarchy of keys entirely; relate the pitches only to each other. Boulez speaks of music leaving the age of Newton and entering that of Einstein.

In Schoenberg's music, we can hear the exact instant this occurs. In 1908, he composed his second string quartet in whose last two movements a soprano voice appears. Clearly, it is a striking moment because singers don't normally turn up in string quartets, but this one is present to draw our attention to a far more significant departure, and to explain it. The first three movements of the string quartet are in the keys of F sharp minor, D minor and E flat minor — just — but the last movement has no key signature, because it has no key. The musical figures scurry upwards, resisting gravity, finally coming to rest on a strange, ambiguous chord. And then the soprano sings words by the poet Stefan George: *Ich fühle luft von anderem planeten* ('I feel the air from another planet'). There are no two ways about it: this is one of the vital moments in the history of music, and the singer is there as a commentator, to describe what is happening.

This music is usually referred to as atonal, even though the term is rather inexact. Schoenberg himself pointed out that atonal music was an impossibility: how could you have music without tones? Even if we allow that the expression implies music without key — without tonality — this assumes that the perception of a tonal centre in music will be the same for everyone, whereas it's fairly clear that it isn't. Tonality is, to a degree, in the ear of the beholder. A better phrase altogether might be 'non-tonal' music, because that implies the avoidance of tonality by the composer, but, accurate or not, the use of 'atonal' is so widespread that I'll use it now.

Atonality was not merely the result of the gradual expansion of harmonic language. Music does not happen in a social vacuum: not only was the early 20th century the era of Einstein, it was also, as I have noted, the era of Freud, and of a form of 'home cosmology' that Thoreau surely never contemplated. Viennese artists at the beginning of the 20th century were drawn to the unconscious mind and its potentially hysterical outpourings, as surely as the Romantics had embraced the natural world, and Classical artists had celebrated the Age of Reason. But to place the responsibility for Schoenberg's abandonment of tonality at Freud's door would be over-simple. If Freud has become a figurehead of the movement we call 'expressionism', it is equally true that his delving into the unconscious world of dreams and nightmares was stimulated by the environment in which he found himself. What was expressionism?

Expressionism happened, very largely, in Austria and Germany and it was the polar opposite of impressionism. Where impressionists painted what they saw, expressionists tended to deal exclusively in the world of the imagination. In particular, they took the unsettling, private images of dreams, and blew them up on a large canvas. If this sounds like an extreme form of late Romanticism — Romanticism gone bad, Romanticism gone mad — then that's pretty close to the mark. Perhaps we could say that expressionism equals Romanticism plus Freud.

Wagner's *Tristan und Isolde*, which isn't even an especially *late* Romantic work, already had some distinctly expressionistic leanings, and were it possible to take the four hours of music and drama in Wagner's opera — all the passion, all the harmonic tension — and somehow compress them into half an hour, one might very well end up with Schoenberg's *Erwartung*. In *Tristan*, Wagner addressed topics that had previously been considered taboo; indeed, they remained taboo even after *Tristan*. These included the violent and sexual aspects of human desire and, significantly, their intersection. The example of *Tristan und Isolde* was so strong, musically and dramatically, that it led, in the 20th century, to operatic manifestations of these same obsessions that include not only *Erwartung*, but also Richard Strauss's *Salome* and *Elektra*, Berg's *Lulu*, Prokofiev's *The Fiery Angel* and even, in a very English way, Britten's *Peter Grimes*. It could be argued that the sixth symphony of Mahler, despite its neutral, generic title, has a similar subject matter.

Because of its very abstraction, it is difficult to be in any way specific about Mahler's underlying thoughts in this work, but the music suggests an agenda beyond the notes on the page, and a terrifying agenda at that. After the rapturous second subject of the symphony's first movement — a theme associated with the composer's wife, Alma — and the tender, bucolic Alpine landscape of the *Adagio* (complete with the evocative clanging of distant cowbells), the purposeful heroics of the finale are violently mocked and ultimately decimated by three hammer blows, each more crushing than the last. It is as though Mahler has deliberately destroyed his own world, and if Alma Mahler's story of her husband, backstage after the first rehearsal, weeping with fear at what he had just heard, is perhaps a little exaggerated, it's not actually implausible.

An act of destruction such as this might be thought of as a

Freudian rejection of parental authority, and Schoenberg's renunciation of tonality might also come into this category. Now, this is notwithstanding Schoenberg's belief in tradition, because Freud tells us that these acts of destruction are as inevitable as Schoenberg felt his own musical direction to be, and of course that (perhaps justly) maligned figure, the historicist, would argue that history itself consists of the regular overturning of established practices. Certainly this was the view of Karl Marx, who with Einstein and Freud was the other towering philosophical presence in turn-of-the-century Europe.

In Schoenberg's *Erwartung*, composed in 1909 and one of his very greatest achievements, tradition, destruction and a singularly Freudian subject all come together. *Erwartung* ('Expectation') is a monodrama, an opera with only one character. The text was written, at Schoenberg's request, by the young poet and medical student, Marie Pappenheim, and in an astonishing burst of creativity, Schoenberg completed the composition and virtuoso orchestration of the half-hour piece in a mere seventeen days. A woman wanders (or dreams she wanders) through a moonlit forest in search of her lover. She fears for his safety, and becomes increasingly frantic. At the climax of the work she stumbles across his dead body (or dreams she has). Perhaps she herself has killed him. From a dramatic point of view, the Freudian implications are instantly apparent.

It is interesting that the action of both *Verklärte Nacht* and *Erwartung* takes place in a moonlit forest: it emphasises the link between the late Romanticism of one and the expressionism of the other. But where *Verklärte Nacht* ended with the lovers' reconciliation, bathed in the silvery gleam of D major, *Erwartung* ends with blood on the floor, and in harmonic limbo. It is no coincidence that atonal music and the nightmare world of expressionist art grew up together; in popular culture they remain linked: listen to the soundtrack of the next horror movie you see.

What makes *Erwartung* such an extraordinary musical accomplishment — aside from its brilliant orchestration — is the form of the work. It is a continuously evolving river of musical ideas — a stream of consciousness, if you like. Malcolm MacDonald has called it 'the most astonishing written-out improvisation in the history of music', and by its very nature it is impossible to analyse by any traditional method. People sometimes talk of the structure of pieces of music as ABA or ABACA; if we apply this terminology to *Erwartung*, we must conclude that its form is A to Z: it contains virtually no repetition; it doesn't even glance over its shoulder. This is perfectly in keeping with the work's atonal harmony. Once the hierarchy of keys had been banished, it became extremely difficult to establish a sense of return — at any rate in harmonic terms — and this led to a problem. How could a composer give a shape to music that had no obvious beginning and end? How could you have moments of tension and release? Tension, conventionally, was created by the use of dissonance, but how could you have dissonance when everything was dissonant? The problem of providing a convincing contour for music without tonality dogged Schoenberg before and after *Erwartung*, but during the burst of white-hot industry in which *Erwartung* itself was forged, Schoenberg did discover a way. How did he do it?

Part of his solution had a parallel in the then-new language of cinema. Schoenberg made good use of a technique that cinematographers call the dissolve. In a film, this is where one shot fades into the next; it is a gradual transformation, rather than a hard edit. Schoenberg employed the dissolve to bring a seamless continuity to *Erwartung*, and it is one of the work's hallmarks. It is most apparent in those portions of the score that lock into an ostinato figure, a holding pattern of notes that repeats over and over. The problem with using an ostinato is that once you have set it in motion it is difficult to stop the thing, and so Schoenberg's use of the dissolve, where the ostinato simply fades from our hearing, is effective. It is effective, too, in dramatic terms, and so is the ostinato itself. An ostinato has an built-in contradiction: the rhythm propels it forward, but the repetition of the same pitches in the same order tends to restrain it. This creates a certain tension, and it is a tension very appropriate to *Erwartung* because it closely resembles that nightmare cliché of running, but getting nowhere. Much of the musical shape and variety of *Erwartung* is provided by its ever-changing texture, but additionally Schoenberg found a solution to the problem of purely harmonic shaping; a replacement for the home key of tonal harmony.

In atonal music, each pitch is given equal importance — at

least, that is the composer's intention. There are twelve chromatic pitches, and in *Erwartung*, Schoenberg establishes harmonic turning-points by gradually piling these pitches on top of each other until all twelve are sounding simultaneously. Having reached the point of saturation, there is, harmonically speaking, nowhere for the music to go except in the opposite direction: the composer can thin out the harmony gradually or abruptly; either way, the piece turns a corner.

After the seventeen-day miracle of its composition, *Erwartung* waited a further fifteen years before it was publicly performed in Prague on 6 June 1924. But other works of Schoenberg's free atonal period were heard, and for the general Viennese public that heard them they were beyond the pale. Unlike Satie and Debussy, Schoenberg never really forsook the dynamism that had characterised Western music for centuries. His music generally surges forward. Schoenberg never became involved with the collages, multiple tempos and conflicting tonalities of Ives, and he never fragmented the melodic line or indulged in rhythmic innovation as Igor Stravinsky was about to do. Schoenberg's small step, logical and — certainly, he felt — inevitable, was to stop using key-signatures and to avoid tonal references. For conservative Viennese concert-goers, however, and for the majority of concert-goers since, such illegal harmonies challenged their listening habits. Perhaps they resented the fact that the very unfamiliarity of the new musical language forced them to listen, rather than merely to overhear. Whatever the reason, they reviled Schoenberg for it.

Once, after attending a performance of Grieg's piano concerto, Schoenberg said to a friend: 'That's the kind of music I'd really like to write.' He may have been half-joking, but it is a touching statement, nonetheless. Obliged by tradition to act in one way, he was condemned for it by audiences. Viennese audiences used to signal their disapproval by whistling on their house keys. It became such a familiar sound to Schoenberg that in 1918 he founded a Society for Private Musical Performance.

Today, when classical music has become a consumer item and is marketed as a fashion accessory, it is hard for us to imagine the fervour with which artistic causes were fought and fought over in the early years of the 20th century. In 1913, in Vienna's Musikverein, a concert of music by Mahler, Schoenberg and his pupils had to be abandoned and the police called out to protect members of the orchestra; only a few weeks later that marvellous French expression *succès de scandale* could be invoked to describe musical history's most famous public stoush during the Paris premiere of Stravinsky's *The Rite of Spring*. There isn't much cheering or booing in our concert halls today, and I've never witnessed a fist fight. Perhaps living through the 20th century has inured us to illegal harmonies. I hope not.

CONFLICT AND REVOLUTION

On 29 May 1913 at the Champs-Elysées Theatre in Paris, Sergei Diaghilev's Ballets Russes introduced a new work. It was choreographed by Vaslav Nijinsky and designed by Nicholas Roerich. The music was by Igor Stravinsky. The ballet was called *Le sacre du printemps* ('The Rite of Spring'), and no sooner was the performance under way than some members of the audience began to hurl abuse both at the stage and at each other. For good measure, they also hurled a few punches. The premiere had, in a word, created a scandal. And yet, if the English word 'scandal' carries Anglo-Saxon overtones of disgrace and dishonour, the French *scandale* has a rather triumphant ring to it. So rapidly spreading news of the opening-night scuffle that attended *The Rite of Spring* instantly assured Stravinsky's place at the forefront of 20th-century music.

The aggressive response to it was provoked at least as much by the convulsive, angular movements of Nijinky's dancers as by the sound of Stravinsky's score. But the music was boldly original, and it remains so today. Its most obvious characteristics are the jagged violence of its sound world and its incessant, almost primitive, rhythmic vitality, but under the surface of the music was a structure that, for its time, was quite as radical as those primitive rhythms.

What Stravinsky sought and found in *The Rite of Spring* was a temporary solution to the problem that beset any but the most conservative composer in the first years of the century. The problem concerned form and continuity — how to hold a piece together; how to make it go forwards — and the problem existed, principally, for those composers who no longer worked with strictly tonal harmony. Yet even those who clung to the language of tonality — and, in 1913, they were greatly in the majority — even those composers felt some sense of the problem.

Gustav Mahler, who died in 1911, in some ways encapsulates the problem with form, if only in the symphony. Mahler's symphonies were grand in scale and sprawling in nature. It was not that they lacked formal discipline — far from it — but these works were about more than music. Mahler made his living as a conductor and especially as a conductor of opera. Although he composed no operas himself — perhaps because of it — his symphonies teem with dramatic incident; themes and motifs stalk through his music like the characters in a 19th-century novel. Where Bruckner's symphonies are exclusive, hermetic, fanatical in their purity of purpose, Mahler's are inclusive, full of humanity. They deal with the world in a manner rather like that of Charles Ives; both composers embrace the everyday as well as the cosmic. Ives incorporated hymns, college football songs and American marching bands; Mahler took folk dances, cowbells and Austrian marching bands. This comparison becomes stronger when we remember that, just before his death, Mahler was making plans to conduct Ives's third symphony with the New York Philharmonic. The major difference between the two composers was in their attitude to the found objects. Ives was an innocent, rejoicing in the raucous cacophony of his musical collages. Mahler must have longed to be an innocent; as it was, he carried the cares of the world on his shoulders. When Mahler took a *Ländler* — a kind of slow, peasant waltz — and put it in one of his symphonies, he did not do so uncritically. Even when the *Ländler* is presented simply and affectionately, as in his *Resurrection* symphony, we can be fairly certain that it's only the calm before the storm. Often the original dance will be deliberately exaggerated: the *Ländler* in Mahler's ninth symphony is a particularly grotesque example, and it also demonstrates some of the internal complexity of the composer's symphonic canon.

Mahler's ninth symphony was immediately preceded by *Das Lied von der Erde* ('The Song of the Earth'). Composed in 1908, *Das Lied* is an hour-long sequence of six songs, settings of poems from the Chinese. The texts were perfect for Mahler because they concerned nature, the seasons and the human spirit. The final song, 'Der Abschied' ('The Farewell'), lasts as long as the previous five put together, and it is one of Mahler's supreme achievements. The leave-taking described in the poem is effectively a farewell to the world: Mahler's heart condition had been diagnosed and he knew he was dying. The reluctance of the poet's departure is reflected in the music. The final word of the piece — 'Ewig' (eternally) — is repeated over and over by the singer on the interval of a falling major second, or a whole tone. In the context, this interval implies a further descent to the tone below — the harmony insists that this is how the music wants to resolve, and in the orchestral accompaniment that is what it does, but the singer continues to repeat the word 'Ewig', finally only managing the first two notes of the sequence, lingering there, trapped, as it were, in the 'sweet sorrow' of this parting.

That same interval of the falling second — I suppose we might call it the 'Ewig' motif — comes at the opening of the ninth symphony, the piece Mahler composed next. The harp and muted brass conjure a rather desolate landscape into which the 'Ewig' motif steps with a degree of purpose; in its new context, the motif no longer implies the sense of closure that it did in *Das Lied von der Erde*; it is as though Mahler is saying, 'I'm still here'. The theme is still troubled, but it is also positive, hopeful. Then comes the second movement, and that country dance. The *Ländler* now takes the same poignant motif and ridicules it by giving the notes to a pair of unusually perky clarinets. It is a moment of black, self-loathing humour, typical of Mahler.

What the symphonies of Gustav Mahler signalled, if it needed signalling after Beethoven, Berlioz and Liszt, was the potential impurity of the form. Much as he resisted his publisher's requests for detailed programmatic accounts of his symphonic works, going so far as to repudiate the explanations he had already written, Mahler could hardly deny that his symphonies had non-musical meanings in addition to their purely musical ones. You simply cannot turn the children's song 'Frère Jacques' into a funeral march — as Mahler did in his first symphony — and not mean something by it. Mahler gave a splendid twist to the 19th-century conceit of the artist as hero. His symphonies *are* heroic, and arguably Mahler himself is the hero of them, but he is a deeply flawed and tragic hero.

For Mahler's younger colleague Arnold Schoenberg and his pupils Alban Berg and Anton Webern, the problem of form grew exponentially with the rejection of the system of keys that had given structure to tonal music. The difficulty of making large-scale forms without a tonal hierarchy was immediately clear. *Erwartung*, Schoenberg's masterpiece of the pre-World War I period, remains an example of how it could be achieved but, for the time being at any rate, it was an isolated example, and as Webern pointed out, Schoenberg had had the advantage in *Erwartung* of a text to 'carry' the music. Schoenberg and his pupils styled themselves the 'second Viennese school' and, more and more, they began to explore small scale forms, some of them very small indeed: all six of Webern's Bagatelles for string quartet, for instance, can be played in about three and a half minutes.

The advantage of the miniature for these composers is plain enough. It allowed them to present and shape a few ideas without the problem of developing them and then controlling that expansion. Yet if there is inevitably a fleeting, rather provisional quality to much of this music, it is important to see the pieces as far more than sketches. Webern's Orchestral Pieces Opp. 6 and 10, and his Six Bagatelles, Berg's Four Pieces for Clarinet and Piano, Schoenberg's Six Little Piano Pieces Op. 19 and the Three Pieces for Chamber Orchestra of 1910 (the last of which, in fact, is incomplete) all explore worlds of extraordinary concision and precision. What is frequently overlooked, however, in considering these works is that the miniature form itself is an aspect of expressionism. In the miniature, the composers of the second Viennese school found a unitary form entirely appropriate to the intense, heightened, nightmarish language of freely atonal harmony.

The last of Schoenberg's Six Little Piano Pieces Op. 19, composed, perhaps appropriately, on his return home from Mahler's funeral, is an essay in claustrophobia. Two chords alternate (they could be tolling bells), a fragment of melody is heard, the chords return ('like an exhaled breath', Schoenberg writes in the score), and the piece is over. The ability of such brief music to create intense poetry suggests the art of the Japanese haiku writer.

In contrast to Schoenberg's piano pieces are the Six Orchestral Pieces Op. 6 composed in 1909 by his pupil Anton Webern. Webern's pieces are a stylistic hybrid. They are miniatures in terms of their length and the compression of their ideas, and yet they deal in Mahlerian gestures and employ an orchestra of Mahlerian proportions. One striking aspect of the music, however, is that the full orchestra is rarely employed: Webern exploits the range of colours available to him from the expanded orchestra, but the textures he draws are mostly of chamber dimensions. This, in itself, was not a significant departure from the late Romantic norm. Wagner habitually filled his opera pit with a large orchestra, but apart from some of the more famous set-piece preludes and interludes, his music–dramas are notable for the intimacy of their instrumental writing; Mahler too, in of all places his eighth symphony — the so-called 'Symphony of a Thousand' — divides and subdivides his massive forces into a profusion of chamber ensembles. Still, in Webern's Six Orchestral Pieces, there is something undeniably provocative about a hundred or more players filing on to a concert platform in order to play music of such brevity.

The dichotomy between massive forces and miniature forms did not last. Certainly Webern never again used such a large orchestra, and in the works that followed the Six Pieces he pursued the small scale form with an equally small scale palette. The Six Bagatelles for string quartet are one of the most celebrated examples of this. This time, not only did Webern opt for just four instruments from the same family, he restricted himself severely in terms of the length of the pieces: the longest is thirteen bars, and two of the movements run for only eight bars each.

In Schoenberg's written introduction to the score of Webern's Six Bagatelles, he focuses on that intensity, and also on the stark difference between this music and the Mahlerian epic. Schoenberg wrote:

Consider what moderation is required to express oneself so briefly. You can stretch out every glance into a poem, every sigh into a novel. But to express a novel in a single gesture, a joy in a breath — such concentration can only be present in proportion to the absence of self-pity.

In Anton Webern's Six Bagatelles, we hear the essence of expressionism distilled, but if we examine the score, we also notice a new approach to pitch. Webern wrote that part of the reason for the brevity of the Bagatelles was that as he was composing the set he had begun to believe that a piece was over as soon as each of the twelve chromatic pitches had been sounded. Here, in embryo, is a musical logic that would ultimately provide the second Viennese school with a means of composing expanded works once more; here is the beginning of serialism, that rigorous methodology that would not be named for another decade but would become a bone of musical contention for the next half century.

Anton Webern is a fascinating case. After their explorations of small scale forms, Schoenberg and Berg began to wrestle once more with the problems of expansion; Webern, however, remained attracted to the miniature. His longest mature piece — his second cantata, and his final work — lasts only fourteen minutes, and it has six movements. The concision and compression of the pre-war miniatures may well have been an act of necessity, both in terms of the difficulty of handling anything larger without the organising principles of tonality, and also as a way of producing a sort of hyper-expressionism, but for Webern it became a way of life. From the listener's point of view, this brevity continues to be simultaneously attractive and problematic. The attraction is obvious enough: small scale forms have an ineluctable delicacy about them. As the Elizabethans knew, the miniature portrait was unrivalled in its intimacy: you could hold it in your hand, view it in the utmost privacy, even carry it around with you. But music and the visual arts are very different matters, because music exists in time. Part of the attraction of the miniature portrait is its ever-presence, but most of the problem with miniature music is its tendency to vanish: sneeze during Webern's Six Bagatelles and you have missed one of them; become distracted and you have probably missed all six.

In 1955, on the tenth anniversary of Webern's death, Stravinsky wrote:

We must hail not only this great composer but also a real hero. Doomed to a total failure in a deaf world of ignorance and indifference he inexorably kept on cutting out his diamonds, his dazzling diamonds, the mines of which he had such a perfect knowledge.

Webern's adherence to the miniature is symptomatic of a great composer's ability to turn adversity into advantage. One thinks of Hector Berlioz, for example, composing with his guitar. It is not a technique any composition teacher would recommend because the tuning of the instrument is so restricting, especially in terms of the available chord structures; but by the force of his musical personality Berlioz made those chord structures a hallmark of his orchestral compositions. Nearer to our own time, the student Iannis Xenakis was sitting in Messiaen's harmony class at the Paris Conservatoire and failing rather conspicuously. Recognising Xenakis's singular imagination, Messiaen advised the young composer to forget about harmony and concentrate on the things he could do well. It was good advice. The result was an utterly individual 20th-century composer. So it was with Webern and the miniature: the compression of musical ideas came to represent a kind of intense purity in his work. In Webern's music it is almost impossible to improve on the finished manuscript. Just finding a note that could be removed or changed is even harder than with Bach or Mozart. This intensity obviated all need to expand his musical structures; that was not what Webern was about.

For other composers, continuity within large scale forms continued to present challenges. In Finland, Mahler's slightly younger contemporary Jean Sibelius greeted the second decade of the 20th century with a work of surpassing grimness, his fourth symphony. It is easy, with hindsight, to say that the symphony somehow presages the world war that was only three years away — similar claims might be made for the rejection of tonality in Vienna, or for the violence of *The Rite of Spring* — but what emerged from the musical cocoon of Sibelius's fourth was a bold, new slant on tonality that has continued to be a characteristic of music in northern Europe right up to the end of the century. We can hear it at work in the compositions of Einojuhani Rautavaara and Arvo Pärt. It is a rather rugged brand of tonality that emphasises the tonic in a manner that suggests

Wagner and Mahler's music might never have happened, let alone the second Viennese school. And yet this was not a retrogressive move on Sibelius's part, and neither was there a hint of nostalgia, except, perhaps, for the folk music of his politically oppressed homeland.

In his Symphony No.5, first completed in 1915, though subjected to numerous revisions, Sibelius made great use of pedal points, simple drones that underpin the musical action. When he did change key, his preferred modulations were not those of Classical music (to the fifth or fourth), but to the keys a third away from the tonic. And since these thirds can be either major or minor, there is more than a whiff of folk-song modality in the fifth symphony.

Sibelius's handling of the flow of the music was just as original. The fifth symphony had begun life as a traditional four-movement work, but during its renovation, Sibelius knocked the first two movements into one. Since they had different tempos — slow and fast — he had to find a way of shifting gear in mid-movement. He opted for a seamless acceleration, beginning shortly after the gently undulating horn call that opens the movement and culminating in the exultant *presto* of the closing pages. It is a virtuoso trick, and the first time you hear the work you are not really aware of how it's done. Even on repeated and closer listening the music speeds up imperceptibly. There are actually two techniques at work. The first consists of the composer's occasional instructions to the conductor gradually to increase the tempo. But the music also accelerates from within. There will be a slow theme in the foreground, with a faster, rocking accompaniment in the background. Gradually, the accompaniment figure gains in prominence until it has become the foreground. In the process, the surface of the music seems to be gaining speed. These devices frequently occur over one of those pedal points, so that the music is harmonically static, apparently without direction, even as the notes themselves are rushing ahead ever more quickly. In the first movement of his fifth symphony, Sibelius is like a musical illusionist. He makes us gasp in admiration at the transition from slow to fast, but he's careful not to let us see how it's done.

Like Mahler, Sibelius insisted that his symphonies had no extra-musical program, but it is tempting to hear the first movement of the fifth symphony as a race against time. In the middle of the century's second decade, the upheaval of the war in Europe and the revolution in Russia was mirrored by political turmoil in Finland. In 1917, Finland declared itself independent of Russia and plunged into civil war. The defeat of the Communist Red Guard by the Finnish-nationalist White Guard in 1918 came just as Sibelius completed his revision of the fifth symphony, and listening to the triumphalism of the finale, it is hard to believe the two are not associated.

Debussy's response to the war was to retreat into a rather cool form of classicism, though who is to say this wouldn't have happened even in peace time. But in the year before war broke out, he produced perhaps his single most innovative score; as with Sibelius's fifth symphony, the innovations concerned form and continuity. *Jeux* was commissioned by the Russian Ballet, better known by its French name of Ballets Russes. Debussy's music evolves via a process of continual variation and renewal. *Jeux* was to be the composer's final orchestral piece, and if we compare it to his *Prélude à l'après-midi d'un faune*, the work that only nineteen years before had consolidated his reputation, we quickly spot some important differences. In *L'après-midi d'un faune*, Debussy's response to a poem by Stéphane Mallarmé, the famous flute theme that opens the work appears again and again throughout the music's brief eight-minute span. The theme stays more or less the same on each appearance, even if its context alters. Now during the fifteen minutes of *Jeux*, nothing returns. The faun's languid (if obsessively priapic) afternoon has been replaced, in *Jeux*, by a kind of restless athleticism, which is nothing if not appropriate to Nijinsky's unlikely ballet scenario.

By the time of *Jeux*, in March 1913, Debussy and Nijinsky were accustomed to controversy; you could argue that they even courted it. A year earlier, Nijinsky had choreographed *L'après-midi d'un faune*, a role he danced himself and brought to a climax — in every sense — with a masturbatory flourish involving a long silk scarf. There was nothing in Nijinsky's dance that couldn't be justified by reference to Mallarmé's original poem, but the event was quickly added to the Ballets Russes's growing catalogue of *scandales*. Unlike *L'après-midi d'un faune*, for which Nijinsky had taken Debussy's existing score, *Jeux* was from the start a collaboration with the composer, who subtitled his music 'poème dansé'. Nijinsky's idea for the ballet concerned a game of tennis. *Jeux* means 'games', though from the outset both Nijinsky and the Ballets Russes's impresario Diaghilev had other games in mind: 'Les jeux de sports, les jeux de l'amour,' Nijinsky wrote to Debussy ('games of sport and games of love'), and by the premiere there were plenty of the latter and precious few of the former.

The scenario of *Jeux* is really about a *ménage à trois* between a boy and two girls, enacted at dusk in a French garden. A tennis ball bounces into view. It is chased by the boy, who is followed on stage by the girls. They are all dressed in tennis whites. The boy parades before the girls, who in turn each dance for the boy, but he plays hard to get. The girls now dance flirtatiously for one another and, realising that they are about to lose interest in him, the boy decides his only option is to have them both. At this point another tennis ball bounces on from the wings and the three dancers run off. What might easily have become yet another *scandale* was received by the first-night audience with frank puzzlement. In addition to the scenario itself, there was the contrast between Léon Bakst's garish modern set in greens and purples, and Nijinsky's deliberately formal, rather classical choreography. And all this was set to Debussy's continuously evolving music.

Nobody much performs the ballet any more; what remains of *Jeux*, and triumphantly so, is the score. Perhaps more than any of the composer's other works, *Jeux* won the respect of the notoriously hard-to-please avant-garde composers of the 1950s and '60s, and the reason was its structure. As with all of Debussy's musical radicalisms, the actual sound of *Jeux* is far less confronting than the contemporary scores of Stravinsky, Bartók or the second Viennese school, and so the originality of the music is easily missed. The novelty of the score lies in the contradiction between its sense of forward motion and its localised structure, comprising a series of discrete 'moments'. It was this that was to prove its fascination two generations down the track. Naturally, composers such as Boulez and Stockhausen took the idea of 'moment form' further, going so far as to allow performers the responsibility for deciding the precise order in which these moments occurred, but the seeds of the technique are found in *Jeux*.

The premiere of Debussy's ballet may have mystified its audience, but a fortnight later they were ready and waiting for the Ballets Russes's next offering: *The Rite of Spring*. Diaghilev first recognised the young Stravinsky's talents when he heard the three-minute orchestral miniature *Fireworks*. He asked the composer for a new piece for the Ballets Russes, and Stravinsky produced an opulent score entitled *The Firebird*. This was in 1910. That *The Rite of Spring* should have followed just over two years later is a miracle of sorts, and it is testimony to the swiftness of development in the composer's skill and, more importantly, in his imagination: Stravinsky himself commented at the time that there seemed to be more like twenty years separating the two pieces. What actually separates them is Stravinsky's second score for Diaghilev, *Petrushka* of 1911.

The precise chronology is this. The score of *The Firebird* was started in late 1909 and completed in the middle of the following year, but even before it was finished, *The Rite of Spring* had begun in Stravinsky's mind's eye. Following the premiere of *The Firebird* on 25 June 1910, Stravinsky began to sketch the score of *The Rite of Spring* but, for whatever reason, he soon interrupted his work in order to compose a concert piece for piano and orchestra. This music became associated in his imagination with a wooden puppet come to life; he called the puppet Petrushka, and it was soon apparent that the music would become another ballet score. *Petrushka* was premiered in 1911, and Stravinsky returned to work on *The Rite of Spring*, completing the score on 8 March 1913 (although he continued to tinker with it right up to 1967).

The intervention of *Petrushka* is significant, because it goes some way towards explaining the changes that came over Stravinsky's music in such a short time. In his first Ballets Russes commission, Stravinsky ingeniously wove Russian folk melodies into the fabric of his score, yet for all its accomplishment, for all its wonderful music, *The Firebird* isn't a particularly radical work: it looks backwards as much as forwards; its debts to Stravinsky's musical precursors are very clear. Tchaikovsky is one: the very idea of a fairytale ballet immediately conjures the ghosts of *The Nutcracker*, *Swan Lake* and *Sleeping Beauty*. Borodin is another and, for me, his influence is even stronger. Even beyond the use of folk songs, there is a Russian accent to *The Firebird* that recalls Borodin. It is true we get a foretaste of *The Rite of Spring* in *The Firebird's* 'Infernal Dance', but here Stravinsky's model was Borodin, too: specifically, the 'Polovtsian Dances' from *Prince Igor*, already in the repertoire of the Ballets Russes. In terms of *The Firebird's* dazzling orchestration, there was a more immediate precursor in the company's repertoire, namely *Sheherazade* by Stravinsky's former teacher Rimsky-Korsakov.

By the time of *Petrushka's* composition, Stravinsky was a confirmed expatriate. Exile tends to confer a degree of objectivity regarding one's homeland, and perhaps that is the reason *Petrushka* contains more than just a Russian story and Russian folk tunes. When Stravinsky used folk material in *The Firebird*, he did it in the manner of a 19th-century composer, weaving the melodies into a lush, sophisticated symphonic tapestry, giving the score as a whole an exotic flavour. This is why it so often sounds like Borodin. But *Petrushka* not only makes greater use of folk song, it actively engages with it. While composing the piece, Stravinsky visited St Petersburg, the city of his birth, and it may be that his more objective eye and ear allowed him to assess his native culture more keenly. At any rate, it is the *sounds* of Russian folk music, quite as much as the melodies themselves, that characterise *Petrushka*. The tunes are no longer bathed in a romantic light, now they are terse, jagged, and pungent: Stravinsky said of the ballet's fairground setting that you could smell the food in the music. Virtually all the innovations in the score have a dramatic rationale, in spite of *Petrushka's* origins as a concert piece for piano and orchestra. Even the piano, which retains its prominence, gets caught up in the drama. Stravinsky had used an orchestral piano in *The Firebird*, but its role there was largely restricted to that of an extra harp, providing occasional flashes of colour. In *Petrushka*, the piano often takes centre-stage, not at all in the sense of the lyrical hero of a concerto by Liszt or Tchaikovsky, but as a mechanical fairground instrument, implacably hammering out its tunes and fragments of tunes.

Before discussing the music of *The Rite of Spring*, it is worth pointing out one basic difference between it and Stravinsky's two earlier ballet scores. *The Rite* uses a far less colourful orchestration than its predecessors. The harps, pianos and tuned keyboard percussion are gone, and although we might think of *The Rite* as a percussion-heavy work, in fact the opposite is true. What the score does call for, however, are two timpani players, and the virtuoso writing for them has no precedent. The wind and brass requirements have grown to include no fewer than five of each woodwind instrument (including their various doublings), eight French horns, five trumpets and two bass tubas. In other words, the predominant sonority of *The Rite of Spring* is a battery of wind instruments, reinforced by timpani writing of compelling savagery.

Turning to the music itself, the first difference between *The Rite* and its predecessors concerns the use of folk song. Stravinsky liked to deny that there were any actual folk melodies in *The Rite of Spring*, though several have since been identified. But in general, it must be said, *The Rite* is not really about tunes as such, folkloric or otherwise. Stravinsky seems to have absorbed the very essence of Russian folk song to the extent that it now imbued his own music. In *The Firebird*, folk song added modal spice to an essentially romantic piece; in *Petrushka* the orchestra impersonated the sounds of Russian folk instruments; but in *The Rite of Spring*, Stravinsky uses the elements that make up folk music. They form the building blocks for his own rhythmic and melodic invention.

The building block analogy carries over into another area of the music: its absence of development. In Classical and Romantic music, composers would state their melodic material and then vary it, subjecting their themes to a process of real-time analysis. But Stravinsky merely juxtaposes his various ideas, like a child playing with different coloured blocks. He makes them into rows, or piles them on top of each other, but the blocks themselves remain essentially unchanged.

Finally, and perhaps most strikingly new, was Stravinsky's treatment of rhythm. In the process of discovering his own voice via the traditional music of his homeland, Stravinsky liberated rhythm from its previously subordinate position. This had already begun to happen in *Petrushka*, but was taken much further in *The Rite of Spring*, where the composer arrived at what was no less than a radical rethinking of musical syntax.

Hitherto, the structure of Western art music had been defined by its harmony; a grand harmonic scheme provided what we might think of as a framework, and the rate of harmonic change gave the music its momentum. Now if we zoom in on the localised activity in Classical and Romantic music, we discover that it's the bar (or the four-bar phrase) that provides the framework, while the notes themselves can be seen and heard in terms of subdivisions of that basic unit. Stravinsky's *Rite of Spring* subverts these relationships. His basic unit was not the four-bar phrase or even the bar, but the single beat, and instead of subdividing, Stravinsky added. So we get groups of two, three or five beats, and their irregular ordering produces intense syncopation.

All these innovations — the absorption of folk music, the lack of development and the syncopation — can be heard early on in the ballet, in the section entitled 'The Augurs of Spring'. It is heralded by an ostinato pattern, played first by pizzicato violins. The three pitches have a pentatonic relationship that is not only fundamental to Russian folk song, but to the indigenous music of virtually every country in the world. In what follows, there is no harmonic development at all; the entire section consists of a single eight-note chord. The pulse remains constant, too, but the composer moves the music forwards by the placing of unpredictable stresses, creating the distinctive syncopation.

At the end of the 'Dance of the Earth' which concludes the first part of *The Rite of Spring*, the syncopations are created by accents occurring in the same proportions as those in 'The Augurs of Spring'. As before, it is rhythm, rather than harmony, that propels it. The music in this section is faster, but the technique is the same: the semiquaver is the basic unit, the repetition of the unit gives the pulse, and this is cut into irregular groupings by strong accents. It is a technique that *The Rite of Spring* shares with the final passage in a novel by a writer with a keen musical ear. It may be mere coincidence, but the novel was begun at the time of *The Rite's* premiere.

In the closing pages of *Ulysses*, James Joyce abandons sentence structure in a manner very similar to Stravinsky's rejection of regular metre. For more than 30 pages, the words run on continuously without paragraphs or punctuation. The voice we hear in this final episode of the novel is that of Molly Bloom. She is lying in bed beside her sleeping husband Leopold, lost in reverie, her mind ranging freely over the events of the day and of her life, particularly her sexual encounters. As her often rambling monologue nears its end, Molly concentrates on what is presumably her first sexual experience and her language becomes increasingly explicit in that it takes on the tone of sexual climax itself, the repetitions of the word 'yes' becoming more and more frequent. The effect of this passage is uncannily close to the music of the 'Dance of the Earth'. For Joyce the unit is the word; for Stravinsky, it's the semiquaver. The words and the semiquavers run on, their incessancy providing the pulse, but the momentum comes from the rhythm formed by Molly's yeses and Stravinsky's accents.

In the first fifteen years of the 20th century, musical style underwent a staggering number of developments. It would be no exaggeration to say that by the outbreak of World War I, Western music was more diverse than at any point in its history, establishing directions that would remain and further expand as the century progressed. Yet almost all these directions were inspired from outside music. The struggle for cultural and, in a few cases, political independence was, at some level, the force behind the music of Vaughan Williams and Sibelius, Bartók and Janáček. Charles Ives's tendency to make collages of Americana was fuelled by his reading of the great trancendentalist philosophers, Ralph Waldo Emerson and Henry David Thoreau; the symbolism that affected Debussy was primarily a literary movement, and Schoenberg's eventual abandoning of tonality went hand-in-glove with his settings of the expressionist poetry of Stefan George. But above all, as for Monteverdi, Mozart and Wagner in previous centuries, it was the theatre that provided the crucible for musical innovation: Debussy's major contribution to French symbolism — symbolism's central musical work — was the opera *Pelléas et Mélisande*; it was via the nightmare scenarios of the stage works *Erwartung* and *Die glückliche Hand*, that Schoenberg expanded his new harmonic language; and it was as a composer of ballet scores that Stravinsky developed his rhythmic idiolect.

The theatre was also responsible, in large part, for another growing trend in 20th-century music: the pop song. Music halls proliferated in the years before radio; along with silent movies, vaudeville was the primary form of urban entertainment, and the popularity of its songs was spread by commercial publishing of sheet music and, increasingly, by the availability of recordings. Significantly, and swiftly, this ushered in the age of the international hit, so that the British composer Michael Tippett could recall hearing, as a child, two local village girls singing Irving Berlin's 'Everybody's

Doing It'. This was in 1911, in rural Suffolk, just down the road from where, six years before, Joseph Taylor had first sung the traditional folk song 'Brigg Fair' for Percy Grainger.

That American popular music should have become more important to Tippett the composer than even folk song is presumably no mere coincidence, but this would not happen for another 30 years. In the meantime, popular culture in general began to have a profound influence on European composers. In Paris, where Erik Satie already worked as a part-time cabaret pianist, Stravinsky and Ravel became fascinated by ragtime, or at least the idea of ragtime. We cannot know just what music they were exposed to, but it seems likely that in 1917, when Stravinsky composed the piece he called *Ragtime*, he was responding primarily to sheet music.

In the United States, early jazz was a fusion of African–American rhythm and blues-inflected European harmonies. Even the instrumentation of New Orleans jazz reflects its hybrid beginnings. On the one hand were the instruments of the cotton plantation: the banjo, jug and home-made string bass. On the other hand were the European clarinet, cornet, trombone and euphonium, which owed their ubiquity to the marching bands of the Confederacy that had vanished after the Civil War, leaving their instruments behind them. Jazz was improvised, but ragtime composers like Scott Joplin sought to give it a kind of respectability; not only was the music indeed composed, it was written down and published as sheet music. The problem that arises from the notation of jazz rhythms is the impossibility of notating with any degree of accuracy that elusive, lilting quality known as swing. Swing is neither a triplet rhythm nor a dotted one; it's somewhere in between. Given that it can only be felt, not written down, it follows that the person who only reads the music, only has a part of the picture. So in Stravinsky's *Ragtime* a rather stilted syncopation emerges, far removed from the true jazz feel of the real thing. Yet the piece is not without its attractions, notably Stravinsky's inspired use of the cimbalom — the Hungarian hammered dulcimer — to lend the music a honky-tonk sonority.

Of all the composers to feel the influence of popular culture, perhaps the most unlikely was Arnold Schoenberg. Schoenberg has a reputation as a high-minded aesthete, but *Pierrot lunaire* owes a lot to the world of cabaret: Pierre Boulez called it *un cabaret supérieur*.

While Stravinsky was working on *The Rite of Spring*, his Viennese colleague was creating something on a far smaller scale that would have a correspondingly massive impact on the music of the century: a setting, for reciter and five instrumentalists of poems about the *commedia dell'arte* character Pierrot. In *Pierrot lunaire*, Schoenberg's text was by the Belgian poet Albert Giraud. The poems had been translated into German from the original French by Otto Erich Hartleben, and it is clear that Monsieur Giraud owed Herr Hartleben a great debt: Hartleben's *Pierrot* poems are a distinct improvement on the originals.

The origins of *Pierrot lunaire* are found not only in cabaret, but also in 18th- and 19th-century German melodrama. As this term suggests, melodrama was a mixture of music and drama, and it was most often a dramatic recitation accompanied by music, a rather overblown art form, giving us our modern expression 'melodramatic'. The single most striking aspect of Schoenberg's piece is its vocal line, derived from melodrama and calling for the reciter to adopt *Sprechstimme* or *Sprechgesang* — literally 'speech song'. It is a form of pitched speech, and it is notated in the normal fashion for a sung vocal line, but with a little cross through the stem of each note. In his introduction to the score the composer is very clear about what he wants from his speaker–singer. She should pitch the note for an instant and immediately begin sliding to the next note. The premiere of the work in 1912 employed an actor, emphasising the link with the melodramatic tradition.

There are 21 movements in *Pierrot lunaire*, and they are divided into three groups of seven. More correctly, perhaps I should say there are 21 *numbers*, because the structure of *Pierrot*, as much as the forces it employs, is indebted to popular music. The musical style of *Pierrot lunaire* is fascinating. It was, and remains today, a provocatively modern score; the American composer and musicologist George Perle has called it a piece one never gets used to. And yet beneath the strongly expressionist and expressive surface of the music, something else is going on. Each of the 21 numbers of *Pierrot* is a parody. Occasionally, Schoenberg owns up to his models in the titles he allocates to the movements. The fifth of them is called 'Valse de Chopin', the eighth is subtitled 'Passacaglia', and the penultimate 'Journey Home' is designated a 'Barcarolle'. But elsewhere

Schoenberg's models range from the popular song styles of the Viennese cafe to Bach.

Bach is a recurrent reference point in *Pierrot lunaire*. The accompaniment to the fourth piece is effectively a chorale; the seventh is a two-part invention. And what is the very opening of the whole work, if not a version of the first prelude from Book 1 of Bach's *Well-Tempered Clavier*? The templates Schoenberg employed in *Pierrot lunaire* enabled its composer to cease worrying, at least temporarily, about the problems of form associated with the absence of tonality: the forms of *Pierrot* were ready-made: found objects, again. But there is another aspect to this, for Schoenberg seems to have intended his models to be understood ironically. In making that reference to Bach's C major Prelude, for instance, Schoenberg can hardly have been unaware of Gounod's earlier wholesale appropriation of the same piece to form the accompaniment of his famous, rather saccharine, 'Ave Maria'.

Poor Pierrot is drunk on 'the wine we drink with our eyes'; he's had too much moonlight and gone mad — in the most literal sense of the word, he is a lunatic. From Pierrot's fevered imagination now streams a succession of bizarre and violent images. This may be tongue-in-cheek expressionism, but it's expressionism none the less: the least rational and most lurid aspects of the human mind are grotesquely inflated. One can see why the piece has gained a reputation for horror, particularly in English-speaking countries. Anglo-Saxon culture has always found it difficult to take Germanic humour when it's as black and occasionally violent as the humour in this piece. In the sixteenth number, for instance, Pierrot bores a hole through the bald head of Cassander, scoops out its contents and fills the cranium with the best Turkish tobacco. He then screws in a cherry pipestem and puffs away.

Pierrot lunaire is often very funny, an idiosyncratic mixture of *Grand Guignol* and satire, but its primary device — musical and dramatic — remains ironic parody. For its final number, Schoenberg adopts the tone of German Lieder. In 'O alter Duft aus Märchenzeit', the antique fragrance mentioned in the title comes in the form of an unexpected waft of tonality. The instrumental accompaniment with its preponderance of thirds hints strongly at E major, and its mood might be mistaken for nostalgia, were it not for a reference in the text whose unintentional significance cannot have escaped the composer. Only four years earlier, in the final movement of his second quartet, Schoenberg had set Stefan George's words about a rather different breeze. The 'air from another planet' had borne on it the seeds of atonality. At the very end of 'O alter Duft', which is also the end of *Pierrot lunaire*, the instrumental accompaniment fades away and the female reciter's voice descends to its bottom register where it half-whispers, half-croaks the word 'Märchenzeit' — mythical times. A joke, perhaps, at the expense of Schoenberg's conservative audience in Vienna, and *Pierrot's* final irony.

The sound of *Sprechstimme* and the hallucinatory nature of its text remain *Pierrot lunaire's* most arresting features, but they were not the aspects of the piece that most influenced the composers who followed Schoenberg. *Pierrot* marks the first appearance of a mixed ensemble of instruments unlike anything that had previously existed in Western art music. Commonplace as it may seem today, the instrumentation of *Pierrot lunaire* was revolutionary. In their chamber music, Classical and Romantic composers had combined winds and strings, winds and piano and strings and piano; there were also pieces for one of each type of instrument, wind, strings and keyboard: the trios of Mozart, Beethoven and Brahms are examples. But Schoenberg's line-up of flute (doubling piccolo), clarinet (doubling bass clarinet), violin (doubling viola), cello and piano — eight instruments played by five musicians — was unique. In effect it was a mini orchestra, and the idea for it came to Schoenberg, like so much else in *Pierrot lunaire*, from the theatre, where small pit bands of versatile players were the norm, and remain so. Its effect on the music of the century has been pervasive. Right around the world, chamber groups specialising in new music came to adopt the '*Pierrot* ensemble' as their basic instrumentation, and it would not be surprising to learn that, in the last 75 years or so, there has been more concert music written for this combination of instruments than for any other.

The premiere of *Pierrot lunaire* took place not in Vienna, but in Berlin, and, for once, it was a success. The work won many admirers, including Puccini, and its influence was quickly felt. Stravinsky and Ravel both got to work on sets of songs with similar instrumentations. Stravinsky even interrupted work on *The Rite of Spring* in order to write his *Three Japanese Lyrics*, while in his *Trois poèmes de Stéphane Mallarmé*, Ravel was affected by more than Schoenberg's instrumentation, composing the most chromatic music of his career in the final song, 'Surgi de la croupe et du bond'. Ravel even proposed a 'scandalous concert' at which *Pierrot lunaire* would appear on the same bill as his own and Stravinsky's songs, although the concert failed to eventuate in his lifetime.

Pierrot is often credited with being the origin of small scale music–theatre, a genre that would exert a considerable pull over the imaginations of the composers of coming generations. Since its premiere, Schoenberg's piece has received many performances that stressed its theatricality, but it would be an exaggeration to describe the original conception as music–theatre at all. Screens concealed the instrumentalists and conductor (Schoenberg himself), so that the reciter, Albertine Zehme in a Columbine costume, was the only performer in view. But apart from these minimal concessions to theatricality, it remained a recitation with music, firmly in the tradition of melodrama. Even so, with its combination of gruesome text, singer/actor and virtuoso chamber ensemble, *Pierrot lunaire* certainly demonstrated the potential for a non-operatic fusion of music and theatre, and it was now Stravinsky who gave the medium of music–theatre its first fully-fledged masterpiece.

It was 1917, and Stravinsky's hitherto glittering career had come to a virtual halt, because of the war. The Ballets Russes had all but ceased performing, orchestral performances were rare, and because of the revolution in Russia, Stravinsky was no longer receiving royalty cheques from his publisher. These privations, together with the composer's temporary exile in Switzerland, made the intimate scale, simple staging and portability of *The Soldier's Tale* obvious advantages. Yet Stravinsky was not treading creative water in this piece; on the contrary, he was establishing a whole new medium.

Stravinsky's piece is scored for seven musicians playing clarinet, cornet, trombone, bassoon, violin, double bass, and a modest assortment of percussion. The little band has a quite different sonority to Schoenberg's ensemble, and the piece avoids both song and *Sprechstimme*: three actors and a dancer now provide the action. *The Soldier's Tale* is more conventionally theatrical than *Pierrot*, from its avoidance of song down to its narrative structure. Its Faustian story tells of a soldier returning home on leave. He meets the Devil disguised as an old man, and sells him his violin in return for a magic book. The book brings the soldier wealth, but he soon tires of it; he plays cards with the Devil, gets him drunk and takes back the fiddle; the sound of the instrument cures a dying princess, whose grateful father, the King, gives her to the soldier in marriage. But there's no fairytale ending. The Devil returns and the soldier is lured away to his doom as the Devil dances in triumph.

Stravinsky thought that by writing a work of such a small scale he would get more performances — *The Soldier's Tale* was eminently suitable as a touring production — but it was not until after World War II that the piece enjoyed much success, and perhaps it was this that deterred its composer from exploring the medium as he might have done. In the 1960s, particularly, the innovations of Schoenberg and Stravinsky began to bear regular fruit in the music–theatre pieces of composers such as Hans Werner Henze, Mauricio Kagel, Alexander Goehr and Peter Maxwell Davies. Stravinsky himself was drawn, again, to the form in his musical play *The Flood*, commissioned by CBS Television in America and first broadcast in 1962. By this time, *The Soldier's Tale* had firmly established its reputation, and in 1966 in New York, the 84-year-old Stravinsky attended an all-star performance of *The Soldier's Tale*, with three composers in the speaking roles. Elliott Carter was the narrator, Aaron Copland the soldier, and John Cage was the Devil.

The first decade and a half of the 20th century had been a period of artistic revolution. But the horrors of World War I brought a change in the attitudes of many artists. For composers in Europe, the war was more than merely disruptive, it seems to have given a context, a sense of perspective to their pre-war endeavours: the nightmare visions of *Erwartung* and the savagery of *The Rite of Spring* were not so shocking set against the hideous reality of trench warfare, hand-to-hand combat, cavalry charges and gas attacks. During the first few years after the armistice some of the leading lights of musical modernism would have changes of heart whose ramifications were felt internationally. It has been argued that the greatest music of both Schoenberg and Stravinsky had already been written by the outbreak of war; for Debussy, who died at the war's end, his final brief period of classical restraint saw a distillation of the composer's aesthetic in a set of piano *Etudes* and a proposed (though incomplete) series of sonatas for various instruments. Debussy's plan was for a sequence of six pieces, the last of which would bring together all the instruments employed in the earlier works. The three that he completed are for cello and piano, flute, viola and harp, and violin and piano.

Stravinsky's musical homage to Debussy also exhibited restraint and a sense of distillation. *Symphonies of Wind Instruments* retains the techniques of *The Rite of Spring* — the discrete blocks of material, laid end to end, or superimposed on one another — but the savage rhetoric has gone. *Symphonies* is a short work and, in spite of its title, it's no symphony: Stravinsky intended the term in its original sense of 'sounding together'. The pulses of *The Rite*, the uneven accents and their attendant syncopations, characterise the new piece, too, but there is a cool, deliberately non-expressive quality about the music — almost an objectivity — that is wholly in keeping with the piece's dedication to Debussy's memory. The blocks of music follow each other, *respond* to each other, like the component parts of a funeral service: now the bells, now the voice of a priest, now the responses of the congregation. In spite of its avowed non-expressivity, the piece is profoundly moving. Perhaps it moves us because of the music's restraint, because we know that this is the work of the composer of *The Rite of Spring*, reining himself in; perhaps it is because we know that this is a funeral oration, modest and respectful, rather than emotive and full of show. But in *Symphonies of Wind Instruments* I also hear a composer who has lived through the Great War and, at least for the time being, feels that grand rhetoric may have had its day.

During and after the war, artists in many fields began to distrust their instincts. Stravinsky had composed *The Rite* at a piano, feeling his way into the music. He would later describe how he had been able to play the concluding 'Danse sacrale' on the keyboard long before he had devised a method of notating it. The image that had sparked the piece — of a sacrificial virgin dancing herself to death — had come to the composer in a dream, and his description of the process of composition ('I am the vessel through which [*The Rite of Spring*] passed') suggests a composer taking dictation, either from some higher being or, at any rate, from the depths of his imagination: 'I heard, and I wrote what I heard,' Stravinsky said.

Schoenberg's creation of *Erwartung* must have been very similar. Just to have copied out the score in not much more than a fortnight would be mildly impressive, but to compose and orchestrate it in so short a time is breathtaking. This, surely, was a man possessed. Neither Stravinsky nor Schoenberg would enjoy this level of sheer spontaneity again.

Both *The Rite* and *Erwartung* had, in a sense, been the products of creative incaution, and one might contend that it was also incaution which had led to the Great War. During the decade after *Pierrot lunaire*, Schoenberg worked on his ambitious oratorio *Die Jacobsleiter* ('Jacob's Ladder') in which the harmonic language of free atonality and the Swedenborgian mysticism of the composer's text were intended as mutually analogous. But the need for order afflicted both music and words from the outset. The Archangel Gabriel's opening peroration is especially ominous in this regard: 'Whether to the right or the left, forward or back, uphill or down, one must carry on . . .' The Archangel might be describing the fundamental tenets of the as-yet-undefined twelve-tone system whose serial procedures involved the use of a row of notes employed forwards, backwards and upside-down. *Die Jacobsleiter* was never completed, and after the war Schoenberg, like Stravinsky, would take creative refuge in compositional models from the past: no more sheer instinct; no more incaution.

After completing *The Rite of Spring*, Stravinsky told Diaghilev that he had composed 'the end of the world'. In a way, he had.

ANARCHY AND ORDER

t is significant that, even after World War II, we still refer to its predecessor as 'Great'. We will never be sure precisely how many lives it took — ten million is the round figure — but most of those who died were soldiers, further advances in technology being necessary before it was possible to kill civilians on that kind of scale. The Great War's deaths occurred on the battlefield, and its hero, as the historian A.J.P. Taylor pointed out, was 'the unknown soldier'. Because it was an old-fashioned war, in that it was primarily about men and horses, tanks, guns and bayonets (as opposed to the more arm's-length warfare of planes and bombs), those who survived it were often permanently scarred, physically or psychologically or both. Many had lost limbs; many more had lost their minds. In the years that followed, the sight of these returned soldiers would be a constant reminder of the human cost of war. The question, then: what price art in the face of such carnage?

It is possible, though doubtless unwise, to view virtually all the musical developments of the 1920s in terms of a response to the war. Certainly there were few composers unaffected by it, even if the actual casualties in the profession were small. In 1916, the young English composer, George Butterworth was killed in action during the battle of the Somme. The same year, returning to Europe from the New York premiere of his opera *Goyescas*, Enrique Granados stopped off in England. Sailing home to Spain aboard the *Sussex* he died attempting to save his wife from drowning in the English Channel after the ship was torpedoed. Ravel, like his former pupil Vaughan Williams, drove an ambulance during the war. Schoenberg, Berg and Webern were all called up. Not only was Schoenberg proud to be undergoing officer training at the comparatively advanced age of 41, he also regarded his service as an escape from the vilification of Vienna's musical public and critics. When some of that city's most prominent artists got up a petition to have him discharged from his military duties, Schoenberg objected: 'The good thing about the war is that I am not being attacked, and I should like to enjoy this peace a little longer.'

However directly or tangentially the war affected composers, the music of the 1920s was markedly different from that of the preceding decade. In specific cases, the effect of the war on individual musical works is clear enough. Ravel's *Le tombeau de Couperin* is more than a homage to the Golden Age of French music; each of its six movements is headed by a dedication to one of Ravel's friends who had perished in the conflict. Significantly, Ravel chose never again to compose for piano alone, though it was his own instrument and it had dominated his output prior to the war. Can it be coincidence that Alban Berg's post-war project, his first opera, has for its eponymous hero the hapless, victimised Private Wozzeck? Surely, the military drum in Carl Nielsen's fifth symphony, relentlessly rattling away to the endangerment of the musical fabric, is not a merely abstract conceit? Perhaps the most moving musical recollection of war, because it is so personal and reflective, comes in the second movement of what Vaughan Williams called *A Pastoral Symphony*. The critic Philip Heseltine, who was sometimes the composer Peter Warlock, dismissed the symphony as 'a cow looking over a gate', but Vaughan Williams's piece has very little to do with English pastoralism. He made his first sketches for the symphony in France in 1916 where, as an ambulance orderly, his duties involved combing the battlefields for wounded men. Twenty years later, he wrote in a letter about the genesis of the piece.

> It's really wartime music — a great deal of it was incubated when I used to go up night after night with the ambulance wagon at Ecoivres and we went up a steep hill and there was a wonderful Corot-like landscape in the sunset — it's not really lambkins frisking as most people take for granted.

From his hill-top vantage point in the fading evening sunlight, Vaughan Williams could hear a solitary bugler practising and, time and again, failing to hit his top note. Whoever he was — the unknown soldier himself, perhaps — Vaughan Williams immortalised him in his symphony.

Although he was 50 years old in 1922, when *A Pastoral Symphony* was first played, Vaughan Williams had a long career still ahead of him, including six more symphonies. But two other great symphonists were moving into retirement. Edward Elgar's Cello Concerto of 1919 was his last major work, although he was not to die for another fifteen years. His two completed symphonies are in their way every bit as great as Mahler's, if not perhaps so ambitious. The death of Elgar's wife, Alice, is usually taken to be the reason for his retirement from composing (although as late as 1933, the year before his death, he was sketching a third symphony), but one cannot help wondering whether after the musical upheavals of Stravinsky and Bartók and the second Viennese school, Elgar simply felt displaced. Jean Sibelius, too, reached a creative crisis in the 1920s. Like Elgar, Sibelius sporadically sketched his next symphonic work — it was to be No. 8 — but in the 30 years up to his death in 1957, he published nothing further.

Leoš Janáček was quite another matter. A few years older than either Elgar or Sibelius, the Moravian composer was just hitting his stride. Virtually all of Janáček's best music dates from his late sixties and seventies: two string quartets, two chamber-sized piano concertos, the *Glagolitic Mass*, the *Sinfonietta*, and half a dozen operas: eleven years of astonishing productivity, apparently fuelled by his unrequited passion for a married woman some 37 years his junior. Janáček's infatuation with Kamilla Stösslová may explain his creative energy at a time of life when others are contemplating retirement, but his very personal musical style was surely also a factor. He had so little in common with most of the period's other major composers, that he remained unaffected by the directions they took.

Musically speaking, I suppose his closest contemporary was Bartók, in that the experience of folk song informs Janáček's work, too. But Bartók and Janáček responded very differently to this stimulus. Janáček seems closer in spirit to the 19th-century Russian Mussorgsky, both in his fascination with the speech patterns of his compatriots and in his ability to turn these rhythms and inflections into melody. As with Mussorgsky, this influence not only affected Janáček's vocal lines, it also found its way into his purely instrumental music, so that even in a work like the nominally abstract *Capriccio* (1926) for piano left hand, flute and brass, one is constantly aware that the terse, angular melodic lines are attempting to speak to us.

Another composer of this generation who did not retire was Richard Strauss. Unlike Janáček, Strauss belonged to the same Austro-German tradition as Schoenberg, and at the beginning of the century, in his operas *Elektra* and *Salome*, Strauss had explored precisely the same richly chromatic harmony as Schoenberg in *Verklärte Nacht* and the monumental cantata *Gurrelieder*. But his younger colleague's ultimate rejection of tonality was too much for Strauss. While Schoenberg dived headlong into the turbulent waters of expressionism, Strauss embraced a sumptuous, make-believe world of 18th-century romance in *Der Rosenkavalier*. He wrote a letter to Alma Mahler stating his position beyond all doubt: 'Only a psychiatrist can help Schoenberg now . . . he'd be better off shovelling snow than scribbling on manuscript paper.'

Mahler's widow conveyed Strauss's sentiments to her friend Schoenberg, as Strauss doubtless knew she would, and a year later, asked to write a tribute to Strauss on the occasion of his 50th birthday, Schoenberg declined with a degree of understandable rancour.

It seems to me that the opinion I . . . have of Herr Strauss as a man . . . and as an artist . . . is not suitable for general publication in honour of his 50th birthday . . . He is no longer of the slightest interest to me, and whatever I may once have learnt from him, I am thankful to say I misunderstood.

They sound like fighting words, but the truth is that, like Strauss, Schoenberg was also troubled by the language of atonality. His essential conservatism and high regard for the tradition of Germanic music left him personally at odds with the apparent lawlessness of the harmonic language he now championed. Schoenberg suddenly lacked the stomach for trailblazing. Instead, he seemed to feel a need to take stock; a need for order. For the moment, however, he too fell silent.

Not everyone was afraid of lawlessness. Perhaps the most appropriate response to the lunacy of the Great War came in the form of lunacy itself. The so-called Dada movement had its origins amongst visual artists in Zürich and Berlin during the last years of the war. Dadaism was inspired, in part, by the Futurism of Italians such as Marinetti and it led, in turn, to surrealism. What all these 'isms' had in common was a broadly absurdist stance, and while on the face of it there might seem to be a connection here with the tortured dreams of German expressionism, in fact Dada was avowedly anti-expressionist. Dada was, if you like, low art; it owed more to cabaret and the circus, than to the concert hall or the opera house. It was also political — which expressionism never was — to the extent that it sought to prick bubbles of official pomposity wherever they began to inflate.

We cannot be sure where the word Dada comes from. It might well have been chosen for its universality, since 'Dada' — or at any rate 'Da' — turns up in practically every European language. Equally, it is one of the first sounds made by a child, and Dada, in many ways, was particularly childish. To say that there's no great Dadaist music is, I suppose, a truism, because concepts of great art were practically anathema to the movement; in any case, it was frequently impossible even to tell whether a Dada performance was music, theatre or poetry. Often it was all of these and none. But there's one famous piece of pure Dada, that in spite of being created by a leading visual artist of the movement, might best be thought of as music; it is even called a sonata.

Kurt Schwitters was based in Hamburg and his visual art consisted of found objects, generally garbage, assembled into collages and large scale installations. His *Ursonate* — really a piece of performance poetry — is essentially a collage, too: to the eye, a collage of invented words and parts of words, laid out by a demented typesetter; to the

ear, a collage of sounds evoking a basic, primeval — in German, 'ur'
— language. Thus, *Ursonate*.

Schwitters first recited the *Ursonate* at the Bauhaus in 1924, but
he continued to add to the work and it wasn't published in its final
form until 1932. This and his other experiments with performance
poetry proved surprisingly durable examples for composers of later
generations. Avant-garde composers in the 1950s and '60s produced
a variety of works for solo voice — John Cage's *Aria* of 1958 is
perhaps the most famous instance — and the *Ursonate* was the model
for many of these, as it was for the sound-text composers of the following generation. The uses of this most portable of pieces have even
extended beyond the theatre and concert hall. The British jazz singer
and art critic George Melly once found himself approached by a
couple of potential muggers in a dark alley. As they came closer,
Melly began a spirited rendition of Schwitters's *Ursonate*. His
assailants exchanged quick glances and fled.

The spirit of Dada spread quickly in post-war Europe, and in
Paris it influenced all of the arts, including the music of Erik Satie
who might be considered a Dadaist before his time. His pieces entitled *Musique d'ameublement* (or 'furniture music') consisted of essays
in early Muzak. They are pieces to be ignored, and at their first performance in a Paris art gallery, Satie, disappointed to find the patrons
falling silent in order to listen, took to striding about urging them to
talk. It was in the theatre, however, that Satie's brand of Dadaism
found its true medium. In 1917, the ballet score *Parade* (to a scenario
by Jean Cocteau and with a set designed by Picasso) included parts
for a typewriter and a revolver. But it was in his last work of all that
Satie unambiguously embraced the Dadaist aesthetic.

The ballet *Relâche* has been described as an act of artistic suicide,
and its title, which means 'tonight's performance is cancelled', does
tend to support the theory: if you paste up the word 'relâche' outside
a French theatre, the audience turns round and goes home. As fate
would have it, the planned premiere of the work was indeed cancelled when Jean Borlin, the choreographer and principal dancer of
the Swedish Ballet, fell ill. When *Relâche* finally opened a week later,
audience members who actually made it into the auditorium were
greeted by a poster advising that 'patrons who aren't satisfied are
authorised to fuck off'.

The scenario of *Relâche* was by the sculptor Francis Picabia, and Satie himself referred to the ballet as 'obscene' and 'pornographic'. In the first act, while a chain-smoking fireman poured water from one bucket to another and back again, another figure slowly took measurements of the stage. The intermission was occupied by a short film, starkly entitled *Cinema*, directed by René Clair. Satie himself had a bit part. The camera shoots through a glass floor above which a bearded man in a tutu (Jean Borlin) attempts ballet steps. A hearse, pulled by a camel and decorated with wreaths made from bread, moves through the streets of Paris; the cortege is gradually gaining speed, and the procession of mourners begins to jog and finally sprint in order to keep up with it. These scenes were accompanied by Satie's specially composed *Entr'acte cinématographique*, a proto-minimalist concoction with eight-bar sections designed to be repeated over and over until the end of each scene. In the ballet's second act, beneath a poster announcing that 'Erik Satie is the world's greatest composer', the male dancers undressed and, at the end of the night, Satie and Picabia drove on stage in a motor car belonging to the conductor Roger Desormière. All this took place at the Champs-Elysées Theatre, where Stravinsky's *Rite of Spring* had had its turbulent premiere a dozen years before. This time, too, there was a riot, and the negative response to *Relâche* brought about the closure of the Swedish Ballet.

Satie's score, also, attracted considerable critical hostility. And it was mainly posthumous hostility, at that, because the composer's motorised stage entrance at the end of *Relâche* was also his final public appearance; a few months later he was dead. The obituaries were not particularly kind, but Satie's former protégé Roland-Manuel didn't even wait for the composer's death before publishing his opinion that *Relâche* was 'the most boring and most stupidly depressing thing in the world' and that Satie himself should now 'hurry away to hell'. Not usually one for heeding a critic's words, on this occasion Satie obliged.

Relâche was arguably the last stand for Dada, though its influence can still be felt. Despite the efforts of his critics, Satie's influence remains, too, and so does his music, even if we tend only to hear a handful of his pieces today and they are generally misunderstood. I wonder how many people who recognise Satie's *Trois gymnopédies*, have any idea of the composer's other work. These simple, modal dances have proved themselves eminently adaptable to the rather narrow demands of background music. In hotel lobbies and elevators all over the world, Erik Satie's *Gymnopédies* have been transformed into what the composer himself called 'furniture music'; they are internationally ignored, and Satie — who knows? — might even have approved.

If Dada was an artistic response to the political uncertainty of the Great War and the post-war years in Western Europe, further east a quite different set of circumstances prevailed. Strangely, in Russia, where during the last years of the war a new political order had been imposed, artists discovered a fresh sense of freedom, albeit short-lived. The revolutions of 1917 had seen the overthrow of a feudal system of government that had been in place since the Middle Ages. The last Tsar, Nicholas II, had abdicated in March of that year and, following the October Revolution, Vladimir Lenin was installed as Soviet leader. Today we associate the Soviet system with artistic repression; we think of careers cut short, and of artists living in fear of their lives, seeking not to offend against the Kremlin's mercurial agenda. We recall Prokofiev and Shostakovich obliged to compose stirring militaristic cantatas in praise of the Heroes of the Revolution. So it is important to remember that not only was the revolution welcomed in many quarters — in Russia and beyond, and not least by artists themselves — but that in the first years of the Soviet system its leaders considered the artistic avant-garde the logical and necessary corollary of a revolutionary attitude. Lenin and Trotsky were committed to the ideals of total revolution, and 'total' included the arts.

Yet it would be a mistake to assume that modernist art in Russia was a consequence of the revolution. As Robert Hughes has pointed out, there had been artists of a modernist persuasion in Russia — particularly in St Petersburg — from the late 19th century. Paintings by Matisse and Picasso were in Russian collections, and modern music was regularly performed there. Neither was the cultural traffic one-way. Many Russian artists visited Western Europe; many lived there. Stravinsky, for example, had been a virtual expatriate since 1910. Strongly opposed to the new regime, he now found himself forced to remain in exile.

At the time of the revolution, composers such as Nicolai Roslavetz, Arthur Lourié and Josef Schillinger were exploring musical languages not so very distant from Schoenberg's free atonality, even though they had reached that language by a somewhat different route. The pioneer of chromatic harmony in Russia was Alexander Scriabin, who had died in 1915, two years before the Communists came to power. Scriabin's view of music was nothing if not cosmic. In connection with his later works, such as *Prometheus*, his 'Poem of Fire' for large orchestra with chorus and solo piano, Scriabin spoke of 'stopped time', 'sonorous silences', the 'astral desert', and 'white sound'. He was fascinated by synaesthesia, the capacity of some to hear specific pitches as colours, and the score of *Prometheus* is headed by a 'line of light' — a theme to be played on a so-called 'colour organ' that would translate the pitches into shafts of coloured light. It's utopian stuff, certainly, even if Scriabin's attempt to build the instrument in question resulted in little more than a rather ordinary-looking harmonium topped off with a row of coloured light bulbs.

Scriabin's experiments directly inspired the next generation of composers and, in post-revolutionary Russia, the musical avant garde flourished, the Association for Contemporary Music receiving official recognition. Besides proving a temporary haven for experimental artists, the Soviet system also became an inspirer of new directions. Scriabin's language had been a very personal one that was firmly rooted in 19th-century Romanticism. If it looked forward, it was not so much to the 20th century as to the apocalypse, to eternity. In building on Scriabin's work, Roslavetz, Schillinger and Lourié took their music into still more rarefied areas whose relationship to political revolution was, at best, theoretical. But there were other composers in Russia who were concerned with the here and now. Younger than his three colleagues, and fired by the spirit of revolution, Alexander Mosolov was far more down to earth. In 1928, he produced what remains the best known musical work of Russian constructivism. It takes about three and a half minutes to play, and it's called *Zavod* or *The Iron Foundry*. The music celebrates the mechanisation of Communist Russia, where the machine that had only recently laid bare an entire continent was now in the process of transforming a medieval economy into a modern industrial power.

You can see why the Soviet authorities initially believed modernist artists to be partners in the revolution.

The mechanical brutalism of Mosolov's *The Iron Foundry* seems to owe a debt to the more barbaric sections of *The Rite of Spring*, but then barbarism was much in vogue among Russian composers, whether tied to revolutionary fervour or not. The first symphony by the brilliant 19-year-old student Dmitri Shostakovich certainly had its share of savagery, and Shostakovich's older contemporary, Sergei Prokofiev, composed symphonies characterised by driving aggression and brilliant colours.

Prokofiev's Symphony No. 3, first performed in 1929, recycles parts of his opera *The Fiery Angel*. While its heady mix of sensuality and barbarism might at first appear to have much in common with Scriabin's ecstatic mysticism on the one hand and Mosolov's *Iron Foundry* on the other, in truth Prokofiev's models were quite different. Strauss's operas *Salome* and *Elektra*, Schoenberg's *Erwartung* and Bartók's *Miraculous Mandarin* are the real precursors of *The Fiery Angel*, both in their music and in their psycho-sexual subject matter. Prokofiev's opera, set at the height of the 16th-century Inquisition, deals with madness, witchcraft and violent sexual obsession. Its central character is the deeply disturbed Renata, a *femme fatale* with bells on. The plot is convoluted and generally rather sordid, but in the final act, our heroine attempts to bring her passions under control by entering a religious order. Unfortunately, Renata's presence in the convent provokes an outbreak of devil-worshipping among the other nuns. An inquisitor is called in, but he and the Mother Superior can only look on helplessly as the nuns whip themselves into a sado-lesbian frenzy. How do you solve a problem like Renata?

The Fiery Angel was not staged until after Prokofiev's death, but it serves to illustrate a fundamental problem facing the Soviet regime. Prokofiev's third symphony contains some of the opera's most fevered passages, albeit stripped of their dramatic context. And yet some of these passages might almost be switched with sections of Mosolov's *Iron Foundry*. The danger here for the Russian authorities was that in a piece with a neutral title like 'Symphony No. 3', you really had no idea what the music was about. You couldn't say with any certainty whether it was inspired by images of heroic industrial advance or of demonic possession and rampant sexuality. That's the trouble with music.

By the 1920s, the Russian Communist Party was already having second thoughts about its encouragement of the new and experimental in art. Terms such as 'formalist' were coined to be applied to any composer whose music appeared to have the potential to undermine the purity of the Revolution. I have never fully understood what 'formalist' means or why it should be particularly dangerous, and I don't imagine the Kremlin did either. Probably it meant nothing in particular, but it was a convenient enough tag. Another was 'naturalistic'. So, armed with their labels of arbitrary condemnation, the Soviet government, often in the name of puppet organisations like the Russian Union of Proletarian Musicians, began stamping out originality wherever they found it. Lourié, who had visited Paris in 1922 and elected to remain there, was declared a 'non-person', and a similar fate befell Schillinger after he became an influential teacher in the United States where his pupils included the young Glenn Miller. Mosolov remained in the Soviet Union until his death in 1973, but eventually even *The Iron Foundry* fell foul of the Soviet censor. It was denounced as 'naturalistic', and thereafter Mosolov's creative powers dwindled as he tried desperately to toe an increasingly hazy Party line. The Association for Contemporary Music was finally dissolved in 1934.

I wonder whether Israel Baline, born in Russia in 1888, ever considered what might have happened to his musical talents had he remained in the country of his birth. As it was, his family had emigrated to the United States even before the Revolution, and Israel Baline — or Irving Berlin as he soon called himself — became perhaps the most successful composer of popular songs in history. The burgeoning success of the Broadway musical and the nature of that success were partly due to new technologies. By the 1920s, gramophone players and radios were features of many homes. In 1927, *The Jazz Singer* was the first talking picture, but, equally, it was the first singing picture. The concept of the 'hit tune' may have had its origins in the sheet-music business, but the ready availability of commercial recordings altered the way the general public thought about music. Sheet music was one thing, a recording of Fred Astaire, Gertrude Lawrence or Al Jolson actually singing the same song was clearly another. Radio, the gramophone and the talkies created a voracious demand for new songs. That demand was satisfied by an explosion of song-writing talent. Besides Irving Berlin, there was Jerome Kern whose *Show Boat* of 1927 was a massive popular success. There was Harold Arlen and Richard Rodgers, and we shouldn't forget lyricists of the sophistication of Lorenz Hart and Dorothy Fields. There was also Cole Porter, who, like Berlin, wrote both words and music.

The degree of technical ability possessed by the Broadway composers varied greatly, but the lack of a formal training was certainly no drawback. Irving Berlin could neither read nor write music and his piano playing was limited to the black keys, yet 'Alexander's Ragtime Band' and 'White Christmas' remain among the most recognisable tunes of the 20th century.

George Gershwin, on the other hand, was a composer of prodigious talent. Together with his brother Ira, George Gershwin produced a body of songs that rival those of Schubert in their range and sophistication. Like Schubert, Gershwin would also die in his thirties. To have written Gershwin's songs would have been enough for any other Broadway composer — even one who lived a good deal longer — but Gershwin was more ambitious. He craved the respectability that he associated with composing for the concert hall, and his knowledge of the European modernists and their music was as extensive as his admiration for them. On 3 January 1924, the bandleader Paul Whiteman announced 'an experiment in modern music' to take place at the Aeolian Hall in New York the following month. Public interest in the event was enormous; the box office at the hall reported that it could have sold the concert ten times over. The star turn on the night was the 25-year-old Gershwin and his *Rhapsody in Blue*, composed very quickly and orchestrated for Whiteman's band by the composer of the *Grand Canyon* Suite, Ferde Grofé. Gershwin himself was the piano soloist. The reviews of *Rhapsody in Blue* were mixed, but the public response to the concert was enthusiastic and the work was immediately recorded. At the end of the same year, George and Ira Gershwin's musical comedy, *Lady, Be Good*, opened on Broadway. In addition to the title song, the show contained such numbers as 'The Man I Love' and 'Fascinating Rhythm', and it was an instant success. By the middle of 1925,

Gershwin had become the first American composer to have his portrait on the cover of *Time* magazine.

The mixed critical reaction to *Rhapsody in Blue*, as well as the positive public response, tended to hinge on the consideration of Gershwin as a jazz composer and the question of how well jazz translated to the extended medium of what was effectively a piano concerto. Lawrence Gilman, the critic of the *New York Tribune* wrote:

> Jazz is basically a kind of rhythm plus a kind of instrumentation. But it seems to us that this music is only half alive. Its gorgeous vitality of rhythm and of instrumental colour is impaired by melodic and harmonic anaemia of the most pernicious kind . . . Recall . . . the *Rhapsody*, and weep over the lifelessness of its melody and harmony, so derivative, so stale, so inexpressive.

In one sense, Gilman's criticisms are shrewd. *Rhapsody in Blue* may be Gershwin's most famous piece, but it's not his best, and both its melodic material and harmonic palette are limited. But the foundation of Gilman's remarks is suspect, because Gershwin was never a jazz composer. The themes of the *Rhapsody* are closely related to Broadway tunes, and as early as 1924 Broadway was beginning to furnish jazz musicians with the raw material for their improvisations — what would eventually become known as 'standards'; but there was some considerable distance between what Gershwin was doing in *Rhapsody in Blue* and genuine jazz played by the likes of Louis Armstrong, Duke Ellington or Bix Beiderbecke. The confusion, however, is understandable, for quite apart from the ignorance of many critics about the exact nature of jazz, Gershwin *played* his music with a rhythmic buoyancy and sheer panache he had learned from jazz musicians. When Ethel Merman introduced 'I Got Rhythm' in the Gershwins' *Girl Crazy* (1930), it was a show tune — indeed, it was a show-stopper — and Gershwin subsequently made the theme the basis of an extended set of variations for piano and orchestra; but to hear a recording of Gershwin himself play the tune as a piano solo, taking subtle liberties with the internal rhythm of the phrases, is to hear a performance shot through with a jazz sensibility.

Gershwin knew many of the European composers of his day. He met Ravel when the Frenchman toured the United States in

1928, and after Schoenberg made his home in Hollywood in 1934, he had a standing invitation to play tennis on Gershwin's backyard court — an invitation he took up on a weekly basis. On trips to Europe, Gershwin visited Kurt Weill, Prokofiev and Berg. Yet if Gershwin might have wished to be a composer of 'serious' music and taken Europeans as his role models, Europe wanted Gershwin-the-American. By 1928, *Rhapsody in Blue* had been choreographed by Anton Dolin of Ballets Russes.

Gershwin, of course, wasn't the only American in Paris. Following the war, it had become a cultural centre for expatriate artists, particularly writers like Ernest Hemingway, F. Scott Fitzgerald, Gertrude Stein and Ezra Pound. This partly accounted for the popularity of jazz in the French capital. Another American composer who made his mark in the city was George Antheil, and his fame was meteoric. Today, we're most likely to encounter Antheil's name on late-night television as the composer of scores for a host of B-grade movies, many of them westerns, but in the 1920s he earned a reputation as a musical renegade, and he had a success in Paris that predated Gershwin's.

Thanks to the patronage of Ezra Pound, Antheil was engaged to provide the music for a film by the Dutch painter Fernand Leger which involved animated mechanistic images of a sculpture by Picabia employing parts of a Model T Ford. The film was called *Ballet mécanique* ('Mechanical Ballet'), and Antheil created his music, aptly enough, for a mechanical piano or pianola. Although the composer's name remains on the credits, the music was never used with the film. Five days after the film's first screening, in September 1924, Antheil's music had a private premiere at the Salle Pleyel in Paris, where the select audience included Hemingway and James Joyce. Antheil immediately set about augmenting the score, adding parts for multiple grand pianos, xylophones and bass drums, a tam-tam, a siren, eleven electric bells and three aeroplane propellers (specified in the score as 'small wooden, large wooden and metal'). The following year, Antheil, still in his mid-twenties, introduced the expanded work at what, by now, had become the only place in Paris to stage such a premiere: the Champs-Elysées Theatre. Predictably, there was a riot.

Aaron Copland, Antheil's exact contemporary, was present and he wrote to his colleague Israel Citkowitz, describing the occasion:

The scene is a beautiful theatre off the Champs-Elysées, filled with an audience of more than 2,000 people among whom one can distinguish James Joyce, Serge Koussevitzky, Ezra Pound, Darius Milhaud, Nadia Boulanger, Marcel Duchamp . . . etc., etc., each and every one buzzing with the excitement and expectation of hearing for the first time anywhere a program which contained — oh marvel of marvels — your only true rival — George Antheil! who proceeded to outsack the 'Sacre' with the aid of a Playela and amplifiers, ventilators, buzzers and other what-not . . . [and] brought forth the usual near-riot so everyone went home content . . .

The Champs-Elysées Theatre was an appropriate venue for the premiere, because the *Ballet mécanique* shared far more with *The Rite* of *Spring* than its opening night punch up. Antheil was fascinated by Stravinsky's music. In his *Jazz Symphony* of 1925 — intended for Paul Whiteman's second 'experiment in modern music', though unaccountably left out — Antheil had quoted *The Rite of Spring* and *The Soldier's Tale*, as well as Scott Joplin's rag, *The Entertainer.* But, as its title suggests, Antheil's 'mechanical ballet' also plundered the music of Soviet constructivism and increasingly, in its presentation, the spirit of Dada. At the American premiere of *Ballet mécanique* at Carnegie Hall in 1927, the piece was elevated to the status of a happening. It was played against a giant backdrop depicting skyscrapers, the instrumental forces were further expanded and now included no fewer than ten pianos, and the conductor, Eugene Goossens, stood on a table in the middle of the stage. The aeroplane propellers blew such a gale in the direction of the audience that its members retaliated by folding their programs into paper aeroplanes and hurling them back at the stage. Of course, it made headlines, but the trouble with happenings is that, by definition, they're unrepeatable. Perhaps the score of *Ballet mécanique* had become irretrievably associated with the sensational, extra-musical trappings of its New York premiere. At any rate, it wasn't heard again for 62 years.

Aaron Copland was present in Carnegie Hall as he had been in Paris, this time as one of the ten pianists. In his letter to Israel Citkowitz after the Paris premiere, Copland had concluded by venturing some strongly worded opinions about Antheil and his music:

I am in all honesty bound to repeat my unshakeable conviction — the boy is a genius. Need I add that he has yet to write a work which shows it. If he keeps on exactly as he has started the sum total of all his genius will be exactly nothing. Voila!

Copland's judgement on his 'genius' fellow composer now seems uncannily acute. And yet Antheil's *Ballet mécanique* remains an artistic bell-weather for the 1920s, fusing jazz and the din of city life, with mechanised, mass-produced clatter, and doing so, moreover, in a manner at once celebratory and ironic.

There is one last aspect of *Ballet mécanique* that has tended to be overlooked, although Antheil himself was well aware of its significance. At the end of the piece, the pianola suffers an on-stage mechanical breakdown. It goes out of control, becoming stuck on a trill, until it stops altogether. There follows a series of measured silences, interrupted by doomed attempts to start the piece up again. The composer wrote to Ezra Pound:

> The *Ballet mécanique*: here I stopped. Here was the dead line, the brink of the precipice. Here at the end of this composition where in *long stretches no single sound occurs and time itself acts as music*; here was the ultimate fulfilment of my poetry; here I had time moving *without touching it.*

These are portentous words indeed, especially for an American composer. Because, crazy as it sounds, Antheil appears suddenly as the link between George Gershwin and John Cage.

Cage himself was still in his early teens when the *Ballet mécanique* had its New York premiere, but the aesthetic milieu that would nurture him as a composer was already in existence. The cosmopolitan Antheil was part of it, as were Dada and the surrealist movements. Satie, perhaps above all other European composers, would be another facet of Cage's make-up, Cage later claiming that 'without Satie we can do nothing'. But the United States also had its own, unique brand of musical experimentalism, dating back to the last years of the previous century.

The figure of Charles Ives was influential for American composers, if not so much for his experimentalism as for his use of non-European material. Even today, Ives's music is less well known in Europe than it should be, and when it is played there it inevitably fails to a degree. As sonic landscapes, of course, Ives's pieces can hardly help but impress — the collage of collisions caused by marching bands playing in different keys, or the superimposition of revivalist hymn tunes still sound modern; but Ives never employed these tunes in an entirely random way. Ives's material had (and continues to have) specific meanings for an American audience that it can't possibly have for a European one which probably won't recognise the tunes, and it is this aspect of his work that makes him such a significant figure in American musical life. By the 1920s, Ives had virtually ceased composing, but musical independence had become an American way of life, and it now took many forms. Carl Ruggles pursued a path not too aesthetically different from that of Ives himself. Ruggles's work may notably lack the collages of found music that typifiy Ives, but there is a tough, outdoor — again, I'm afraid I have to say 'macho' — quality to his work that does seem to derive from the older composer.

You could also use the word 'macho', albeit a sensuous kind of macho, to describe the work of Edgard Varèse. Born in France, and referring to himself as a Burgundian peasant until the day he died, Varèse sailed for New York in 1915. The sounds of his adoptive city at once suffused his compositions; his first mature work — the monumental orchestral composition *Amériques* — pounds away relentlessly, the rebarbative writing for brass and percussion occasionally supplemented by the wailing of police sirens. In a series of pieces composed during the 1920s, Varèse displayed a healthily inclusive attitude to sound. Schoenberg may have claimed to have liberated dissonance; in much the same spirit, Varèse could justifiably claim to have liberated noise. Again, it is music that would not have sounded this way without the example of *The Rite of Spring;* Varèse took Stravinsky's ideas in that piece almost to their extreme, both in terms of rhythmic propulsion and also of blocks of contrasting material that refuse to develop, but are simply placed alongside or layered on top of each other.

Rhythmic vitality of a quite different nature is one of the hallmarks of the music of Ruth Crawford Seeger. Here is an utterly original voice, whose complex view of rhythm now seems to be a premonition of the later work of Elliott Carter, Conlon Nancarrow and György Ligeti. In the first movement of Crawford Seeger's string quartet, for example, the four voices are metrically independent of each other in ratios of 3:4:5:7. *The Rite of Spring*, yet again, is a precursor of sorts for this music, but, like Varèse, Ruth Crawford Seeger takes Stravinsky's technique further, making it the entire basis of her first movement.

Such radicalism was a long way from where Igor Stravinsky found himself in the years after World War I. He was engaged on *Les noces*, the last of a series of works, beginning with *Petrushka* and including *The Rite of Spring*, *Renard*, and *The Soldier's Tale*, that are sometimes referred to as the composer's 'Russian period', by which commentators mean those works that are explicit in their use of Russian folk tales and music. *Les noces* is conspicuous in taking these tendencies to their limit, and no less so in its scoring for chorus and soloists, four grand pianos and six percussion. It was not a sound that came to the composer quickly. Originally scored for full orchestra, then rewritten for an ensemble including pianolas, it only found its final form in 1923, by which time Stravinsky had embarked on a quite different journey that would occupy him for the next 30 years.

Pulcinella (1920) was Diaghilev's idea and at first Stravinsky resisted it. The impresario presented Stravinsky with a selection of songs and instrumental pieces attributed (at the time) to the 18th-century Neapolitan composer Pergolesi, but, in spite of his initial reluctance, Stravinsky soon became caught up in making the arrangements Diaghilev had requested. Once one recovers from the shock of hearing this music from the pen that wrote *The Rite of Spring*, one begins to appreciate that *Pulcinella* is covered in Stravinsky's finger prints. The project was successful because the composer's confrontation with Pergolesi's music had the effect of placing in a new — or, rather, old — context, gestures and techniques that were already an established part of Stravinsky's own creative palette. The ornamented melodic lines and motor rhythms that are so typical of baroque music were also typical of Stravinsky: *The Rite of Spring* is full of them. However naturally *Pulcinella* came to Stravinsky, it is hard to escape the conclusion that in the neoclassical style to which this project led, Stravinsky was inventing a new sense of order — one might almost say a type of civilisation —

in which all the elements of his earlier music were tamed and house-trained.

Searching for order also continued to preoccupy Arnold Schoenberg. Between *Pierrot lunaire* of 1912 and the Five Piano Pieces Op. 23, completed in 1923, Schoenberg produced only one new work, four brief songs for soprano and orchestra. Eleven relatively unproductive years was an eternity for a composer who had completed *Erwartung* in seventeen days. Some of those years were taken up with his war service, but, back at his work desk, Schoenberg had reached a crisis. It was the same old crisis that had been going on since 1908 — how to create a convincing musical structure without the tonal hierarchy of keys — but whereas the 35-year-old composer of *Erwartung* could blast his way beyond such difficulties in the spirit of exploration and creative exuberance, the middle-aged Schoenberg was more self-critical. He sought a means of imposing order on what looked very much like chaos. Part of the answer was serialism.

When Anton Webern was composing his Six Bagatelles around 1913, he had noticed that in order to achieve maximum chromaticism, to avoid tonality as completely as possible, he had reached the point where each of the twelve available chromatic pitches was being employed only once. He even went so far as to write out the twelve pitches, and cross each one off as he used it.

> I had the feeling, 'When all twelve notes have gone by, the piece is over.' Much later I discovered that all this was part of the necessary development. In my sketch-book I wrote out the chromatic scale and crossed off the individual notes. Why? Because I had convinced myself, 'This note has been there already.' It sounds grotesque, incomprehensible, and it was incredibly difficult. The inner ear decided quite rightly that the man who wrote out the chromatic scale and crossed off individual notes *was no fool* . . . In short, a rule of law emerged; until all twelve notes have occurred, none of them may occur again. The most important thing is that each 'run' of twelve notes marked a division within the piece, idea or theme.

This is serialism in embryo. The two key phrases in Webern's exposition are 'inner ear' and 'rule of law'. That serial composition involves rules of law is well known and the fact has been used as the basis of criticism of the twelve-tone technique ever since its inception: serialism is artificial; it is a musical straitjacket; it denies creative spontaneity. But what about that reference to the 'inner ear'? This suggests that serialism was not an invention, but a discovery; and so it was.

There is a direct parallel here with the way in which sonata form evolved in the middle of the 18th century. Contrary to what we often read, sonata form was not a set of laws handed down, Moses-like, to the composers of the 'first Viennese school': Haydn, Mozart and Beethoven. It was the outcome of working in the harmonic language of the day, which was as fiercely diatonic as the language of the second Viennese school was atonal. In dealing with diatonicism and in seeking to display it as boldly as possible, Classical composers evolved a formal template that clarified and indeed celebrated the twin harmonic poles of tonic and dominant. That template was sonata form. In contrast, atonal harmony requires that no one pitch should emerge as more important than any other: if tonal relationships occur they will sound wrong. In striving to avoid tonal references, Schoenberg, Webern and Berg arrived at serialism. It was a matter of instinct.

Once a procedure has evolved, of course, it can be codified; it can become a 'rule of law'. So is serialism a straitjacket? It probably depends who's using it; certainly there were composers later in the century who felt pressured into being serialists when their natural instincts lay in other directions altogether. They must have found the twelve-tone system horribly restrictive. But for the members of the second Viennese school, although each of them pursued it in his own personal manner, the system was liberating. Put most simply, serialism provided atonal composers with a formal logic for deciding which note to write next, and for an essentially traditional composer like Schoenberg, this must have seemed like a life-line.

How does serialism actually work? To begin, you need a series of pitches, otherwise known as a tone row. The row is usually made up of twelve tones, comprising the notes of the chromatic scale. Finding the order for the pitches is the composer's job. In his very last work, the Violin Concerto of 1935, Alban Berg employed a twelve-tone row which emphasised triads, so that an illusion of tonality permeates the work, but the normal practice in serial pieces is to emphasise atonality; after all, that is why serialism developed in the first place. So the pitches are organised into a sequence that is as atonal as possible, often with internal correspondences such as the two halves of the row mirroring each other. This order is now inviolable. The series can be played forwards or backwards; it can be transposed, so that it begins on another note; it can be inverted. But it always retains its internal structure. In fact the term 'twelve-tone system' is a little misleading, because it is not the tones that are fixed in the series, but the relationships between them.

So, how do you turn a tone row into a piece of music? The series works a little like a medieval *cantus firmus*, a melodic line, repeating over and over, as the music that is built on it varies and develops. In a medieval motet, the composer often disguises the presence of the *cantus firmus* by passing it from voice to voice, losing it in the polyphonic texture. The *cantus* becomes like the foundations of a building: you're not aware of the foundations as you walk through the building, but if they were not there the whole thing would fall down round your ears. And so it is with the row in twelve-tone music. It's not a theme; you can't easily hear it: the only way you can be certain if a piece is serial is to dig beneath the surface and inspect the foundations.

Between 1920 and 1923, Schoenberg was experimenting with serial tendencies. Where Webern had recognised the sense of completion that the sounding of all twelve tones brought to his miniatures, Schoenberg now employed the row as the basis of musical unity, deriving all the notes of his pieces from it. He concentrated on short dance-like movements, producing, piecemeal, three separate opuses. Two of them were works for solo piano — the Op. 23 pieces and the Suite Op. 25 — the other was the Serenade Op. 24 for chamber ensemble. Although it was the Suite that was the first fully serial work, all the movements deriving from the same twelve-tone row, it was the final movement of the Op. 23 set that was the first serial piece. And here's the rub: though the musical technology was new, the form of the work was not. In his first serial piece, Schoenberg glances wistfully back to Old Vienna. He writes a waltz.

Schoenberg's use of waltzes, gavottes and minuets would later attract much criticism from those who viewed the composer's failure to invent new musical forms for his serial techniques as little short of cowardice. In *Erwartung*, Schoenberg had been attempting to control the volatile language of free atonality, and produced a formal solution that was breathtakingly original. Now, with the new technology of serialism at his disposal, he was apparently abandoning structural experimentation, content to settle for the tried, true and, arguably, trivial. One explanation of this paradox is to see Schoenberg's attitude to form as another manifestation of neo-classicism. But we mustn't forget that Schoenberg had been using antique models in his work at least since *Pierrot lunaire*. The difference was that, in *Pierrot*, the models were subject to parody.

There is an important parallel here between Schoenberg's changing attitudes to form and to the language of atonality. Just as he continued to use baroque models long after abandoning his parodic intent, he stuck by atonality even though his impulse to create feverish nightmare scenarios had been vanquished by the Great War. Stripped of its expressionist aesthetic, atonality had lost its rationale. With the mathematical elegance of serialism, Schoenberg found it a new one. Given the cool logic of the twelve-tone system, did it not, at one level, make sense to adopt structures that were equally devoid of expressionist angst? And what could be better than centuries-old dance forms?

Schoenberg considered his discovery of serial procedures a turning point in the history of music. The system, he announced, would ensure the supremacy of German music for the next hundred years. Well, as we now know, he was quite wrong about this. Furthermore, his Führer-like prediction was, to a degree, responsible for a dogmatic attitude on the part of certain later serial composers that would polarise contemporary music into warring camps.

In 1920s Germany there was already another music being composed that had little to do with Schoenberg and his twelve-tones, but everything to do with the politics of the Weimar Republic. Kurt Weill, in partnership with the poet and playwright Bertolt Brecht, had created a style of performance that had its origins in cabaret, in the music hall, in jazz, and in works like Stravinsky's *The Soldier's Tale*. And yet it was thoroughly distinctive and thoroughly German. *The Threepenny Opera* — an adaptation of John Gay's 18th-century *Beggar's Opera* — was music-theatre as political critique, simultaneously serious and populist. Its deliberately down-market appeal was underlined in the scoring for instruments such as saxophones, piano accordion, banjo and drum kit, and its ironic title — for *The Threepenny Opera* is anything but operatic — was driven home by the use of actors to do the singing.

The Threepenny Opera and Weill's music in general made clear the divide that was opening between popular music and so-called 'serious' music. It was a divide that, in many ways, was enhanced by the growing ubiquity of radio and gramophone records, and it seemed that the intellectualism of the second Viennese school and the populism of, say, George Gershwin now appealed to very different audiences, notwithstanding Schoenberg and Gershwin's own mutual admiration.

There is a Gershwin story which may well be apocryphal, since I've heard it told in relation to Stravinsky, Ravel and Schoenberg. One day, Gershwin plucked up the courage to ask his European counterpart for lessons. The other composer enquired how much money Gershwin earned from his music in a year. On learning the amount, the European is supposed to have replied that perhaps he ought to be the one taking lessons from Gershwin.

DEPRESSION AND OPPRESSION

n 1930, one of the top American orchestras marked its 50th anniversary by commissioning five eminent European composers. Paul Hindemith wrote his Concert Music for Brass and Strings, Roussel and Honegger both provided new symphonies, Respighi offered his *Metamorphosen*, and Stravinsky composed one of his very greatest works, the *Symphony of Psalms*, dedicating it, with an admirable blend of humility and pragmatism, 'to the glory of GOD and . . . the Boston Symphony Orchestra'.

Coming some ten years after the composer's first neo-classical work, the *Symphony of Psalms* marks a kind of exaltation of the style. But what does this term 'neo-classicism' really mean? Its detractors would claim that it implies the aping of 18th-century mannerisms, a sort of musical costume drama, and certainly that describes the worst of it. But, in Stravinsky's hands, neo-classicism was considerably more than that. It is a confusing tag, because the neo-classical composers of the 1920s and '30s did not, on the whole, look to classical music for their models. Yes, in Stravinsky we find the flourishes and driving crescendos typical of early Classicism — the so-called

'Mannheim sky-rockets' and 'Mannheim steamrollers' — but in general it was late baroque music that drew their attention, and particularly the music of Bach, which is why the neo-classical movement, in so far as it *was* a movement, is sometimes referred to as 'Back to Bach'.

Stravinsky and his admirers held up Bach's music as an exemplar of lucidity of form and objectivity of utterance. They rejected the often blatant emotionalism that had come to characterise music in the early 19th century, escalated wildly in the work of the later Romantics, and reached a sort of crisis in the first years of the 20th century in pieces as various as Schoenberg's *Erwartung* and Stravinsky's *The Rite of Spring*. Neo-classical composers attempted to remove their feelings from their music, seeking a form of rationalism, devoid of overt emotional display.

Now, the fact that Bach's music was thought to embody such values might seem odd to us when, as much as anything, it is the expressive nature of his work we value most. But we have only to listen to historical recordings of Bach — a bracing reading of one of the *Brandenburg* concertos from a full symphony orchestra will do — to realise that it was possible for composers in the 1920s and '30s to reach a different conclusion. The vigour of these performances is strongly reflected in the motor rhythms of much neo-classical music, and it typifies Stravinsky's approach to neo-classicism.

Perhaps the first thing that strikes us about the *Symphony of Psalms* is its instrumentation, most notable for what it lacks. There are no high strings — no violins or violas — in this orchestra. At the time, Stravinsky considered these instruments too expressive for his music; the objectivity he required was better served by wind and brass and, in the case of the *Symphony of Psalms*, by two pianos. Then there is the *lingua franca* of the neo-classical style: the chugging motor rhythms; the angular motifs; the little blocks of material, repeated and rearranged. The mechanical nature of Stravinsky's piano writing serves all of these well. But if the description sounds familiar, it is because it holds equally good for much of this composer's earlier music. The piano, for example, had featured in Stravinsky's orchestra for twenty years — decoratively in *The Firebird*, as an occasional soloist in *Petrushka*, and (multiplied by four and stiffened with percussion) as the orchestra itself in *Les noces.* And there is nothing particularly new, either, about Stravinsky's use of motor rhythms and bold motifs: they are recurrent features of *The Rite of Spring*. We are frequently led to suppose that Stravinsky's long career falls into mutually exclusive periods — the so-called 'Russian' period, followed by 30 years of neo-classicism, and finally, in the 1950s and '60s, serialism. But there is no exclusivity. Stravinsky might not have become the neo-classicist he did without Diaghilev's prompting to compose *Pulcinella*, but equally he would surely not have embraced the style so completely had it not suited his musical temperament. For Stravinsky, neo-classicism was not an abandonment of his earlier enthusiasms; on the contrary, it was a distillation both of his technique and his stylistic tendencies. All that was abandoned were the grand gestures of late Romanticism, and one could argue that he had ditched these immediately after *The Rite of Spring*.

Another misconception about Stravinsky's neo-classicism is that the composer somehow stopped being Russian. It is a theory supported by the incidental evidence of his biography. He was a cosmopolitan expatriate, now in Paris, now in Switzerland, before finally emigrating to the United States in 1939. But as the third movement of the *Symphony of Psalms* amply demonstrates, his Russian heritage never left him. The final pages of the score contain music at once static and ecstatic. The Psalm speaks of praising God with cymbals, but there is nothing so vulgar as a cymbal to be heard in Stravinsky's *Symphony*. The voices that sing of cymbals appear to have entered a trance-like state, their triple meter gently floating above a four-note ostinato pattern from timpani, harp and pianos. It is as though we have entered, not so much a Russian Orthodox church, as Russian Orthodox heaven.

The rapt spiritual quality that characterises the closing moments of Stravinsky's *Symphony of Psalms* was also in evidence in the music of a young Frenchman. Early in 1908, the poet Cécile Sauvage wrote a series of verses entitled *The Burgeoning Soul*. They were addressed to the child with whom she was then pregnant. She knew the child was male, and that he would be an important artist. And she was right. When he was eight, Olivier Messiaen's Christmas presents included the scores of Mozart's *Don Giovanni* and Berlioz's *The Damnation of Faust*; soon after, he began to compose. His first published work was for his own instrument, the organ. It is called *Le banquet céleste* ('The Heavenly Banquet'), and Messiaen wrote it at the age of nineteen.

For all that late 20th-century listeners have become familiar with the sustained, slow-moving, sometimes transcendent music of composers such as Arvo Pärt, Henryk Górecki and Sofia Gubaidulina, *Le banquet céleste* remains an unusual work. Perhaps its most notable quality is the way in which it seems to make time stand still. One remembers *Le banquet* as a long piece, but in clock-time it takes a mere seven minutes. More surprising, to anyone unfamiliar with the score, is the fact that *Le banquet* consists of only 25 bars. When it was first published, the piece was written in 3/4 and had no metronome mark, just the indications that the tempo should be 'very slow' and the mood *extatique*. In the revised score of the second edition, however, all the note values have been doubled and a tempo of 52 quavers to the minute specified, as though Messiaen were saying to his prospective performers: 'Yes, I really do mean it to be *that* slow'.

And yet the languid ecstasy of *Le banquet céleste* is only partly a result of its tempo. The tendency of the music to drift, apparently without aim, is also a function of its harmony. Ravel had achieved something similar in his piano solo of 1901, *Jeux d'eau* ('Fountains'), where the sense of weightlessness was achieved partly by the music's concentration in the upper range of the keyboard, and partly by the simple expedient of refusing, for long stretches, to sound the tonic notes of his chords, rendering them literally rootless. Debussy had created similar effects by avoiding major and minor keys altogether, or at least by making their identities ambiguous. He also used the whole-tone scale, which has no root at all. And this brings us back to Messiaen.

The whole-tone scale is an example of what Messiaen called a 'mode of limited transposition' ('mode' being just another word for scale). What Messiaen meant by this is perhaps best demonstrated by a comparison with the standard major scale. If you place your finger on a piano keyboard at middle C and play the notes ascending from it — all of them, white and black — you will encounter twelve pitches before you reach the next C. This is the chromatic scale. The scale of C major uses just seven of those pitches, and as it happens they're the white ones. Now the structure of the scale of C major is the same as that of the major scales beginning on the other eleven pitches — an irregular arrangement of whole tones and semitones — but each of those scales has a different permutation of seven pitches from the twelve that are available. So we say that the major scale can be fully transposed. But the whole-tone scale is limited to one transposition only. It is a six-note scale and, as its name suggests, it comprises only intervals of whole tones. If you start on middle C again, but this time only play every other note as you ascend, you'll produce one of these whole-tone scales. It does not matter which note in that scale you begin on, you'll still get the same six pitches. You will find the other possible whole-tone scale if you play the notes you left out the first time. But that's your lot. While there is a full complement of twelve major scales, there are only two whole-tone scales. The whole-tone scale, then, is the first of Messiaen's 'modes of limited transposition'.

Messiaen, in fact, avoided blatant use of the whole-tone scale, simply because when he did use it his pieces always ended up sounding like Debussy. By the same token, more recent composers have tended to avoid the other modes of limited transposition, lest their work seem a pale imitation of Messiaen. In *Le banquet céleste*, Messiaen employed his second mode, an eight-note scale made up of alternating intervals of semitones and whole-tones. This mode is limited to just two transpositions and, as with the whole-tone scale, there is no hierarchy, so no root, no sense of gravity. The chords seem to float freely, and Messiaen achieves his promised ecstasy.

For Olivier Messiaen, composition was an act of divine worship. He was a Catholic. He said he was born with his faith, and it never left him. We should not be surprised, then, that his harmonies seem to want to float upwards, to sever contact with a system of keys that would only drag them back down to earth, nor that the composer now looked for a rhythmic equivalent for these harmonies. The torpid tempo of *Le banquet céleste* had itself created a sense of rhythmic dislocation — with music that slow, it is hard to hear rhythmic patterns — but Messiaen also wanted to rid his music of the regular metres that had characterised Western music pretty much since the Renaissance. For Messiaen, rhythm meant the avoidance of repeated patterns; truly rhythmic music, he said, 'finds its inspiration in the movements of nature, which are free and of uneven length'. His primary example in Western music was *The Rite of Spring*. Just as Messiaen had built on the harmonic language of Debussy, particularly *Pelléas et Mélisande*, he now set out to expand Stravinsky's concept of rhythm. He turned to Greek and Hindu rhythmic patterns in order to establish a theoretical basis to his investigations. Some of the texts he consulted have since been found wanting in scholarly credentials, but this is probably not important: Messiaen was not seeking academic respectability, he was attempting to define his personal rhythmic language, and in this regard a bogus text would arguably have served him quite as well as a reliable one. Anyway, by the early 1940s, the importance of textbooks to Messiaen's rhythmic development would diminish, as the composer who believed that musical rhythm should reflect that of nature increasingly looked for inspiration to the decidedly non-academic world of birdsong.

The rhythmic and melodic freedom that resulted from the composer's early experiments can be heard very clearly in his song cycle of the mid 1930s, *Poèmes pour Mi* ('Poems for Mi') — the 'Mi' of the title being Messiaen's first wife, Claire Delbos. The poems, which are by Messiaen himself, are addressed to Claire at the outset of their married life. By modern standards, the sentiments embodied in the texts seem very old-fashioned. *Poèmes pour Mi* is the 20th-century equivalent of Schumann's *Frauenliebe und -leben*. It represents a man's view of how his wife should live — particularly regarding her relationships with him and with God — and one might easily feel ambivalent about a piece that can coolly maintain that 'the wife is an extension of the husband'. But Messiaen's music — like Schumann's, for that matter — is profoundly inspired and original, and a significant element of its novelty stems from Messiaen's approach to rhythm.

Messiaen's rhythmic structures sound free, in that they do not fall into familiar and perceivable metric patterns; yet frequently they are rigorously organised. One typical device is the superimposition of unequal sequences of chords. In the accompaniment to the first song there are two sequences sounding simultaneously. One of these has nine chords, the other ten. Naturally the nine-chord sequence finishes and begins again before the ten-chord sequence is quite over, and the longer they continue, the more out-of-phase they get. But after 90 beats — giving us ten repetitions of the nine-chord sequence and nine repetitions of the ten-chord sequence — they are both back to where they started. It is really quite a simple conceit, but it yields considerable harmonic and rhythmic richness; it is both strictly controlled, yet, because of the independence afforded to the individual lines, it offers a sense of freedom. Again, the parallels between Messiaen's music and his Catholic faith are hard to avoid.

The free floating vocal part of *Poèmes pour Mi* is characterised both by the rhythms of speech — the influence of Debussy's *Pelléas*, once more — and by soaring arabesques, usually linked to passages of religious ecstasy, such as the expanded 'Alleluias' that conclude the first song. Nothing quite like this had ever been heard in the concert hall; when we listen to this music, we are present at the birth of one of the true originals of 20th-century music.

Messiaen was not the only young composer to come to prominence in the 1930s. Across the English Channel, Benjamin Britten was attracting much attention, although his personality could scarcely have been more different to Messiaen's. In place of the Frenchman's unquestioning faith, for example, there was Britten's agnosticism; and in contrast to the uxorious Messiaen, Britten was a homosexual: this, at a time when homosexual practices were still illegal in the United Kingdom. Even had that country's laws been more liberal, it seems unlikely that Britten would ever have felt genuinely at ease with his sexual orientation, for he was very much a product of the provincial English middle-classes; in Rupert Christiansen's words, Britten 'deeply wanted' tea at four and socks for Christmas.

His first composition teacher was Frank Bridge, whose own music had been influenced by Alban Berg. Possibly because of this, Britten himself developed an enthusiasm for the Viennese composer and later, at the Royal College of Music in London, he tried to persuade the authorities to let him go to study with Berg. The idea was vetoed, apparently on the grounds that Berg — perhaps because he wrote twelve-tone music — was in some way morally reprehensible.

That Britten did not go to Berg leaves us with one of the great 'what-ifs' of 20th-century music. But there was little stopping Britten's progress. He completed his formal studies in 1933, at the age of twenty. The following year he had a series of performances and broadcasts that established him as a significant new voice, not only in English music but in Europe. Symbolically, this same year saw the deaths of three of the old guard of English music: Elgar, Delius and Holst. Among Britten's new pieces of 1934 was the *Simple Symphony* whose premiere he conducted. By the end of 1939, the 26-year-old was in the United States with his lover and companion for the rest of his life, the tenor Peter Pears. He had completed concertos for piano and violin, and the song cycles *Our Hunting Fathers* and *On This Island* (both to words by W.H. Auden), *Les illuminations*, which set poems by the turn-of-the-century French symbolist Arthur Rimbaud, and the *Seven Sonnets of Michelangelo*.

Britten's choice of texts was always significant. The poets of these early cycles were all themselves homosexual, and Auden, just six years older than Britten, was to become an important influence. By late 1940, Britten and Pears were sharing a house with him at Brooklyn Heights in New York. It belonged to the writer, George Davis, and it was effectively a commune, other residents including the novelist Carson McCullers, the composer and novelist Paul Bowles and the stripper Gypsy Rose Lee. For a short time, they were joined by a chimpanzee and its trainer. The callow Britten was easily shocked and he found plenty to shock him in Auden's menagerie. The poet appointed himself house-mother, collecting the rent and organising meals; he also took on the role of Britten's mentor and set about inculcating in the composer a political conscience that would never leave him. Across Europe and United States there was profound economic depression; Hitler and Mussolini were beginning to flex their political muscles, and 1936 had seen the start of the Spanish civil war in which Auden, briefly, attempted to involve himself. That year, the poet had also provided Britten with the text of a song cycle, and Britten's setting of it showed how well he had absorbed Auden's influence.

The text of *Our Hunting Fathers* was only partly written by Auden. The rest of it was culled from Elizabethan sources. On the face of it, *Our Hunting Fathers* is an essay in animal liberation, but in the fourth section of the song cycle Thomas Ravenscroft's poem about hawking becomes a metaphor for the rise of fascism in Europe. The singer begins by reciting the names of the hawks, a kind of magical incantation, punctuated by cries of 'Whurret!', urging on the hunting birds. Britten's music is brilliantly orchestrated and full of energy as the hunt apparently reaches the kill. But then comes a twist. Among the names of the hawks are 'German' and 'Jew'. The words are not next to each other in Ravenscroft's poem, but Britten quietly and ominously juxtaposes them at the end of the song. Although it has tended to be overshadowed by Britten's later music, *Our Hunting Fathers* remains an impressive achievement, and, at many levels, a most moving one.

The swift development in the early careers of Messiaen and Britten was far from being the norm among 20th-century composers. Indeed, it might be argued that with the growing complexity of music, in terms of styles and techniques, many more composers have had to struggle to find their personal voices. Two others who would eventually develop into leading individualists of the post-World War II era, and who were both older than Britten, had barely begun to show their worth prior to the war. Michael Tippett, Britten's fellow Englishman, produced his first really distinctive music in 1938, by which time he was 33. The American Elliott Carter, just a day younger than Messiaen, had to wait longer still. It was not until 1948, the year Carter turned 40, that he composed his Cello Sonata, showing the first signs of the rhythmic intricacy we now associate with him.

Dmitri Shostakovich, however, was a prodigy through and through. Like Britten and Messiaen, he displayed a precocious teenage talent. He composed his first symphony as a student and flourished under a political system that equated radical politics with artistic daring. It was an attitude as enlightened as it was temporary. When the Stalinist purges began in 1934, with their trumped-up charges and show trials, no genuine artist could any longer feel safe in the Soviet Union. That same year, the premiere took place of Shostakovich's second opera *The Lady Macbeth of the Mtsensk District*.

The opera was based on a dark, Dostoyevskian tale by Nikolai Leskov. It concerns Katerina Ismailova, who lives with her husband, an unpleasant fellow called Zinovi, and his foul and lecherous father, Boris. While the husband is away on business, Katerina climbs into bed with a third man, every bit as revolting as the other two; this one is a servant called Sergei. Her father-in-law catches them, beats up Sergei, and then himself tries to seduce Katerina; so she feeds him rat poison. When her husband returns, she and Sergei murder him too, hiding the body in the cellar. By now, like the original Lady Macbeth, Katerina is half mad and even beginning to see visions of her victims. A servant discovers the husband's body and, just at the moment of Katerina and Sergei's wedding, the police arrive to arrest the murderers. On their way to a Siberian labour camp, Katerina learns that Sergei now despises her, and has transferred his affections to a younger woman. Katerina pushes her rival into an icy river, then jumps in herself. They both drown.

By all accounts, the premiere of *The Lady Macbeth of the Mtsensk District* was a big popular success, so much so that the Bolshoi mounted a new production of it at the end of 1935. By this time, the show trials were at their height, and on 26 January 1936 Shostakovich was ordered to attend a performance of *Lady Macbeth*, because Stalin himself would be present. It has been suggested that the Soviet leader's response to the work was partly governed by the fact that his box in the theatre was directly above the orchestra's brass section. Shostakovich's brass writing was always bold, and in *Lady Macbeth* particularly so; for pages on end it blares away, and a tuba-induced headache cannot have done much to placate the Soviet leader. Another possible source of Stalin's irritation was the figure of the corrupt police chief in the opera: there seems to be little doubt that it was intended as a lampoon of the Soviet authorities, if not of Stalin himself. A third possibility is that Stalin objected to the overt sexual references on stage and even in the music: in a scene in which the loathsome Sergei leads a failed attempt to rape Katerina's cook, his consequent detumescence is accompanied by downward sliding trombones. Whatever the provocation, Stalin and the rest of the official party had left the theatre before the final act.

Two days later, *Pravda* published an editorial vilifying Shostakovich. At the time many believed it was written by Stalin himself. Under the headline 'Muddle in Place of Music' the anonymous author listed the grievances against Shostakovich's opera: 'From the first minute the listener is confused by a deliberately disordered, chaotic stream of noise . . . This is a transposition and amplification of the most negative qualities of the "Meyerhold-manner" into opera, into music.'

Shostakovich was now effectively an 'enemy of the people'. His fourth symphony was almost completed and its premiere had been announced, but after the first rehearsals, the composer withdrew the piece on the advice of the conductor, who was presumably in fear of his life. Instead, Shostakovich began work on his fifth symphony, which acquired the subtitle, 'A Soviet Artist's Response to Just Criticism', although this was not the composer's doing.

Whether the simple forms of the fifth symphony were intended ironically, or whether they represent political toadying, is a question that has absorbed musicologists, critics and historians of Soviet Russia ever since, and the matter has been debated more fiercely since the posthumous publication, in 1979, of the composer's contested memoirs. If we accept that Shostakovich was in no sense a 'true believer' in the Communist cause, the symphony can be interpreted in only two ways. Either it is bureaucratic boot-licking on a grand scale, or it is continuously ironic. The latter view has become fashionable in the West: here was wily old Shostakovich pretending to atone for his 'formalist' sins, but actually putting two musical fingers up to the Grand Panjandrums of official Soviet art. And what's more, they fell for it. It is an interpretation that the music can certainly support, especially if one concentrates on the arrogant militarism of the symphony's finale. But if Shostakovich's fifth symphony was just irony, of how much lasting musical interest would this be?

The problem of divining Shostakovich's motives and meanings is that virtually all the evidence is hearsay, and one quickly learns to distrust hearsay from Soviet Russia. What we ought to be able to trust, of course, is the music itself. In proposing a third interpretation, then, let me confess that I can find little biographical support for it. It is based solely on an emotional response to the music, and I raise the matter gingerly. Perhaps Shostakovich meant it. Perhaps he was neither a furtive critic nor a boot-licker, but rather someone who was making a desperate, last-ditch attempt to believe in the utopian ideals of the Revolution, confronted, on a daily basis, by the grotesque reality of Stalinism. He may have suffered official persecution, and like many artists and intellectuals he kept his bags packed in the hallway, but perhaps, in spite of it all, he really wanted to believe in communism. He certainly continued to believe in Russia.

It is unfashionable, but I rather resist the claim of some, that Shostakovich's life's work was a satirical attack on totalitarian dogma and vainglorious officialdom: it was surely more than that. Listening to the slow movement of the fifth symphony, I hear a heartfelt struggle between the composer's private and public self, his pessimism and idealism. There are even positive qualities in the fourth symphony, which finally saw the light of day in 1961, 25 years after its timely withdrawal. It is a gargantuan thing: two massive movements, almost half an hour apiece, framing a shorter, lighter, scherzo-like episode. What does one say about music that deals so comprehensively in violence, horror, desolation and bitterness? There is no solace in Shostakovich's fourth, no acceptance, no reconciliation; the hushed coda of the finale resolutely refuses to resolve. Even if one lacked all knowledge of the circumstances under which it was composed and then *not* played, it would be hard to avoid the conclusion that this was the work of a profoundly tormented composer. And yet if its contents remain disturbing, the sheer size of this piece, it seems to me, offers some sort of hope. That anyone, at any time, might compose this highly original music, and on such a scale, is testimony to the endurance of the human spirit; that Shostakovich should have done so during the Stalinist Terror was an act of personal creative defiance in the teeth of despotic philistinism.

The persecution of composers and artists in general proceeded apace during the 1930s, and not only in the Soviet Union. Jewish composers fled Nazi Germany and Austria, many of them settling in the United States. Still more of them never escaped, however, and in the 1940s the Third Reich would destroy the careers of hundreds of artists, many of whom perished in concentration camps. In Hungary, Béla Bartók was not personally under attack, but he was increasingly preoccupied with the descent of Europe into totalitarianism. He held great fears for his own country and eventually he too would end his days in America. But the 1930s did see the composition of some of Bartók's greatest music, and in particular his Music for Strings, Percussion and Celesta.

It is scored for two string orchestras separated on the concert platform by a percussion section that includes prominent parts for xylophone and timpani. This group of players is given added colour by the presence of a piano, a harp and the celesta of the title. It is a fascinating piece in many ways, and not least because in it we can hear the extent of the synthesis its composer had now achieved between eastern European folk music and his own style. In fact it is impossible to separate the two. Bartók had absorbed so much from the folk traditions of his own and neighbouring countries that their melodic inflections and rhythms now defined his own style. Music for Strings, Percussion and Celesta includes no direct borrowings — it is pure Bartók — yet it could not have been written without an intimate knowledge of these ethnic musics.

Quite clearly, the two quick movements both contain rhythms that derive from the composer's experience of folk dance. But it is the slow movements that are the most celebrated in this piece. The first is a complex fugal structure, while the third has a slow lamenting theme played against one of Bartók's 'night music' soundscapes, where insects buzz and frogs croak; the composer's use of his two string orchestras and various percussion is exceptionally resourceful here. The impression this work gives to the listener is one of variety: four contrasting movements that add up to a powerful, almost symphonic structure. And yet a little digging around in the score will demonstrate that Music for Strings, Percussion and Celesta is partly so powerful because of an intense unity: thematically, virtually everything that happens can be traced back to its first movement.

The theme of the fugue is made up of four phrases. Later on these will come back much developed in the second movement, nostalgically quoted in the third, and as a full-blown, harmonically altered recapitulation in the fourth. Some analysts have gone further in their attempts to demonstrate the degree of calculation present in Bartók's piece. As the third movement's insect-infested 'night music' attests, in a descriptive, poetic manner, the composer was attracted to nature. But what we find in the first movement of Music for Strings, Percussion and Celesta, is evidence of proportions that occur throughout the natural world. One of these is the so-called 'Golden Mean' or 'Golden Section'; the other is the related Fibonacci series. Fibonacci was a 13th-century mathematician and in the series that bears his name each number is the sum of its two predecessors: 1, 2, 3, 5, 8, 13, 21, 34, and so on. These proportions can be found in arch structures, but equally they turn up in nature: many snail shells, for example, can be reduced to Fibonacci. In Bartók's first movement, the

climax commences at bar 55 — a Fibonacci number — and the movement concludes with bar 88, which is one short of being the next
number in the sequence. Coincidence? Since the lengths of the bars
vary so greatly in this movement — they have anywhere from five to
twelve quavers in them — I am not particularly impressed by this line
of reasoning.

The argument for the Golden Mean, however, is a little more
persuasive. The Golden Mean is where a line is divided in such a
way that the ratio of the smaller part to the larger is the same as that
of the larger part to the whole. If you divide a line this way, you cut
it a bit less than two thirds along: 0.618, to be precise. Leonardo da
Vinci knew about this proportion, and if you examine landscape
paintings from the Renaissance on, you find the horizon usually
equates with the Golden Mean. Counting the quavers in Bartók's first
movement, we discover that the climax occurs at 0.63 of the way
through the piece, which is close enough to the Golden Mean to give
us pause for thought.

Did Bartók do this deliberately? We don't know. The evidence is
pretty strong, and there are similar proportions elsewhere in his
music: we need search no further than the one-note xylophone solo
that starts the third movement of Music for Strings, Percussion and
Celesta for an audible example of the Fibonacci series, as the figure
speeds up and slows down. I am inclined to believe that had Bartók
been consciously employing these structures he would have made
them exact. As it is, they are only approximate, and their presence
probably results from the composer's innate sense of balance, perhaps
derived from his nature studies. Immanuel Kant pointed out that it
was not mathematicians that put the mathematics into nature, but
nature itself.

The lyricism that pervades Bartók's Music for Strings, Percussion
and Celesta, his sixth and final string quartet (1939), and indeed all
his late music, has a natural counterpart in the last works of Alban
Berg. Similarly, the expressivity of Bartók's music allied to often complex structures, is another a feature of the Viennese composer's work.

Berg's second and final opera, *Lulu*, was begun in 1929.
Together with the Violin Concerto of 1935, *Lulu* represents the
climax of the composer's career and a frustrating indication of what
he might have achieved had he lived beyond the age of 50; for 1935

was also the year of Berg's death. Berg is popularly regarded as the romantic of the second Viennese school, the most approachable of the twelve-tone trinity, and there is some justification for the view, although it fails to tell the whole story. For one thing, it is just as valid to view Schoenberg as a romantic, not least for his almost blind faith in what he created. And if, by 'romantic', we mean the more schmalzy Viennese trappings of Berg's music, it must be admitted that even Webern never managed to shrug off a degree of *Sehnsucht*, in those sighing Mahlerian phrase patterns. Above all, the second Viennese school remained Viennese; its music was always, at one level, an extension of late Romanticism.

What we do find in Berg — and this is uncommon in the music of Schoenberg and wholly absent in Webern — is an engagement with popular culture. There are many echoes in *Lulu* of Kurt Weill and the other cabaret composers of the Weimar Republic, and Berg's openness to this is probably another legacy of Mahler, whose symphonies are full of references to the music of the world around him. But Berg went further than Mahler: he brought about a genuine synthesis of styles in his late works, and it is worth dwelling at some length on the last two.

In his first opera, *Wozzeck*, Berg had taken an incomplete play by Georg Büchner as the source of his libretto. Büchner's *Wozzeck* can only be successfully staged when a theatre company somehow completes it; it needs to be given a convincing shape. At the very least, this involves making certain choices about ordering and linking the scenes, finding a kind of dramatic sellotape that will make the play seem whole. Every production of *Wozzeck* is by definition provisional and experimental. In Berg's opera, the music provides the sellotape.

With *Lulu*, Berg opted for a different approach. Instead of taking an unfinished torso, he took two complete plays by Frank Wedekind, and knocked them into a single opera. Berg had long known Wedekind's work, reading it as a student and, in 1905, at the age of twenty, attending a small scale production of one of the plays that would later form part of his libretto. The playwright's own reputation as an anti-establishment pornographer was everything he might have wished it to be and this was doubtless part of the appeal to the young Berg. Wedekind's first major play was *Frühlings*

Erwachen ('Spring Awakening'). It was published in 1891, though not produced until more than a decade later, and it deals in the hormonal stirrings and furtive fumblings of a group of teenagers, much to the consternation of their elders — and to the horror of respectable German audiences. His next plays were *Erdgeist* (or 'Earth Spirit') and *Die Büchse der Pandora* ('Pandora's Box'), they took the playwright's fascination with sexuality further, and both had the character of Lulu at their centre. The simplest description of Lulu is that she is a *femme fatale*, and that has certainly been the preferred interpretation of directors and critics over the years. But the events of Wedekind's original plays and Berg's opera are far more complex than is allowed by the cliché of a nymphomaniac luring unsuspecting men to their dooms.

In the first part of the opera (which is Wedekind's *Earth Spirit*), Lulu in turn marries three men: a medical specialist, a painter and a newspaper editor. The specialist dies of a heart attack when he discovers her in the arms of the painter. The painter slits his throat when he learns from the newspaper editor, Dr Schön, that Lulu has lied about her past. Dr Schön himself (husband number three) accuses Lulu of bringing him into disrepute and hands her a revolver so she can do the decent thing; instead of shooting herself, however, she shoots Dr Schön. There are other admirers in Lulu's life besides her three husbands: Dr Schön's son, Alwa, is the most notable, but there is also an athlete, a schoolboy and an asthmatic old man called Schigolch who returns from Lulu's past and whom she seems genuinely pleased to see. He may even be her father, but probably isn't.

The other principal female character, besides Lulu, is the Countess Geschwitz. Geschwitz is a lesbian, and Lulu is the focus of her unrequited affection. After Dr Schön's murder and Lulu's arrest, the Countess changes place with Lulu in the isolation ward where she is being treated for cholera, allowing her to escape. In the second half of the opera, based on Wedekind's *Pandora's Box*, Lulu, recovered from her illness though physically very weak, runs first to Paris and then to an attic in London where she is joined by Geschwitz, Alwa, and Schigolch. Lulu now becomes a whore and is visited in turn by three clients (played by her three husbands from the first half of the opera). The last of these, formerly Dr Schön, is now Jack the Ripper. Jack murders Lulu.

These are the bare bones of the plot of Alban Berg's *Lulu*. Put thus simply, you can see why the eponymous heroine has that *femme fatale* reputation, particularly in the first act which she spends marrying men and then bumping them off. Equally it is easy enough to appreciate why some feminist critics have viewed the second half of the opera as the work of a misogynist. But it's not that simple. Musically and dramatically, this is a richly complex work whose very strength is that it is open to so many different interpretations. *Lulu* is an opera about the idea of the *femme fatale;* it's also an opera about misogyny; but the opera itself is always critical of the male characters who populate it.

For all these men, Lulu is a construct, really a series of constructs. They idolise her to the point of reinvention, and these reinventions are always to their own specifications. The painter even refuses to call Lulu by her real name, variously preferring Nelly or Eva. He also paints a highly subjective portrait of her, dressed as Pierrot, and the canvas turns up in each successive scene of the opera, its presence relentlessly mocking Lulu's physical deterioration in the final act, like Oscar Wilde's *The Picture of Dorian Gray* in reverse.

We feel no remorse for the dead men, indeed we feel no special sympathy for anyone in this opera until the last scene. Wedekind, an early and powerful influence on Bertolt Brecht, was at pains to keep his audience from identifying with these characters; time and again, he refuses to allow us to suspend our disbelief. In the prologue to *Earth Spirit* (which is also the prologue of the opera), Wedekind has a circus ring-master in top hat and tails present the characters as animals under his command; Lulu is the serpent. The ring-master's introduction is archetypically misogynist, but this is not necessarily Wedekind's view, and it's certainly not Berg's. The music subtly, yet comprehensively, reinforces Wedekind's distancing and the critical attitude towards the characters. *Lulu* is possibly the most musically thorough opera ever composed. As in *Wozzeck* (and Schoenberg's *Pierrot lunaire*), Berg uses existing formal models throughout the score, and he intends them ironically, the forms often mirroring the motivations of the characters. In Scene 1, for example, when the painter, sexually aroused by his model, is chasing Lulu around his studio, the music is a canon, in which a duplicated melodic line chases itself (in Berg's canon the distance between the two voices becomes shorter and shorter). When Dr Schön tells Lulu — who is now married to the painter — that he, Dr Schön, must stop seeing her because he seeks respectability, he does so to the accompaniment of a gavotte and a musette, courtly dances of a bygone age. In Act 3, a Marquis attempts to blackmail Lulu, offering his silence about her identity in exchange for Lulu's agreement to work for him in a Cairo brothel. While this is happening, a solo violin plays a cabaret song. The tune is actually by the playwright Wedekind and was part of his own cabaret act; the subject of the song is pimping, and it turns up again played by the full orchestra in the interlude that precedes the final scene in London, by which time Lulu is indeed on the game.

The entrances and exits of the characters (detailed in the score) are always accompanied by musical mottos and instrumental sounds that make Wagner's use of the *leitmotif* seem half-hearted. The athlete (fleet of foot but feeble of intellect) is represented by thumping forearm clusters from the piano; Schigolch, the asthmatic, is associated with an ensemble of wind instruments; Alwa is accompanied by the saxophone, an instrument Berg had by now made his own, so introducing an element of self-parody. Wedekind's Alwa was a poet, but Berg turned him into a composer: Alwa's name is, after all, very close to Alban. Towards the end of the first act, Alwa wonders aloud whether the events of Lulu's life might make a good opera (meanwhile the orchestra quotes the opening of *Wozzeck*), but he decides the plot is too far-fetched: no audience would ever believe it.

There are dozens of examples in *Lulu* of the musical underlining of characters, their motivations and their actions, but the two most brilliant are not really borrowings from existing forms but actual inventions of Berg's. The first of these is an insistent rhythm in the scene of the painter's suicide. Berg called it a monorhythm and he set it in motion at the beginning of this scene on which it functions like a clamp, imposing itself on the music and the action, getting faster and louder until it reaches its brutal and horrific climax as the painter cuts his throat. The monorhythm then begins to slow and fade and finally, at the end of the scene, it stops as abruptly as it had begun. It works rather like film music: the painter's death occurs off-stage, but the score tells us that something dreadful is happening. The same rhythm returns at the deaths of Dr Schön and Countess Geschwitz.

Berg's other stroke of sheer brilliance comes in the middle of Act 2. *Lulu* is a three-act opera, but it is also a work of two halves, and dramatically these halves mirror each other, hence the three husbands of the first half playing the three clients of the second. The centre of the opera is marked by a hectic orchestral interlude, lasting just two and a half minutes, during which Berg envisaged the showing of a film depicting the events of Lulu's trial and imprisonment for Dr Schön's murder, her transfer to the cholera ward and her escape, stage-managed by Countess Geschwitz. In order to emphasise the centrality of this episode, both the film and the music are cast in the form of a palindrome: the two halves are mirror images of each other.

Berg was extremely precise about the incidents shown in the film. In terms of the general sweep of events, the first half shows Lulu's arrest, her detention pending trial, the trial itself, and the prison door shutting. In the second half, the prison door opens, she faces a medical council, is moved to an isolation ward, and escapes to freedom. But Berg also lists precise images that mirror each other in the film's two halves: the faces of the courtroom in the first half and those of the medical council in the second; a revolver in the first, a stethoscope in the second; bullets and phials; chains and bandages; a closeup of punctuation marks in the legal documents and cholera bacilli in a Petri dish. All of this, remember, in two and a half minutes. The music, which is literally palindromic, reaches its central pivot as the cell door closes. The piano has a rising figure, a chord is softly held. This is the centre of the interlude: from this moment, the music plays back on itself and we get the first half of the interlude in reverse. The piano now plays a falling figure (the rising figure backwards) and the cell door opens.

The key to *Lulu* is the character of Countess Geschwitz. She is the only one capable of real love and Berg's portrait of her is sensitive and compassionate (it may be relevant that his own sister was a lesbian). In the final scene of the opera she comes into her own. I'm not thinking of her vow to return to Germany, study law and fight for women's rights: an expression of fine sentiments, of course, but dramatically a bit clumsy. The most significant moment, for me, is when she is spotted by Jack the Ripper. The scene is played out like slow-motion cinema. Jack turns up at the attic door. He and Lulu haggle protractedly over the price of Lulu's services; in a moment of black humour that is also curiously touching, Jack points out that he needs enough change for the bus home. Even if we know what he is about to do to Lulu, Jack can seem an oddly sympathetic character in the context of this opera; he is also observant. Geschwitz has come in for a lot of stick in the first two acts: Dr Schön has called her 'the devil', and even Lulu (who, after all, owes Geschwitz her freedom) barely tolerates the Countess. When Jack sees Geschwitz, he asks Lulu who she is. Lulu says, 'She's my sister.' But Jack stares at the Countess. 'She's not your sister,' he tells Lulu, 'she's in love with you.' And he adds the words, 'Armes Tier!' ('Poor beast!'). And then he takes Lulu into an adjoining room and murders her.

That Jack the Ripper should turn out to be the only genuinely perceptive male character in Berg's opera is a chilling realisation. It gives the lie to the *femme fatale* interpretation. This opera is about how men view women, and far from being misogynistic, *Lulu* is actually close to being a feminist opera. 'Lulu! Mein Engel!' sings Geschwitz, after she too has been stabbed by Jack and lies dying. 'Lulu! My angel! Let me see you once more. I am always near you.' In what might be taken as an echo of the end of Mahler's *Das Lied von der Erde*, the Countess's final word is 'Ewigkeit' ('eternity'). The monorhythm returns, like Geschwitz's faltering heart beat. It stops suddenly and the opera is over.

Berg did not live to hear *Lulu*, nor even to finalise the score. It was first performed in 1937, minus its third act, thus making non-sense of the symmetrical structure. Berg's widow, Helene, tried to interest Schoenberg in the job of completing the opera, but he declined. He is said to have found the portrayal of the banker in the third act anti-Semitic, but in any case it is hard to imagine Schoenberg being terribly enthusiastic about the sordid subject matter: his own operatic project, *Moses und Aron*, was on a far loftier philosophical plain. Helene Berg now became convinced that the opera could not and should not be completed, and for the next 40 years, up until her death, it was performed only as a two-act torso. But secretly, Berg's publisher had commissioned a completion from the German composer Friedrich Cerha, and in 1979 *Lulu* finally had its full premiere, conducted by Pierre Boulez at the Paris Opera.

In the months leading up to Berg's death, he wrote another work that he would never hear: his Violin Concerto. Perhaps subconsciously reflecting the final words of *Lulu*, the concerto is dedicated 'to the memory of an angel'; the angel was Manon Gropius, the daughter of Mahler's widow Alma and Walter Gropius, the architect of the Bauhaus. Manon had died at the age of nineteen, and Berg, greatly affected by the news, composed his concerto very quickly.

There are many remarkable things about it, including quotations from a Carinthian folk song and a Bach chorale, and the fact that, as with *Lulu*, the piece constantly implies tonalities. Why should these things be remarkable? There were, after all, plenty of composers whose work amply demonstrated the continued viability of tonality — Britten and Shostakovich, to name two — and quotation was becoming commonplace in 20th-century music. The remarkable aspect in all this is that the Violin Concerto was a broadly serial composition. Berg structured his series so that it consisted of interlocking major and minor triads, related, in turn, both to the cycle of fifths that underpins tonal harmony and to the tuning of the open strings of the solo violin. He also employed his series thematically: Berg's Violin Concerto is one of the few twelve-tone works in which we can actually hear the row.

The final four notes in Berg's row are B, C sharp, D sharp and F — a succession of whole tones — and these form the first phrase of Bach's chorale *Es ist genug* ('It is enough. Lord, if it is thy pleasure, relieve me of my burden'). Perhaps this was coincidence and occurred to Berg after he had begun work on the concerto; perhaps he planned the row that way. At all events, the appearance of Bach's funeral chorale in a concerto that is also a requiem is appropriate. Berg allows his soloist to play each phrase of the chorale, after which the same phrase is repeated in Bach's own harmonisation played by the woodwind, sounding astonishingly like a small chamber organ.

In his Violin Concerto and in *Lulu*, Berg consciously attempted to bring about a synthesis between the essentially hermetic twelve-tone system and the world beyond his work desk. His conspicuous success in these endeavours makes his premature death, to me, the most regrettable single event in 20th-century music.

George Gershwin might well have agreed. He was one of Berg's greatest admirers, and he had been present at the American premiere of *Wozzeck*. A few months before the Austrian composer's death, the premiere took place, at the Colonial Theater, Boston, of a work that for many reasons deserves to stand shoulder to shoulder with Berg's own operas. The influence of *Wozzeck* on Gershwin can be heard in the opening minutes of *Porgy and Bess*, even before a note is sung. The bustling overture quickly self-destructs to be replaced by an on-stage bar-room piano which draws us into the action on Catfish Row. Not only is it an example of the musical found objects that litter Berg's opera, it is a direct steal from the on-stage piano in *Wozzeck*'s pub scene.

In Gershwin's pub, Crown, a stevedore, is full of alcohol and 'happy dust' that he has bought from the drug dealer Sporting Life. He gets into a brawl and kills a man called Robbins. Crown's woman, Bess, warns him that the police will come and so he goes into hiding, while Bess seeks comfort with Porgy. Porgy is crippled, he has no use of his legs, and he gets around on a cart pulled by a goat. When the police arrive, a detective accuses Peter, the Honey Man, of the murder, and, frightened, Peter denounces Crown. Porgy and Bess pledge their love for each other, but at a picnic on Kittiwah Island, Crown appears. He is still on the loose and he wants Bess back. When he comes to Catfish Row to get her, Porgy kills him. Porgy is taken away by the police to identify the body and Sporting Life seizes his chance with Bess, telling her that Porgy will not be coming back, and that she will have a better life in New York. When Porgy does return, it is to learn that Bess has gone with the drug dealer. Porgy vows to bring her back and sets off to New York. The passion and violence of *Porgy and Bess* are as strong as anything in Berg's operas, but Gershwin was a very different sort of composer. In lieu of Berg's intricate, through-composed score, Gershwin wrote songs.

Before beginning work on the opera, the composer visited the author of the original book, DuBose Heyward, in Charleston, South Carolina, where he lived with his playwright wife, Dorothy. Dorothy Heyward had turned the novel into a Broadway play in 1927, and it had met with considerable acclaim. Gershwin's first-hand experience of the gullah dialect, of African–American spirituals and of gospel shouting, strongly affected his musical style in the opera. It also made him determined that *Porgy and Bess* must always be sung by an all-black cast, a stipulation the Gershwin estate still tries to enforce. The only non-black characters in the opera are authority figures such as police officers and lawyers, and they never sing. When the detective questions first the Honey Man, then Porgy, about the death of Robbins, his spoken interrogation contrasts, line for line, with the sung denials. It is moments such as these that make Gershwin's opera so compelling: as with Berg's *Lulu*, in a complete performance of *Porgy and Bess*, it is very hard to separate the music from the drama, notwithstanding the proven ability of individual songs to have active lives of their own. The figure of Bess herself is also not unlike Berg's Lulu, in that men — Crown, Sporting Life and even, in a sense, Porgy — project their own personalities onto her. In her responses to these men Bess often seems more passive than Lulu, but she has a degree of self-knowledge that Lulu lacks. She knows that she cannot resist Crown for long, any more than she can resist Sporting Life and his 'happy dust'; she also recognises that Porgy, try as he might, will probably never understand her, that, in her own words, he's 'too decent to understand'.

Gershwin compared *Porgy and Bess* to Bizet's *Carmen* and Wagner's *Die Meistersinger von Nürnberg*. The latter comparison might seem a little obscure — Gershwin was referring to the role of the chorus in *Die Meistersinger* as well as the sense of community that Wagner creates in his stage Nuremberg — but the comparison with *Carmen* is more obvious. What *Porgy* and *Carmen* have in common is their songs, indeed their hit songs. Gershwin was primarily known as a songwriter at the time of *Porgy*, and there has long been a sort of snobbish stigma about his opera. The popularity of some of *Porgy*'s numbers — 'Summertime', 'I got plenty o' nuttin' and 'It ain't necessarily so' — has tended to militate against the work's acceptance in the opera house. But Irving Berlin, generous colleague that he was, had it right when he remarked that 'the rest of us were songwriters. George was a composer'. Gershwin's friend Arnold Schoenberg agreed, adding that, for Gershwin, music was his 'native language'.

By the time of *Porgy*'s composition, Gershwin was at the height of his powers, and who is to say he wouldn't have gone higher, had he lived longer. In his early symphonic works, he had employed orchestrators, but now he orchestrated his own music and did it with immense skill and originality. We can find traces of formula in some of those orchestral works — compare the endings of *Rhapsody in Blue*, *An American in Paris*, and the outer movements of the piano concerto, and you will discover they are virtually identical — but the music of *Porgy* is varied and resourceful, and much of the time, as with any great opera, it is the music that carries forward the drama, the music that makes us feel for and believe in the characters.

In Act 3, Porgy's decision to follow Bess to New York and bring her back is faintly quixotic. His chances of success are surely slim; we picture this innocent and his goat cart arriving in Times Square and we shudder at the likely consequences. But there's something about his determination — and about Gershwin's music — that makes us share his misplaced optimism and will him on.

Two years after the opera's premiere, Gershwin, like his hero Porgy, was on his way 'to a Heav'nly Land', and *Porgy and Bess* the opera — as opposed to *Porgy and Bess* the symphonic suite, or *Porgy and Bess* the Miles Davis album, or any of the other manifestations of this remarkably flexible music — would have to fend for itself. That it remains one of the most gloriously dramatic scores of the 20th century should have assured the opera's future, but it was not as simple as that. *Porgy and Bess* is both serious and popular, and increasingly these qualities seemed mutually exclusive. Berg had not believed them to be, and clearly Gershwin hadn't, but they were now dead. Over the next couple of decades, art music and pop music would grow to have less and less in common.

OLD DREAMS AND NEW DEALS

Richard Strauss's *Metamorphosen* is an old man's music, the music of someone who has lived too long and seen too much. Strauss was 80 when he made his first desultory sketch for the piece. In 1943, following the bombing of the National Theatre in his home town of Munich, the composer had written to his friend and biographer Willi Schuh, describing his utter dejection at the burning down of a building that had held so many memories for him:

> [This was] the place consecrated to the first *Tristan* and *Meistersinger* performances, in which 73 years ago I heard *Freischütz* for the first time, where my good father sat for 49 years in the orchestra as first horn, where at the end of my life I experienced the keenest sense of fulfilment of the dreams of authorship with 10 Strauss productions — this was the greatest catastrophe that has ever been brought into my life, for which there can be no consolation and in my old age, no hope . . .

Strauss produced just 24 bars of music which, at the time, presumably led him nowhere; but we now recognise them as the germ of *Metamorphosen*. Meanwhile he continued to work on other pieces. The 1942 horn concerto — hardly 'an old man's music' — had heralded a last brief creative period in Strauss's life. He wrote two woodwind serenades, whose title of *Sonatina* belies their scale, even if it reflects rather well their easy-going manner. As he made sketches for the pieces at Garmisch in the Bavarian Alps, he learned of the continuing destruction of Germany's great buildings and monuments in Allied bombing. The Berlin Lindenoper had been bombed, and with the horrific raid on the city of Dresden, in February 1945, the last remaining major opera house in Germany was destroyed. The razing of opera houses and theatres was not only of national cultural significance, it was personally distressing for Strauss as he had worked in many of these buildings as a conductor, and knew some of them intimately. The Dresden house had witnessed many premieres of his work. The following month, the site of the Vienna State Opera was destroyed, and by now Strauss had begun work in earnest on *Metamorphosen*. The music came quickly, and on 12 April it was finished, its designation 'for 23 solo strings' distinguishing the piece from the wind *Sonatinas* that preceded it, not that the nature of the music itself really required such underlining.

It is impossible not to be moved by Strauss's *Metamorphosen*. It is filled with despair, but it is also cathartic. Towards the close of the piece, the insistent, dotted rhythm that had been present in the first bar of the original sketch, and which dominates the finished *Metamorphosen*, undergoes a subtle, barely perceptible transformation, becoming the funeral march of Beethoven's *Eroica* symphony. Strauss said the quotation was unplanned, that the phrase just 'escaped' from his pen, and perhaps it did, but it seems like a small miracle when it happens. It is as though the elderly Strauss is summoning the spirit of Germany past, reassuring himself and the world at large, that, in spite of the horrific events of the previous decade, in spite of the evil of the Third Reich, Germany had once produced such generous creative talents as Beethoven, and might do so again. Strauss's *Metamorphosen* may begin as the personal response of an old man to the destruction of his world, but somewhere along the line it achieves a kind of apotheosis; it becomes universal. Music that sets out as an expression of grief, tinged with nostalgia, ends as a tentative affirmation of the human spirit: metamorphosis indeed.

The reference to Beethoven's *Eroica*, however, has a darker significance, even if Strauss himself was unaware of it. Beethoven's symphony had once borne a dedication to Napoleon which the composer later scratched out when it became clear to him that his hero was a tyrant. Hitler was never a hero for Strauss, but the composer's decision to remain in Germany under the Third Reich has left him open to the charge of being a Nazi sympathiser. Richard Strauss was not a political man: with the exception of the paying public, he viewed everything to do with the outside world as an irritation: he was a composer and should, he reasoned, be left alone to compose. In 1933, shortly after Hitler came to power, Strauss was appointed president of the Reichsmusikkammer, the state's official music body. He wasn't consulted about the appointment, and he wouldn't have wanted the job in any circumstances because it took time away from writing music, but he thought it prudent to accept. When the conductor Bruno Walter, a Jew, was compelled to resign from his post with the Berlin Philharmonic, Strauss stepped in to conduct a concert; when Toscanini refused to conduct at Bayreuth, Strauss led a performance of Wagner's *Parsifal* in Hitler's presence.

But Strauss was no Nazi. At worst, he was guilty of massive ingenuousness. Strauss seems to have believed that the Nazis, in contrast to their governmental predecessors, were serious about culture — and of course, in a way, they were. He also hoped that by accepting an official post, he might be able to help people. Strauss's publisher was Jewish, his former librettist Hofmannsthal had been Jewish, and so was his successor, Stefan Zweig. Furthermore his daughter-in-law was Jewish and, therefore, his grandchildren. Perhaps by playing along with the Nazis, Strauss could protect these people. It required turning a blind eye to the political events going on around him, but he had always been rather good at this. Strauss's great tactical error was in assuming that Hitler and Goebbels were gentlemen, and that their word could be trusted. Strauss and Zweig's opera *Die schweigsame Frau* ('The Silent Woman') was scheduled for premiere by the Dresden State Opera in 1935. The printed programs omitted all reference to the Jewish Zweig, and on noticing this a couple of days before the opening night, Strauss angrily insisted they be redone. It was a measure of his naivety. A letter from Strauss to his librettist was intercepted and shown to Hitler. In the letter, Strauss wrote of 'miming out' his presidency of the Reichsmusikkammer 'in order to do good and prevent greater mischief'. The premiere of *Die schweigsame Frau* went ahead, but after its second performance the opera was banned and Strauss officially disgraced.

Richard Strauss was lucky, of course. He was Germany's most famous living composer — a grand old man, whose music was known all over the world. Life could be made very difficult for him and his family, and it was; but his personal welfare was more or less assured by his renown. And he was not, himself, Jewish.

Berthold Goldschmidt was a Jew, and so his denunciation in the same year as Strauss was a far more serious matter. Goldschmidt fled Germany, like so many other composers deemed 'degenerate', either on account of their musical tendencies or their racial characteristics. Nazism, indeed, altered the geography of modern music, directly or indirectly causing the emigration of a host of artists from various European countries. In the main, they headed for the United States, but many also ended up in Asian countries, in Australia and New Zealand. Some quickly disappeared into their new surroundings, others took their fame with them or indeed found fame in their adoptive homelands. By the end of the war, the United States could number among its resident composers Schoenberg and Stravinsky, Korngold (who now devoted himself almost exclusively to film music), Kurt Weill, Bartók, Krenek, Martinů, Milhaud, and Hindemith, while its orchestras were led by the likes of Toscanini and Walter.

But even they were lucky in comparison with those who did not escape. The Nazis' persecution of so-called 'degenerate' art and music was as relentless as it was capricious. Jewish ancestry was, of course, likely to damn any artist as 'degenerate', but there were many others who ended up on the abandoned scrap-heap of Nazi disapproval. In 1938, the Third Reich staged in Düsseldorf an exhibition called *Entartete Musik* ('Degenerate Music'). It was mounted to demonstrate precisely which composers were a threat to the future of the Aryan race. In a remarkably selfless act of solidarity, Béla Bartók, who had learned that his own work was not on show along with the other 'degenerates', wrote from Hungary demanding to be included.

What precisely did the Third Reich claim to object to in music, besides the authorship of a Jew? Broadly speaking, there were two categories, 'atonality' and 'jazz', and since these were arguably the principal areas of interest for European composers in the 1930s, the restrictions put a lot of people at risk. The Nazis never actually banned jazz, but they placed conditions on its performance among which were the outlawing of scat singing, brass mutes, drum breaks longer than half a bar, and wire brushes: all were deemed 'alien to the German spirit'. Double basses were to be bowed and not plucked, and saxophones replaced, wherever possible, with cellos, violins or some other 'suitable folk instrument'. Major keys, optimistic lyrics and brisk tempos should replace 'Jewishly gloomy' slow blues, but care must be taken that the music did not become too fast, thereby undermining 'the Aryan sense of discipline'. 'Negroid excesses in tempo' (so-called hot jazz) were not to be tolerated. Above and beyond this, there were upper limits of ten per cent and twenty per cent respectively for syncopation and swing in bands' repertoires (how this was to be measured is anyone's guess). It's almost laughable — it *is* laughable: it's like saying that atonal music is okay as long as most of it is in C major. But of course, such regulations gave the Third Reich the wherewithal to arrest just about any musician they felt like arresting, and someone like Erwin Schulhoff was a sitting duck.

Schulhoff was Czech. He had been active as a Dadaist in the 1920s, since when he had become fascinated by jazz, filling his works with jazz rhythms. It is easy enough to hear why the Nazis felt threatened by music like Schulhoff's. It is original, innovative, humane, out to have a good time; and you can't goose-step to it. But Schulhoff was also Jewish, and if that wasn't bad enough, his reaction to the rise of Hitler was to join the Communist Party. He nearly got away with it. Following the Munich agreement between Stalin and the Third Reich, Schulhoff sought citizenship of the Soviet Union. Two weeks after it was granted, Hitler invaded Russia and Schulhoff was arrested. He died in the Wülzburg concentration camp in 1942.

For Jewish musicians, the most notorious camp was in Bohemia, about 60 kilometres north-east of Prague. Terezín, or Theresienstadt as it was called by the Germans, was set up as a kind of model Jewish ghetto, the Third Reich's equivalent of an apartheid township. Artists and intellectuals were brought to Terezín from Prague, Brno and Vienna. In reality it was little more than a transit camp, a stopping-off point on the way to Auschwitz, but the Third Reich used it as a public relations exercise to divert the world's attention from the death camps themselves. The Nazis claimed to those who would listen that the residents of Terezín were encouraged to express themselves artistically (which was true), and that they were self-governing (which, up to a point, was also true). An official inspection by the International Committee of the Red Cross found the Terezín residents attending plays and concerts and reading their own local newspaper in which these cultural events were even reviewed. The official music critic was Viktor Ullmann, who was also one of many composers at Terezín. They included the Czechs Hans Krása, Pavel Haas and Gideon Klein. Klein was self-taught but greatly influenced by the music of Janáček and, later, by Berg. His compositions involving quarter-tones are testimony to the fact that even under the duress of internment, creativity and experimentation may flourish.

Certainly, Viktor Ullmann found he was more prolific than ever following his arrival at Terezín in 1942. There was some extraordinary music composed in the camp, but Ullmann's *Der Kaiser von Atlantis* ('The Emperor of Atlantis') was Terezín's masterpiece. The one-act chamber opera is such a fierce satire on the Third Reich that it is hard to imagine how Ullmann and his librettist, fellow prisoner Peter Kien, thought they might get away with it. The piece owed much to the political cabarets of Brecht and Weill, both in its musical styles and its instrumentation for small orchestra, including saxophone and banjo, but it is a work very much of its time and place. It opens with a voice blaring from a loudspeaker, introducing the characters. The loudspeaker is a faceless, dehumanised version of the ringmaster in Berg's *Lulu*; it was also, of course, an everyday feature of life at Terezín. Needless to say, Ullmann's fellow prisoners never got to hear the opera. After an unexpected visit by the Gestapo to one of the final rehearsals, the production was cancelled — it had been noticed that the megalomaniacal Emperor bore an uncanny resemblance to Hitler. Whether the visitors also noticed the distorted rendition of 'Deutschland über alles' is unrecorded. On 16 October 1944, just three months after the Red Cross committee had made its inspection of the model Jewish town of Terezín, Ullmann and the other musicians completed their journeys to the gas chambers of Auschwitz and Furstengrube. *Der Kaiser von Atlantis* had its first performance in Amsterdam in 1975.

World War II seems to have inspired (if that's the word) far more music than World War I. Schoenberg's *A Survivor from Warsaw* was not composed until 1947. This was because, after the war, it took some time for details of many of the worst atrocities to come to light, and news of the violent suppression of the uprising in the Warsaw ghetto did not begin to reach Schoenberg until that year. We may guess the impact the reports had on him, a Jew in exile, because he composed the text and music of *A Survivor from Warsaw* very quickly. It's a strictly serial composition, yet it avoids the academic characteristics of much of his other serial music. *A Survivor from Warsaw* is one of World War II's most urgent musical utterances, and, I think, its most horrifying. The urgency is created partly by the hectic pace of the music — the work lasts a little over seven minutes — and partly by the narrator's first-person account of the events. His account is in English, but the reported speech of the soldiers is mostly in German, in itself a striking dramatic device. The climax of *A Survivor from Warsaw* comes when, in an act of musical defiance, a men's chorus enters, singing the Hebrew *Shama Yisroel*: 'Hear, O Israel: the Lord our God is one Lord . . .'.

The choral conclusion of Schoenberg's post-war statement is perhaps only equalled in its sheer power by another choral work, this time *a cappella*, composed in 1943 in occupied France by Francis Poulenc. *Figure humaine* ('The Human Form') sets words by the unofficial poet of the French Resistance, Paul Eluard. The texts in the early part of the work are bleak and bitter in tone, but as it progresses they become increasingly resilient in nature. In the last part of the work, Poulenc sets Eluard's famous poem *Liberté*. Published anonymously in Algiers in 1942, it was secretly read at Resistance meetings in France throughout the rest of the war and thousands of copies of it were parachuted into occupied areas by the British air force. In 21 four-line stanzas, Eluard lists places, objects and creatures, familiar and exotic, concluding each verse with the line 'I write your name'. It reads like a love poem, and so it is; but the object of his desire — the name the poet writes — is 'freedom'.

Poulenc's musical response was appropriately ardent. The choral writing is restless and exuberantly chromatic as the singers enumerate Eluard's tireless litany.

> On my schoolboy's copy-book
> On my desk and on the trees
> On sand and snow
> I write your name
>
> On all pages read
> On all blank pages
> Stone blood paper or ash
> I write your name
>
> On the gilded images
> On the arms of warriors
> On the crown of kings
> I write your name
> . . . .
> On health returned
> On vanished risk
> On hope without remembrance
> I write your name
>
> And by the power of a word
> I begin my life again
> I was born to know you
> To name you
>
> Liberty.

Even before the end of the war, copies of Poulenc's piece were in circulation. It was rehearsed by a Belgian choir in advance of the liberation of Paris, though the identities of both poet and composer still had to be kept secret. But on the day the liberation came, Francis Poulenc hung the French tricolour in his front window and beneath it he placed a music stand bearing the score of *Figure humaine* for all France to see.

Dreams of liberty were nothing new to Dmitri Shostakovich, and during the war he was called upon, once again, to demonstrate his fervent allegiance to the Soviet cause. His Symphony No. 7 was begun shortly after Hitler invaded the Soviet Union on 22 June 1941. It is a large scale work and its first movement contains a theme whose many repetitions and gradual crescendo have reminded some listeners of Ravel's *Boléro*. The symphony was written very quickly, the first three movements took Shostakovich just nine weeks, after which the composer and his family were evacuated from Leningrad with the approach of the German army. It was completed in December 1941, and the first performance given in March of the following year. This was followed by further performances in the Soviet Union and then, in June, the symphony's London premiere. In July, Toscanini conducted the work's first American performance and it was broadcast across the United States. By now, the piece had taken on a kind of mythical status: the relentless march of its first movement coming to represent a defiant Soviet Union, refusing to bow to fascism. When the symphony was performed in besieged Leningrad itself, the myth making really took off. Shostakovich's piece requires a large orchestra, but the Leningrad Philharmonic had been evacuated, and the Radio Orchestra was down to fourteen members. Retired former players, musically trained soldiers and talented amateurs came together and the Leningrad performance was given by a full-strength, if motley, band on 13 August 1942.

Béla Bartók listened to Toscanini's radio broadcast of Shostakovich's *Leningrad* symphony at his home in New York. Bartók recognised hollow rhetoric when he heard it, and he heard it now. He set about lampooning the self-important first movement theme in his Concerto for Orchestra. The parody comes in the fourth movement of Bartók's piece, designated an 'Interrupted Intermezzo' — the interruption is courtesy of Shostakovich. The *Leningrad* theme is given a kind of fairground treatment, speeding up, becoming out of control and crashing. The trombones blow dismissive raspberries, and Shostakovich's tune starts up again, this time complete with a passable imitation of its orchestration. It comes unstuck a second time, and a third, and then the whole thing fizzles away. What Bartók can hardly have known is that 'hollow rhetoric' was more or less what Shostakovich had intended. The music that was now being held up as a symbol of plucky Mother Russia, that was apparently inspiring its listeners to acts of personal heroism, was nothing of the sort. Shostakovich had written it in response to the pointlessness of the conflict. As he told his friend Isaak Glickman, 'this is how I hear the war'. So Bartók was actually one of the few people to get the point of the piece.

If Shostakovich's seventh symphony failed to endear itself to his Hungarian colleague, it did wonders for the Russian composer's stocks in his own country where it seems never to have occurred to anyone that Shostakovich wasn't just being patriotic. Bartók's stocks, on the other hand, were particularly low. Although a towering figure in Europe, his music was not widely known or appreciated in the United States where he now made his home; neither was he in demand there as a concert pianist. Bartók was ill with leukemia and very short of cash when he was visited by the conductor Serge Koussevitzky. Koussevitzky knew of the composer's situation and came with a cheque for $1000 as payment for a new work for the Boston Symphony of which he was conductor. Bartók accepted the commission, but refused the cheque, saying he wanted no payment until the work was complete. The piece in question was the Concerto for Orchestra.

Aside from its send-up of the *Leningrad* symphony, Bartók's Concerto for Orchestra epitomises its composer's late music. Like late Beethoven, Bartók's final works deal in melody more than ever before. Some commentators have concluded that he was going soft, but I think something rather more profound is occurring in these scores. The Piano Concerto No. 3, for example, opens with a long, winding E major tune played in octaves by the soloist. The only comparable moment in Bartók's music is the beginning of the second violin concerto, but even that does not have quite the same untroubled air to it. It seems that out of the blunt, fiercely argued discourse of his works of the 1920s and '30s, Bartók has discovered a hard-won lyrical simplicity. Yet whatever the outward musical trappings of this work, it surely did not reflect Bartók's state of mind.

The other major piece of Bartók's final years is the Sonata for Solo Violin. Though no less lyrical than the piano concerto, the sonata never emulates the concerto's easy-going nature and so seems to reflect more accurately the composer's personal troubles. The sonata was written for Yehudi Menuhin, whom Bartók had heard play his second violin concerto. The composer knew that it was ambitious to sustain a solo violin for the sonata's duration of almost half an hour; it was equally ambitious considering Bartók's dwindling reserves of energy. And yet he managed to complete the piece before his death, even if, as with the piano concerto, he could not manage the final editing for publication. If the concerto suggests late Beethoven, the sonata pays homage to Bach. The long first movement may be a rather strict sonata form, but it is 'in the tempo of a chaconne', recalling Bach's great D minor partita for solo violin. The second movement is a fugue, and the finale is a comparatively light-hearted dance, though it does not employ rhythms that would have occurred to Bach. The baroque composer would also have been surprised by the finale's use of quarter-tones.

Perhaps the best known concert piece to come out of World War II was composed by Olivier Messiaen. At the outbreak of war, Messiaen had been called up and served as a medical orderly, having been excused active military service on account of his poor eyesight. In the middle of 1940, in the wake of von Runstedt's push into southern France, Messiaen was captured by German troops, and interned in Stalag 8A at Börlitz in Silesia, now a part of Poland. As at Terezín, those in charge of the camp were prepared to allow the prisoners to occupy themselves creatively. Unlike at Terezín, however, there seems to have been no obviously sinister motive behind this official encouragement. Messiaen was provided with pencils and manuscript paper by the commandant, and locked in a wash-house each day with a ration of bread so he could compose. The music he wrote was ambitious in intent and proportion — *Quatuor pour le fin du temps* ('Quartet for the end of time') lasts the best part of an hour. It was scored, of necessity, for the players and instruments available. Messiaen's friends in the camp included a violinist and a clarinettist who both had their instruments with them, and a cellist who, not surprisingly, didn't. A three-stringed cello was provided, again by the commandant, and the first music Messiaen wrote was for this trio. Once a rather ravaged upright piano had been discovered, Messiaen expanded the original trio and some months later produced the completed, eight-movement work.

There are many striking things about the *Quatuor*, not least the presence, for the first time in Messiaen's music, of birdsong. The composer had notated the songs of birds since his childhood in Provence, and from now on they would provide him with the rhythmic, melodic and sometimes even harmonic material of much of his music. In the first movement of the *Quatuor*, the clarinet is a blackbird and the violin a nightingale. As they chirp away, the cello and piano present independent material. The cello repeats cycles of a rhythm of eighteen beats. It is palindromic and superimposed on the piano's cycle of 29 fixed chords, distributed over seventeen rhythmic units. Nothing develops, then; the cycles simply repeat and, since they are of different lengths, they become out of step with each other. If these cycles were allowed to play themselves out to the point at which they all reached their beginnings again at the same moment, the movement would last around two hours. In fact, the first movement of the *Quatuor pour le fin du temps* is just a couple of minutes long; the rhythmic cycles repeat, the birds sing above them, then, almost arbitrarily, the composer stops the music, having allowed us a glimpse of eternity.

For Messiaen, birdsong was linked to his Catholicism. Here was God's own creation, nature, praising him in song. But birds are also universal symbols of freedom and so it's surely no coincidence that they should make their first appearance for Messiaen in this piece, composed under these circumstances. At the head of the score appears a long inscription from the Book of Revelation:

> And I saw another mighty angel come down from heaven, clothed with a cloud: and a rainbow was on his head, and his face was as it were the sun, and his feet as pillars of fire.
>
> And he set his right foot upon the sea, and his left foot on the earth.
>
> And the angel which I saw stand upon the sea and upon the earth lifted up his hand to heaven.
>
> And sware by him that liveth for ever and ever that there should be time no longer.
>
> But in the days of the voice of the seventh angel, the mystery of God should be finished.

Such apocalyptic visions seem to call for music of extremes, and Messiaen provided it. The *Quatuor pour le fin du temps* is virtually the only chamber music Messiaen composed, and it is hardly typical of the medium. The movements range in length from just over one minute to well over ten, and the nature of the music varies correspondingly. Only half of the eight movements employ all members of the quartet, and in one of those the instruments play in unison. The third movement is for solo clarinet, and the fourth and eighth are long, slow meditations for cello and violin respectively, accompanied by gentle piano chords. Messiaen gave titles to each of the eight movements. The clarinet solo is the 'Abyss of the birds'; the spiky, syncopated unison movement is the 'Dance of fury, for the seven trumpets' (that's the six trumpets of the apocalypse, plus the trumpet of the seventh angel); the two rapt meditations are songs of praise to the 'eternity' and 'immortality of Jesus'. Music of such strong contrasts, bearing so little resemblance to earlier classical music and lasting nearly an hour, might well be expected to test the patience of the average audience. As Roger Nichols puts it, the *Quatuor* 'cannot be appreciated by, and could not have been written by a man in a hurry'.

Well, this composer and his audience were in no hurry. On 15 January 1941, with Messiaen himself playing the upright piano, one of the most unusual concerts in musical history took place. In a prefabricated building, the size of a small aircraft hanger, and in sub-freezing temperatures, five thousand prisoners-of-war attended. Wounded men from the camp hospital were brought in on stretchers and carried to the front of the stage. The audience was of many nationalities, predominantly Polish, Czech, and French; there were carpenters, school teachers, shop-keepers, mechanics, bank managers and kitchen hands. Messiaen said his music was never listened to so attentively, before or since.

Messiaen's war ended a few months later with his repatriation. He was appointed professor of harmony at the Conservatoire in occupied Paris, and responding, perhaps, to his academic surroundings, the 33-year-old composer set to work writing a treatise entitled *The Technique of My Musical Language*. Messiaen never formally taught composition, but he soon began to give informal and, by all accounts, extended analysis classes at his home, and these eventually won the official recognition of the Conservatoire. Among his earliest pupils were the composer Pierre Boulez and the pianist Yvonne Loriod, who in 1959 would become Messiaen's second wife. Loriod had been a child prodigy; by the age of twelve, her repertoire included both volumes of Bach's *Well-Tempered Clavier*, as well as all the Mozart concertos and Beethoven sonatas. Messiaen was impressed by her ability to play any music he put in front of her, and he now began composing a mammoth orchestral work in ten movements which included a suitably intimidating solo part for Loriod. He also wrote a part for an electronic instrument known as the ondes Martenot. The ondes is a primitive synthesiser with an otherworldly tone, a little reminiscent of the violin's artificial harmonics but potentially far louder. It wasn't the first time Messiaen had used the instrument, but its inclusion here alongside Loriod's piano seems especially appropriate, because their combined sonorities come to symbolise the spiritual and sexual aspects of love which are the music's principal subject.

The composition of *Turangalîla–symphonie* occupied Messiaen for two years. Its title combines two Sanskrit words — *turanga* is movement and time, and *lîla* is love, physical and metaphysical — underlining the fact that the piece is unusual for this composer in having no obvious theological program. On the contrary, *Turangalîla–symphonie* belongs to a triptych of works from the 1940s that rejoice in human carnality; the others are the soprano song cycle *Harawi* and the *a cappella* choral piece *Cinq rechants*. Messiaen took his inspiration for these three works from the ancient Cornish myth of Tristan and Iseult, best known to us today from its retelling in Wagner's opera *Tristan und Isolde*. The idea of a unity between love and death is also found in Shakespeare, and in Renaissance poetry in general, where death is frequently a metaphor for orgasm. The French still sometimes speak of orgasm as *la petite mort* — 'the little death'. In Wagner's *Tristan*, the lovers long for eternal night as a means of sealing their love, making it invulnerable to the interference of others. Something very like this is wished by Pelléas and Mélisande in Debussy's opera, a formative influence on Messiaen. So the notions of time, timelessness and eternity allied to human sexuality in *Turangalîla* carry all these connotations. The 17th-century English poet Andrew Marvell expressed similar sentiments at the conclusion of the poem, 'To His Coy Mistress':

Now let us sport us while we may,
And now, like amorous birds of prey,
Rather at once our time devour
Than languish in his slow-chapped power.
Let us roll all our strength and all
Our sweetness up into one ball,
And tear our pleasures with rough strife
Thorough the iron gates of life:
Thus, though we cannot make our sun
Stand still, yet we will make him run.

The structure of *Turangalîla* consists of three interlocking cycles of movements. One cycle celebrates sexual love: we might call them the *Amour* movements. Another has the titles *Turangalîla I, II and III*: these form the intellectual crux of the piece; they are the movements in which the mechanics of the music are most fully explored. Finally, a cycle of sorts consists of the introduction, the fifth movement and the finale; they also provide a frame for the work as a whole. These movements combine music associated with both the *Amour* and *Turangalîla* cycles, the introduction setting out the principal themes and showing off the potential sound world of the orchestra, the later movements serving as jubilant conclusions to the first and second halves of the symphony.

There is no getting away from the extravagance of Messiaen's *Turangalîla*. Even today, when the piece is quite often performed and well represented in the record catalogue, and when Messiaen's orchestra doesn't seem so very large — even today, there is something in the nature of the music that is undeniably excessive. This is especially true of the *Amour* movements, and when, in the sixth movement, the *Turangalîla–symphonie* reaches its moment of repose, it turns out to be a lush and rapturous version of rest. The movement is entitled 'Jardin du sommeil de l'amour' ('The garden of love's sleep'), and in it, listless added-note chords drift gently across a musical landscape in which time seems finally to have stood still; above, the solo piano and percussion chirrup songs associated with European garden birds and with night — the nightingale, the blackbird and the garden warbler.

'Time-obliterating' is how the musicologist Wilfrid Mellers

described *Turangalîla*; 'brothel music' was Pierre Boulez's verdict. As a former student, Boulez owed Messiaen much, and in his later conducting career he would be Messiaen's chief advocate, but to this day he has never conducted a complete performance of the symphony, restricting himself to the three, rhythmically complex *Turangalîla* movements, and avoiding the *Amour* music.

Whether one is able to share it or not, there is an indisputable sense of joy and celebration about Messiaen's *Turangalîla* and these are characteristics to be found in much post-war music. In the United States, where in 1948 Leonard Bernstein conducted the world premiere of *Turangalîla*, the mood of the piece suited the prevailing climate well. Bernstein's own hugely successful musical, *On the Town*, had opened on Broadway a couple of years earlier. The music struts with post-war American confidence. The bucolic counterpart of *On the Town* was Rodgers and Hammerstein's *Oklahoma!*, which celebrated an uncomplicated way of life straight out of a Norman Rockwell painting, piling on the corn until it was as high as an elephant's eye.

Of course, the musical mythologising of America had begun much earlier. The celebration, often the sentimentalisation, of place had been typical of the American popular song, even in the 19th century, whether in Stephen Foster's 'Swanee River' and 'Old Kentucky Home' or in Civil War tunes such as 'Dixie'. Tin Pan Alley and the Broadway musical continued the tradition in the early 20th century, as 'San Francisco' opened its Golden Gate, 'Stars fell on Alabama', and 'Manhattan' was transformed into an 'isle of joy'. And the phenomenon was not restricted to commercial music: just as commonly, the blues and other folk music took American place names and enshrined them in song. By World War II, then, the United States of America was the most sung-about country in the world. It had the most sung-about states, the most sung-about cities, and in the case of New York, the most sung-about streets.

This musical patriotism also found its way into the work of the composer Aaron Copland. Copland's early works had tended to fuse a rather tense kind of neo-classicism with strong jazz flavours, but during the Depression years of the 1930s, he had begun to feel a political duty to speak more simply and more directly to what he called 'the Common Man'. He was not alone in this. Elliott Carter and Virgil Thomson, for example, followed Copland's path, as did the slightly younger Alan Hovhaness. In the hands of a less gifted composer, what Copland was proposing might easily have become an exercise in musical condescension, but Copland was immensely gifted. The first result of Copland's vernacular style was his orchestral showpiece *El salón México*, composed in 1936. It proved instantly popular and Copland felt vindicated. Two years later, there followed the ballet *Billy the Kid*, the first of three dance pieces to explore aspects of American history and folklore. The others were *Rodeo*, first performed in 1942, and then a score for the choreographer Martha Graham, whose working title was simply 'Ballet for Martha'. It was Graham's idea to call the piece after a line in Hart Crane's poem, *The Bridge*. She admitted to the composer that it had nothing in particular to do with her scenario, which concerned an early 19th-century pioneer celebration, but Copland liked the title *Appalachian Spring* as much as she did.

Although *Appalachian Spring* quotes only one American tune, the Shaker song 'Simple Gifts', the music radiates a sense of the nation's heritage. Indeed the title of the Shaker song might be considered an apt description of the composer's overall approach: the music of *Appalachian Spring* is surprisingly simple, relying on common diatonic chords, often moving in a hymn-like manner. And yet as the opening of the ballet demonstrates, these familiar materials produce a strikingly original effect. How did Copland do it? It's hard to say. The original score is for just thirteen instruments — flute, clarinet, bassoon, piano and nine strings — and this certainly produces a translucent quality in the music; but Copland also achieved the same effect in his later version for full orchestra. The chords themselves are first inversions, which is to say the root of the chord is at the top instead of on the bottom. Now there's nothing so very out of the way about a first-inversion chord, but Copland presented these chords almost as freestanding objects, and they sound immensely fresh. Well, they did. Partly thanks to Copland's own involvement in writing film scores, harmonies such as these were to become, in very short order, clichés of the Hollywood Western.

Copland's ballet scores have been called nationalistic. But if so, this was a rather different brand of nationalism from those that had typified European music at the beginning of the 20th century.

Composers like Sibelius and Janáček had used their music to advance the causes of Finnish and Czech independence: *Finlandia* is virtually a call to arms. Copland, clearly, had no need for this sort of manifesto — the USA was the most powerful country in the world — but, in purely musical terms, the distinctive harmonies of his ballets and the quotations of American folk tunes certainly assisted with the process of divorcing his country's music from its European roots.

The second half of the 20th century was to witness the continued and increasingly rapid decentralisation of Western music. In 1900, the year of Copland's birth, there had been lone figures such as Charles Ives working outside Europe, but by the late 1940s, something like a centrifugal force had overtaken music. Now composers of real importance sprang up not just in the United States, but in Canada, South America, South Africa, the Indian sub-continent and South-East Asia, in Australia and New Zealand. In many cases, they took a leaf out of Copland's book, turning to the indigenous music of their countries, to their folk songs and dance rhythms. Others simply looked around them, drawing fresh stimulation and creative impulses from their native landscapes. One such was Benjamin Britten.

It might, at first, seem odd to include the British Isles in a discussion about the migration of classical music from Europe, but from the Middle Ages, British music had always been somewhat apart from Continental practices. Since the death of Purcell in 1695, though London flourished as one of the world's great musical capitals, its composers were marginalised. European figures such as Handel, Haydn, Mendelssohn and Dvořák were welcomed to the British capital, but British music was ignored in Europe, and for the most part, rightly so. Even in the 20th century, the likes of Elgar and Vaughan Williams failed to establish themselves in the concert repertoires of non-English-speaking countries, so the advent in England of a truly international composer was news indeed.

Benjamin Britten's music had travelled well for more than a decade, but the 1945 London premiere of his first full-length opera marked the start of a major career. During the next three years there were productions in Stockholm, Basle, Antwerp, Zürich, Milan, Hamburg, Berlin, Brno, Graz, Copenhagen and Budapest; Bernstein conducted the American premiere at the Tanglewood Festival, and there were further productions in New York and California. What seems strange about this international acclaim is that the subject matter of *Peter Grimes* is more parochial than anything in Elgar and Vaughan Williams. Yet it was precisely the evocation of small town life that had inspired some of Copland's music, and for that matter *Oklahoma!*. The small town that is the setting for *Peter Grimes* may have been alien to Britten's non-English audiences, but its ways were familiar enough. And it is these ways that separate *Grimes* from the cosy, down-home worlds of Copland and Rodgers and Hammerstein.

The character of Peter Grimes first appeared in a long poem called *The Borough* by the 18th-century Englishman George Crabbe. Grimes is a fisherman and a sadist. He derives sexual pleasure from torturing the small boys who are his apprentices:

> Some few in town observed in Peter's trap
> A boy, with jacket blue and woollen cap;
> But none inquired how Peter used the rope,
> Or what the bruise, that made the stripling stoop;
> None could the ridges on his back behold,
> None sought him shiv'ring in the winter's cold;
> None put the question, — 'Peter, dost thou give
> The boy his food? — What, man! the lad must live:
> Consider, Peter, let the child have bread,
> He'll serve thee better if he's stroked and fed.'
> None reason'd thus — and some, on hearing cries,
> Said calmly, 'Grimes is at his exercise.'

Like George Crabbe, Britten came from East Anglia. Indeed, after the success of the opera, Britten settled in Crabbe's home town of Aldeburgh, on the Suffolk coast. Not only had Crabbe himself lived there, it had been his model for the Borough. To the extent that the character of Peter Grimes was an outsider, rejected by society and partially formed by its indifference, Britten empathised with him; he too felt he was an outsider. So the Grimes created by Britten and his librettist Montagu Slater is rather different to Crabbe's. He's a more sympathetic figure whose cruelty to his apprentice is the result of a short fuse, rather than out-and-out perversion. Arguably, the leading character in Britten's opera is the citizenry of the Borough — people who 'live, and let live and look', but keep their hands to themselves; in other words, sanctimonious, tut-tutting hypocrites, capable in a moment of turning into an angry mob. I think we know these people.

In *Peter Grimes*, Britten's gifts as a melodist are very much to the fore, yet the music is always at the service of the drama, and it is this aspect of the opera, above all, that is so impressive. *Grimes* also abounds in found musical objects; we might call it 'real music' — music that is essential to the story. Britten's operatic model here — like Gershwin's in *Porgy and Bess* — seems to have been Berg's *Wozzeck*, with its marching band, pub piano and snoring barrack room. In *Grimes*, the patrons of the local inn sing a shanty; the music from the dance hall spills out into the street; a fog horn wails: these are music and musical sounds that would be necessary even if *Peter Grimes* were just a stage play.

One of the most vivid examples, both of 'real music' and of the fundamental connection between music and drama, is the scene outside the church. It is Sunday morning, and the bells ring (albeit in patterns reminiscent of a Balinese *gamelan* whose music Britten had just discovered). The schoolmistress Ellen Orford arrives at the church with Grimes's new apprentice who seems shy and taciturn. Ellen decides that they should not follow the churchgoers in, but sit outside in the sun and talk. As she tries to draw the boy out, we hear a hymn from within the church. Suddenly, Ellen notices a tear in the apprentice's coat and questions him about it, fearing that Grimes has maltreated the boy. This takes place to the ironic accompaniment of the General Confession: 'Almighty and most merciful Father, we have erred and strayed from Thy ways like lost sheep.' Grimes himself now appears, telling Ellen that he has sighted a shoal of fish and that he needs the apprentice to come and work with him. By now, the parson and his congregation have reached what Anglicans call the *Benedicite* — 'O all ye works of the Lord, bless ye the Lord' — and this forms an animated counterpoint to Grimes and Ellen's quarrel. Ellen calms him for a moment, and he tells her that if she will believe in him, they could be free (this to the congregation's recitation of the Creed), but he soon loses his temper once more. As Grimes, finally, strikes Ellen, the on-stage confrontation and its unseen liturgical accompaniment also collide. The congregation sings the 'Amen', to which Peter Grimes hurls his reply: 'So be it. And God have mercy upon me.'

It doesn't stop there. The pitches to which Grimes sang his sardonic parting shot now come to dominate the music. The church-goers emerge from their service and reprimand Ellen for having stood by Grimes so long, and they sing the 'God have mercy' theme to the phrase from Crabbe's original poem 'Grimes is at his exercise'. In other words, the collision is complete, dramatically and musically. Grimes has sung the congregation's words, 'God have mercy upon me', and Britten leaves us in no doubt that they apply more to Grimes than anyone else on the stage. And the congregation has taken the music from these words and turned it into music of crowing, self-righteous glee. It is the repellent chorus that has this opera's most powerful music, and that's as it should be. In the final act, when the good townspeople of the Borough decide to go and get Grimes, Britten unleashes the opera's musical body blow. The citizens egg each other on into a frenzy of vengeance in a fugal chorus, repeating their threat — 'Him who despises us we'll destroy' — like a malevolent mantra. Finally, in a climax of civic hatred, they run out of words, whooping orgiastically as they prepare for the outsider's annihilation.

The music of *Peter Grimes* is hugely assured for a composer still in his early thirties. It is tonal, yet completely modern; like Copland, whom he had got to know in the United States, Britten had the capacity to work in a familiar language and seemingly reinvent it as he went along. Two celebrated moments from the opera illustrate Britten's musical resourcefulness. Grimes's aria 'The Great Bear and Pleiades' is sung virtually on one note — only the harmonies change — whereas Ellen's 'Let those among you without fault', is nothing more than a descending major scale. Likewise there are familiar dramatic set pieces. Besides the correspondences with Berg's *Wozzeck* already mentioned, it is worth pointing out similarities between the operas' last minutes. Both Wozzeck and Grimes drown themselves at night as two other characters look on, and in each case the drowning is followed by an orchestral interlude leading to a brief final scene that takes place the next morning. Britten's capacity for creative re-cycling, then, extends to the drama of *Peter Grimes* as much as the music. What was new about *Grimes* was its covert social agenda; as Philip Brett has pointed out, Britten demonstrated an argument concerning the individual and the crowd that would become crucial to modern society, yet he gave it, in Britten's words, the appearance of 'a rattling good repertoire opera'.

John Antill had no specific social agenda, but he had a subtle political one. Antill completed his ballet score *Corroboree* in 1944, while Copland was working on *Appalachian Spring*, and although Antill himself never received the kind of support afforded to Copland, and so never flourished as he might have done, *Corroboree* itself occupies a place in Australian music similar to Copland's ballets in the United States. As with Copland's 'vernacular style', there was a political dimension to *Corroboree*. In the 1930s and '40s, many Australian artists of European descent had turned for inspiration to the Australian landscape and Aboriginal art. They became known as the Jindyworobaks, taking their name from an Aboriginal word meaning a 'joining': in this case, a joining of cultures. It was a conscious attempt to escape what they perceived to be a colonial mediocrity in the arts, and nowhere was it more deeply felt than in music. For generations, musical establishments in Australia — colleges, university departments, cathedral choirs, the Australian Broadcasting Commission — had been run by third-rate Englishmen who would have been virtually unemployable had they stayed at home. Australian musicians of any talent generally fled the country. Composers like Percy Grainger and Peggy Glanville-Hicks had both headed to Europe for their training, and both settled in the United States, though Glanville-Hicks returned to Sydney in old age.

At first hearing, Antill's *Corroboree* seems to employ the rhythms and melodic patterns of Aboriginal music, but in truth there is little in *Corroboree* that is authentically indigenous: Antill was no ethnomusicologist. The composer himself admitted that the piece was mostly concerned with recollections of corroborees witnessed in his childhood. It is perfectly possible that there are some genuine Aboriginal rhythms in the piece — perhaps Antill's boyhood memories were particularly acute — but what *Corroboree* does have are Aboriginal instruments. The trora, or clapping sticks, are one of the work's characteristic sounds, and the bull-roarer also makes an appearance. Antill describes the bull-roarer as 'a cigar-shaped wooden flat, attached to a cord at one end and twirled about the head rapidly'. The resulting sound, as you might expect, is not unlike a roaring bull.

Corroboree is in seven sections. The opening scene, the 'Welcome Ceremony', is danced by 'Witchetty Grub men' together with 'members of the Emu totem', the following section is a 'Dance to the Evening Star' performed by 'the Thippa Thippa and Bell Bird people', while the final 'Procession of Totems and Fire Ceremony' involves 'representatives of the Lace Lizard, Cockatoo, Honey Ant, Wild Cat and Small Fly totems' with 'much usage of boomerang, spear and fire stick'. One suspects that the choreography that accompanied Antill's score at its first staging might today be considered politically insensitive; certainly, the idea of white ballet dancers impersonating Aborigines and their rites is barely conceivable. But the music remains compelling. The cross rhythms that are established with trora sticks, bass drum and low strings, slowly produce a sensuous melodic line that drops away from the drone-like continuum.

It is pretty clear that Antill's compositional models were European, but it is significant that they were contemporary. Most other Australian-based composers of this time were still being influenced by Brahms, often filtered through the examples of late 19th-century British composers such as Hubert Parry and Charles Villiers Stanford. Perhaps because he had access to recordings, thanks to his day job at the ABC, Antill was in touch with more recent stylistic developments. Like Messiaen's far more elaborate *Turangalîla–symphonie*, *Corroboree* draws heavily on the example of Stravinsky's *The Rite of Spring*, particularly in its use of polyrhythms. So the work is doubly significant. Not only did *Corroboree*, musically speaking, signal Australia's entry to the 20th century, but in its subject matter it also marked a turning away from Europe, with a genuine, if at times clumsy, homage to Australia's traditional inhabitants.

While non-European composers were beginning increasingly to look for musical inspiration in their own backyards, a new generation of Europeans was fomenting revolution from within. Out of the rubble of war came a wholesale rejection of the past, and for these composers, most of them still in their twenties, this meant nothing less than a new musical language. The unofficial leader of this group and its principal polemicist was Pierre Boulez. In 1948, he produced his Piano Sonata No. 2, a half-hour work of exceptional complexity and often confrontational violence. To think that it was composed in the same year Richard Strauss wrote his valedictory Four Last Songs still beggars belief. But the wild discrepancy of style is as much generational as ideological: Boulez was 23 and Strauss was 84.

Pierre Boulez once suggested that 20th-century music really began in 1894, with the first performance of Debussy's *Prélude à l'après-midi d'un faune*. Nineteenth-century music might be said to have ended in 1948, with Strauss's Four Last Songs.

THE **ZERO HOUR**

W e seem suddenly to be in a different world. And in many
ways, we are. Music changed in the years after World War
II; priorities changed. Theodor Adorno famously spoke of
the impossibility of poetry after Auschwitz, but even for those who
allowed art a future there was a sense that the events of the war
necessitated new beginnings. So far as jazz was concerned, Glenn
Miller had disappeared (literally), to be replaced by Charlie Parker,
Miles Davis and Dizzy Gillespie. In the process, jazz ceased to be the
pop music of the day, typified by the big band swing of the 1940s,
and became, in comparison, the province of the musical gourmet. It
was much the same in the concert hall. By 1950, Richard Strauss
had died. So had such crowd pleasers as Rahkmaninov and Manuel
de Falla, together with early modernists like Bartók, Webern and
Kurt Weill. And by the end of the following year, as Pierre Boulez
was swift to point out, Schoenberg, too, was dead.

Boulez's own development as a composer was rapid, to say the
least. In 1944, aged 19, he had joined Messiaen's harmony class at
the Paris Conservatoire, and he was soon attending the famous

private analysis sessions. Here, for a select group of students, Messiaen pulled apart the rhythmic structure of *The Rite of Spring*, and Boulez was introduced to Debussy's *Jeux* and Berg's *Wozzeck;* at a concert conducted by René Leibowitz the following year, he heard his first piece of serial music, the Wind Quintet of Schoenberg and, like Schoenberg before him, became convinced that serialism was the future. Only twelve months later, Boulez composed his *Sonatine* for flute and piano, and over the next two years the music poured forth: the first piano sonata, two ambitious cantatas to words by the surrealist poet René Char, and, in 1948, the massive, *Hammerklavier*-like second piano sonata. Boulez was still only 23.

Along with his precocious talent and fierce intelligence, Boulez was also developing a devastating line in polemicism. Fired with something akin to revolutionary zeal, he was a tireless activist on behalf of the music in which he believed. Boulez had nothing but scorn for the neo-classicism of Paris's prominent composers, including Francis Poulenc, Arthur Honegger and Darius Milhaud. Stravinsky, 25 years a neo-classicist, was also high on Boulez's hit list. An admirer of Stravinsky's music up to about 1920, Boulez viewed pretty much everything Stravinsky had composed since as unacceptably retrogressive. In 1945, over three decades after *The Rite of Spring*, another Stravinsky premiere was booed at Paris's Champs-Elysées theatre. This time the objection to the music was not its challenging modernity, but rather the opposite. The piece was Stravinsky's *Danses concertantes*, and leading the hecklers was the young Boulez.

Schoenberg was not to be spared either. The Wind Quintet may have opened Boulez's ears to serial music, but he was dismissive of Schoenberg's academicism. As part of a tribute to the late composer, the magazine *The Score* commissioned an article from Boulez for its issue of February 1952. His eulogy came in the form of a diatribe, bluntly entitled 'Schoenberg is Dead'. What Boulez meant was that, in the metaphorical as well as the literal sense, this composer had had his day. Schoenberg had chickened out. With serialism, he had pioneered a new musical language, but along with this advance came a simultaneous retreat, because he had failed to adopt an equally bold attitude to structure. In appropriating baroque dance forms such as gavottes and musettes, Schoenberg, in Boulez's view, had poured new wine into old vessels.

I think his objections are understandable, and if it was conceivably in poor taste to voice them in the form of an obituary, it was typical enough of the young composer's firebrand mentality. Boulez believed the late 20th century had to find new structures that reflected the language of serialism, and he was in no doubt that this was the only valid language, believing that any composer who failed to recognise the need for it was scarcely worthy. Yet if Schoenberg was now rejected, his one-time pupil Anton Webern was practically canonised by Boulez and his colleagues. Webern's death alone might have provided him with this status: at the end of the war, in American-occupied Austria, he was shot by a trigger-happy GI.

At one level, Boulez's elevation of Webern makes little sense, for Webern employed historical forms almost as frequently as Schoenberg had done. The surface of Webern's work, however, was quite different from Schoenberg's. Webern's music had undergone a severe transformation in the inter-war years. His pieces were as short as ever, but they were stripped of instrumental effect: no more of those whispering string harmonics, mandolins or celestas; Webern had become interested primarily in pitches and durations. It was like the change that occurred in the painting of his contemporary, the Russian-born Wassily Kandinsky. If you look at Kandinsky's work prior to World War I, you are struck by the bright colour and energy of the paintings; there is a sense of abandon. In the 1920s and '30s, however, the colour and energy no longer burst off the canvas; they are controlled, harnessed, directed inwards. So it was with Webern's music.

Webern systematically exploited what Schoenberg had described as *Klangfarbenmelodie* — a melodic line made up of instrumental colours. In Webern's later music, the timbre or colour of a note came to define its position in a melody, just as much as the pitch itself; and the timbre was governed both by the instrument that played it and the octave in which it was played. If you write out one of Webern's melodic lines, bringing all the pitches within the span of a single octave, and then play the line on a single instrument, it will still sound atonal, but it will have the recognisable contours of a conventional melody. But if, as Webern did, you spread the melody over several octaves and you allocate the first two notes to a clarinet, the next to a harp, the next three to a muted trumpet, and so on, then you fragment it: it's like writing a word and using a different colour pen for each letter. You can hear the process very clearly in Webern's orchestral arrangement of the six-part Ricercata from J.S. Bach's *A Musical Offering*. Not a note of Bach's music is changed, but it is subjected to the principals of *Klangfarbenmelodie*, so that the familiar theme is now passed around between several instruments. What one hears, by virtue of Webern's orchestration, is a simultaneous performance and analysis of Bach's music; the changing instrumental timbre highlights the motivic structure of the Ricercata, and this is also true in Webern's original compositions. Webern's use of instrumental colour may no longer have been atmospheric, but it remained essentially expressive. It brought a sharp clarity to his compositions; it served to explain the notes; it helped the music to express itself.

The idea that a row of pitches might be tied to its own analysis appealed to the new generation of European composers. Besides Boulez, they included Bruno Maderna, Luigi Nono, Hans Werner Henze and Bernd Alois Zimmermann. Their regular meeting place was at Darmstadt in Germany, where a summer school and festival of new music was held each year. All of them admired Webern, and one of the reasons was Webern's attempts in his very last works, especially the second cantata, to find a way of employing the twelve-tone row so that it worked vertically as well as horizontally. Early serial music had applied the techniques to melodic lines, but just how these lines sounded together — the harmony — was often a matter of chance. Webern reasoned that if you were going to control pitch in a piece of music, you had to apply those controls thoroughly; you couldn't just use the technique to generate the melodic lines, and let the harmony go hang. But the Darmstadt boys went further. If pitch were to be rigorously systematised in a piece of music, was it good enough to leave all the other musical decisions up to the mere whim of the composer? Couldn't the series also be used to dictate the relative loudness and lengths of notes?

The first European step in the direction of total serialism came, not from Boulez or even one of his generation, but from Messiaen, in his *Quatre études de rythme* (Four Studies in Rhythm) for solo piano. The second of these pieces, actually composed at Darmstadt in 1949, was called *Mode de valeurs et d'intensités* ('Mode of Values and

Intensities'). As its title suggests, the music was constructed from a chart that allotted each pitch a preordained duration, style of articulation and dynamic, ranging from a heavily accented *fff*, to a barely audible *ppp*. Middle C, for example, is always played *fortissimo*, with an accented attack and held for five crotchet beats; the B flat above the treble stave is always *pianissimo* and five semiquavers in length. As it happens, *Modes de valeurs et d'intensités* was not a serial piece — Messiaen chose the pitches freely from his chart — but the fact that a pitch came with its own length and set of dynamic parameters gave each note a separate existence, almost an individual personality. The fragmentation of melody that had begun with Webern was now complete. The pitches in Messiaen's piece twinkle independently, like the stars in the night sky, and it was precisely this quality that impressed one of Darmstadt's newest recruits, when he heard the piece in 1951. 'Fantastic star music,' Karlheinz Stockhausen called it.

Stockhausen recognised in Messiaen's music, not the kernel of some new method, so much as the opening up of a universe of sonority. This 'fantastic star music' could be heard as random points of sound, but as with real stars, it was also possible for the listener to make mental connections between them, to discover constellations among the flickering pitches. When he heard the piece, Stockhausen was still a student, turning out solid if unremarkable choral settings of Verlaine and a rather dull little *Sonatine* for violin and piano; so it's a testament to his ears and to his imagination, that the confrontation with Messiaen's music should have transformed him, virtually overnight, into the composer of *Kreuzspiel*.

In *Kreuzspiel* — ('Cross-play') — Stockhausen took the isolated pitch events of Messiaen's 'star music', and created a structure for them that was complex yet, at one level, immediately obvious. The music is still concerned with individual pitches, but the composer helps us to hear the constellations by joining the dots. *Kreuzspiel* is scored for oboe, bass clarinet, piano and three percussionists. Stockhausen divides the twelve chromatic pitches into two groups: six and six. One group descends from the very top of the piano keyboard, the other works its way up from the very bottom. As they approach each other, they arrive at the middle four octaves whose range encompasses the oboe and bass clarinet, and these instruments now join in. As the two groups of pitches cross over each other they are sounded more frequently and the music gets louder. Then the process is reversed, the six pitches from the top move down to the bottom, and the six from the bottom rise to the top. The percussionists have a dual role in *Kreuzspiel*. They create a continuum of sound, gently tapping out pulses that 'measure' the distances between the pitches; but they also have their own *fortissimo* attacks which sometimes coincide with the pitches of other instruments, and when this happens the pitch turns up in the 'wrong' octave. The percussion, then, both clarifies the musical process that Stockhausen has set in motion, and attempts to derail it.

Stockhausen now moved to Paris where he joined Messiaen's class, but in many ways his apprenticeship was already over. *Kreuzspiel* had been an epiphany. I can think of no other composers who have revealed themselves so suddenly and so completely in a single early work. Almost all Stockhausen's musical personality is present in *Kreuzspiel*. In his use of astronomical imagery we discover his belief that music is not about human beings expressing their emotions, but about human beings exploring the universe. Very quickly, this became an altogether more mystical view of music as something coming from outer space, perhaps from God, with the composer acting as a kind of radio receiver. But *Kreuzspiel* is also a good example of Stockhausen's delight in casually tossing spanners into the intricate machinery of his music (when one of the percussion parts interferes with the smooth running of one of the other parts). Music may originate somewhere else, but it still has to be realised by humans, so it is bound to go wrong from time to time, or at least be subject to human limitations, and Stockhausen would continue to build these moments into his pieces, often humorously.

Human frailty was of small concern to Pierre Boulez in 1951. What Boulez had learned from Messiaen's *Mode de valeurs et d'intensités* was not about the stars, but about organisation, and in his new work for two pianos, given the stark and significant title of *Structures*, he moved ever closer to total serialism. The desire for maximum organisation is not hard to understand. It is perfectly possible to view it as a response to the values of previous generations. Too much will, too much individual ego had resulted in global catastrophe. Whether Boulez was thinking in such socio-political terms is debatable — I rather doubt it — but certainly, behind his commitment to serial procedures there was a desire to be done with romantic attitudes. Total serialism aimed to give music a mathematical infallibility — something last wished for in the Middle Ages. Every sound would be subject to analytical avouchment, free from the moment to moment vagaries of human volition. And from this 'zero hour' it would be possible to forge musical languages for the future.

It is interesting to compare the musical activity centred on Darmstadt, with contemporary developments in the United States. As early as 1948 — before Messiaen's groundbreaking piano piece — the American composer Milton Babbitt had developed his own form of total serialism. At the time, his music was still unknown in Europe, and what Babbitt came up with was both more and less advanced than the European models. In his Three Compositions for Piano, Babbitt had applied serial procedures to pitch, duration, dynamics, timbre and register, so he had gone further down the path of total serialism than anyone in Europe, at least until Boulez's *Structures*. For Babbitt, this degree of organisation seems to have arisen from his wish to integrate all the elements of music, hence his preferred term 'integral serialism'. You only have to compare Babbitt's piece with Boulez's second sonata, composed the same year, to hear that the instability and sudden eruptions of sound that characterise Boulez's piece scarcely feature in Babbitt's; it's impossible to imagine Babbitt writing into his score (as Boulez does, at the climax of his sonata's last movement) the instruction to 'pulverise the sound'. Babbitt was after cool, rational objectivity in his music. Even his titles reflected this. Following the Three Compositions for Piano, came Composition for Four Instruments and Composition for 12 Instruments, and, in 1950, Composition for Viola and Piano. It amounts to a conscious avoidance of anything too obviously poetic.

From an aesthetic point of view, John Cage was very close to his compatriot Babbitt. Cage aimed to remove his ego from the act of composition. But where Babbitt attempted objectivity through calculation and carefully wrought charts and systems, Cage did it by tossing coins. Cage's commitment to 'chance procedures' was partly inspired by Eastern philosophy, particularly Zen Buddhism, and it only grew stronger as Cage grew older. In 1950, his colleague and pupil Christian Wolff gave him a copy of the *I Ching* — the Chinese 'Book of Changes' — and Cage recognised the possibility of using it to generate the details of his music. The following year, he employed it in a work for solo piano, composed for the contemporary music specialist David Tudor. *Music of Changes* has many of the crystalline sounds and complex rhythmic patterns of Boulez's first book of *Structures* — there are passages that might be interchangeable — yet for all the sounding similarities between Cage's music and Boulez's, a philosophical gulf had opened. The central issue, in a word, was control. For Boulez, composition was an act of calculation; for Cage it was a matter of chance, albeit chance operating under the rigorous discipline of the *I Ching*.

Besides David Tudor and Christian Wolff, the other members of Cage's expanding coterie included the composers Earle Brown and Morton Feldman. Their world was one in which the influences of literature and dance, and especially the visual arts, was stronger than that of other music. By the early 1950s, this group of New York composers had effectively set itself up as the loyal opposition to its European colleagues who visited Darmstadt each summer. In 1952, the year after *Music of Changes*, Cage abdicated responsibility for the sound of his music more thoroughly than ever before.

Without a doubt, Cage's most famous piece is 4'33" for solo piano: surely a musical zero hour beyond Boulez's wildest imaginings. It is in three movements, and each is marked 'tacet', which is the word that appears in an orchestral player's part telling them not to play. In 4'33", the pianist comes on stage, acknowledges the applause, sits, raises the keyboard lid, goes to play, but doesn't. After a minute or so, the pianist relaxes; perhaps a page is turned. The pianist goes to play once more, but still doesn't. This happens a third time. After four minutes and 33 seconds, the pianist closes the lid, rises, acknowledges any further applause there might be, and leaves the stage. The debt to Satie and the Dadaists is obvious, and Cage, it must be said, had an excellent sense of humour. If I were to suggest that 4'33" is one of the most important pieces ever composed, I imagine I'd be laughed at. But I'm not joking, and neither was Cage.

In order to appreciate 4'33", one needs to 'hear' it, in the presence of an innocent audience. Today, that's pretty hard to do, because the piece has gained a certain notoriety and audiences generally know what's coming. But imagine one that doesn't. At the outset of the piece, the audience is all expectation, as before the start of any piece. The members of the audience fall quiet; perhaps some of them edge forward in their seats; there is an air of concentration. In 4'33", of course, this pregnant pause soon goes over term. The audience wonders what's happening. Is it witnessing an artistic tantrum? Is the pianist waiting for complete silence? Perhaps the lighting isn't quite right. Some audience members, by now, will be holding their breath. The silence will, as they say, be deafening.

But is it silence? In such circumstances, the merest shuffle of feet becomes an event. One audience member whispers something; everybody hears. A dropped program is shockingly loud. Watches tick. Breathing patterns alter. Perhaps we register distant traffic noise; we had never noticed the traffic was audible in here before. How often do we listen this intently? Would our attention be so rapt if the pianist were actually playing? Cage teaches us in this piece that there is no such thing as silence. If we will only be still, for a few moments, we will hear many sounds we would ordinarily blot out. By virtue of our attention to them, the sounds become music.

Cage would have argued that the act of listening was all that was necessary for sound to become music. If we find his definition too extreme, we should bear in mind that as we listen, we probably start to rank the sounds we hear; we seek out patterns; we impose our own senses of order; we make connections between the sounds. In other words, perhaps we, the listeners, make the sounds into music. And if so, perhaps the opposite can also be true: if we ignore Beethoven's fifth symphony, if we go about our business as it plays on the radio, it is possible that it ceases to be music and becomes mere sound.

Cage later revised 4'33". In its second version, a piano was no longer specified: the piece could be played by any instrument. It could also be shorter or longer than 4'33". Cage had now removed the only two stipulations he had ever made regarding the piece.

By the time Boulez completed the first book of *Structures*, he had said all he needed to say about total serialism. The second book, which he worked on at the end of the 1950s, was a radically different piece allowing the two pianists a good deal of freedom, especially in the later stages. In between the two books of *Structures*, however, Boulez had written a masterpiece. In it, he abandoned the monochrome world of the piano keyboard and unleashed a kaleidoscope of colour.

Le marteau sans maître ('The Hammer Without a Master'), for contralto and mixed ensemble, takes its title and its texts from a volume of poems by René Char. *Le marteau's* reputation as one of the seminal pieces of the post-war avant garde is well earned, but not everything about the work is without precedent. There is no doubting, for instance, the debt to Schoenberg's *Pierrot lunaire*. It's everywhere, from the scoring for female voice and ensemble, to the continually varying instrumentation, to the presence of one movement for voice and flute alone, to the division of the work into three cycles. But the differences outweigh the resemblances. *Pierrot* has 21 movements, compared to only nine in *Le marteau*, and Boulez uses the singer in just four of these. Also where Schoenberg opted for three consecutive cycles of seven poems in *Pierrot lunaire*, Boulez offers a more complex solution. He may have dubbed Messiaen's *Turangalîla–symphonie* 'brothel music', but Boulez was not above borrowing ideas from his former teacher. For the structure of *Le marteau sans maître*, Boulez turned to the old brothel-keeper himself, creating three interlocking cycles of movements that recall the similar arrangement in *Turangalîla*.

As in *Turangalîla*, these cycles are unequal in length and discrete in character, and, in *Le marteau*, each is related to one of René Char's poems. The first is 'L'artisanat furieux' ('Furious Artisans'). Boulez allocates three of *Le marteau's* movements to this poem: a simple vocal setting (this is the one with the flute) and two brief but frantic ensemble pieces, forming a prelude and postlude. He places the prelude first in the work, the vocal setting third, and the postlude seventh. Next comes Char's bleak, three-line poem 'Bourreaux de solitude' ('Hangmen of solitude'), and this has four movements associated with it: the vocal setting and three instrumental 'commentaries', notable for their often pugnacious use of unpitched percussion. The vocal setting is placed sixth, the commentaries come second, fourth and eighth. Finally, there are two very different versions of 'Bel édifice et les présentiments' ('Beautiful building and the premonitions'). Six lines long, this is the most extended of the three poems. Both settings of it are vocal and they form the central fifth movement and the last one.

This mixing up of the sung texts and their instrumental commentaries is more than just capricious, and though the idea may have been sparked by Messiaen's *Turangalîla*, it also reflects the poetry rather well. For René Char, a collection of poems was like a group of islands, an archipelago. And within a single poem, the various images are also islands. The reader hops from one island to another — like on a Greek holiday — in the process, creating his or her own personal experience. By interleaving the three cycles in an apparently random way (actually it's not random at all), Boulez offers a musical counterpart to Char's poetic manner.

> The footstep has receded the walker is silent
> On the dial of Imitation
> The Pendulum sets in motion its load of reflex granite.

Char's poems contain unpredictable dream images of pent-up violence, and Boulez responds to them with music of great variety. His instrumental ensemble of six players is divided, like the movements, into three uneven groups. The first consists of three melody instruments — alto flute, guitar and viola — one blown, one plucked, one bowed (though the viola also plays *pizzicato* from time to time). What unites these three is their alto register which, of course, they share with the singer. Next come two keyboard percussion instruments, the vibraphone and the xylorimba — one metal, one wooden and both struck with mallets. The solitary sixth player has a wide range of unpitched percussion, but Boulez employs it sparingly, asking for it in only five of the nine movements, and restricting certain sonorities to individual movements — the large gong and the tam-tams, for instance, are saved up for the closing moments of the piece.

This suggests a burgeoning dramatic sensibility on Boulez's part, but it's only one aspect of the significance of *Le marteau sans maître*. The vocal line is extremely lyrical. The contralto has to perform athletic melismas, ornate arabesques that decorate the often greatly elongated vowels: I can't think of any vocal music before *Le marteau* that makes quite these demands. But it's the ensemble that really dazzles us in this piece. As with the vocal line, the writing is virtuosic — even today, a performance of this work requires a great deal of rehearsal. The instrumentation itself has some of the qualities of a modern jazz combo, particularly because of the inclusion of guitar and vibraphone, but we shouldn't make too much of this. What Boulez achieves is a sort of 'world music' ensemble, involving Chinese gongs, African drums and shakers, and the xylorimba, whose origin is also African though here, in company with the vibraphone, it produces sonorities more reminiscent of an Indonesian *gamelan*. The alto flute, by turns, sounds vaguely Indian and then like a Japanese *shakuhachi*, and even the guitar, more often than not, is made to sound like a koto. What is very clearly not intended, however, is any assimilation of Eastern musical styles. The use of 'exotic' instruments was presumably another debt to Messiaen, and it opened up to Boulez a multitude of sonic possibilities. As for other sorts of cultural borrowings, including Messiaen's use of Greek and Hindu rhythms: Boulez regarded them as a form of neo-colonialism.

The ensemble of *Le marteau* proved as influential as that of *Pierrot lunaire* before it, though in a slightly different way. Where the *Pierrot* ensemble was appropriated, lock, stock and barrel, *Le marteau's* line-up was a bit too distinctive to become so ubiquitous. But keyboard percussion as a component of chamber music quickly established itself. By the 1970s, it was virtually a cliché, prompting one university music department to consider banning the vibraphone from student compositions.

I suppose the final significance of *Le marteau sans maître* was that it turned its composer into a conductor. Since the mid 1940s, Boulez had earned his keep conducting a theatre orchestra. When the great French actors Jean-Louis Barrault and Madeleine Renaud left the Comédie-Française to establish their own company at the Marigny theatre, they came across the young Boulez who was recommended to them as a performer (though it now seems unlikely, Boulez had been the resident ondes Martenot player at the Folies-Bergères). Barrault and Renaud liked Boulez and appointed him musical director of their company, and so he learned the basics of conducting in the Marigny's orchestra pit, though the experience can scarcely have equipped him for the task ahead. Boulez was unhappy with the standards of the early performances of *Le marteau sans maître*. Such were the complexities involved even in beating time, that accuracy was continually compromised. Boulez decided to acquire the necessary technique to conduct it himself, and his success soon earned him offers of work from orchestras and opera companies around the world. By 1971, he was simultaneously chief conductor of the New York Philharmonic and the BBC Symphony Orchestra in London, and his composing career was effectively on hold.

Le marteau sans maître typifies the post-war composer's desire to discover new sonorities, as well as new forms, but not every composer was content to approach the problem instrumentally. The invention of the tape-recorder allowed composers to combine all manner of sounds that had little to do with musical instruments. In New York, Edgard Varèse was by no means the first composer to work with a tape-recorder, but his case demonstrates better than most the way in which these machines fulfilled an urgent need.

Varèse's heyday had been the 1920s and '30s, and his preferred medium was the expanded, percussion-heavy, chamber ensemble. In many ways, one can hear such works as *Hyperprism* and *Intégrales* as precursors of the ensemble in *Le marteau sans maître*, though Varèse's concerns were quite different to Boulez's: for Boulez, sonority was of great interest, certainly, and the sound of *Le marteau* is one of its most attractive features, but the hectic counterpoint and serial procedures are the guts of the piece; for Varèse sonority was an end in itself. Varèse's work room was filled with percussion instruments, suggesting that he needed to listen to their sounds, that the physical presence of this gong or that drum was essential to the act of composition. His work, then, was a riot of noise, generally presented in blocks laid end to end or superimposed. It was a technique that owed much to *The Rite of Spring*, and it might have been Stravinsky's own direction had he not headed off down the neo-classical path.

In 1936, Varèse composed *Density 21.5* for solo flute. The title gives the specific density of platinum, the metal from which the flute of the first performance was made. It has become a classic — perhaps the classic — of the 20th-century flute repertoire, and it's typical enough of Varèse in terms of its repeated blocks of sound, only slightly varied. It was quite atypical, however, in its medium. *Density 21.5* was the only solo piece Varèse composed, and after it he fell silent for nearly twenty years. He left the noise of New York City behind him and moved for a time to Santa Fe in New Mexico. Varèse's period in the wilderness has been movingly described by Henry Miller in his collection of essays, *The Air-Conditioned*

Nightmare; out of the silence came a piece for large ensemble, with the standard battery of percussion, but with far from standard interpolations for tape-recorder. It was called, appropriately enough, *Déserts*.

It is not hard to understand Varèse's attraction to the tape-recorder. Given his propensity in instrumental music to work with blocks of sound — terminating one idea and replacing it with another; chopping that one short, and returning to the original material — the tape-recorder might have been invented for him. Razor blade in hand, he found in magnetic tape a medium that matched his technique. And in that medium he was able to control sonority completely, and to fix it in time and space. Varèse's tape for *Déserts*, and for the later *Poème électronique*, consisted of recorded sounds, often industrial in origin. The only thing electronic about the music was its mode of performance. This was *musique concrète* (concrete music), a term coined in the late 1940s by another pioneer in the area, Pierre Schaeffer. The first stormy performance of *Déserts* took place in Paris at the Champs-Elysées theatre, whose fabric was by now, surely, inured to musical scandal.

Although Varèse's complete works total barely a dozen, his importance in the history of 20th-century music is enormous. He was one of the few composers to take Stravinsky's pre-World War I ideas further; he gave percussion instruments equal status with their orchestral neighbours; and he brought about the apotheosis of noise. When he died, in 1965, it fell once more to Pierre Boulez to provide a eulogy. This time, he was rather more generous. If Schoenberg's death, to Boulez, was symbolic of the dwindling influence of his music, Varèse's was almost the opposite. 'Farewell, Varèse,' Boulez concluded his obituary, 'Your time is finished and now it begins.'

The tape operator at the premiere of *Déserts* was Stockhausen. The 1950s was an astonishingly fertile period for this composer. The impressionable youth who in 1951 had listened over and over to Messiaen's *Mode de valeurs et d'intensités*, before writing his own *Kreuzspiel*, now went on to compose a series of impressive and important works with a degree of alacrity and single-minded determination that made Boulez look almost lazy. By the end of the 1950s, he had written the first eleven of his *Klavierstücke* (piano pieces); the brilliant, cerebral wind quintet *Zeitmasze*; *Gruppen*, an astonishingly inventive work for three orchestras; the percussion solo *Zyklus*; and, building on his experience of *Gruppen*, *Carré* for four choirs and four orchestras. In the course of this hyperactivity, he had moved towards total serialism and come out the other side; *Gruppen*, for example, contains music whose dramatic impulse is frequently of far greater import than any theory; and in *Carré* there are passages that are not conventionally notated. These works are important for many reasons, not the least of which is the way Stockhausen deploys his sounds in space. The audience at a performance of *Carré* is surrounded by the four choirs and orchestras, and at the climactic moments, Stockhausen makes the music swirl around his listeners. These experiments with the spatial elements of music had their origins in a work that predates both *Carré* and *Gruppen*, and one that employs no instruments at all, but the new multi-track recording technology.

During his studies with Messiaen, Stockhausen had been increasingly fascinated by the possibilities of electronic music. In 1953, he was appointed a creative collaborator at the new electronic music studio set up at Cologne Radio under the direction of Herbert Eimert. It was here that much of Stockhausen's electronic music took shape. Unlike Pierre Schaeffer's Paris studio, whose achievements were largely in the area of *musique concrète* — acoustic sounds, recorded and edited — Eimert's studio was geared to the invention of sounds by electronic means, and therefore to a genuinely electronic music.

Stockhausen, however, was never going to be satisfied with a sine-wave oscillator; his commitment to the machine was always likely to be balanced by his abiding interest in the human performer. In the electronic piece *Gesang der Jünglinge* ('The Song of the Young Men'), a boy soprano provides a link between the new technology and the most basic of musical instruments, the human voice. This confluence of ancient and modern is further underlined by the boy's text. He intones the words from the apocryphal Book of Daniel, sung by Shadrach, Meshach and Abednego as they prepare to be thrown into Nebuchadnezzar's 'burning, fiery furnace' — 'All ye works of the Lord, praise ye the Lord'. They were the same words, coincidentally, chanted by the hypocritical congregation in Britten's *Peter Grimes*, but there was nothing ironic in Stockhausen's use of the text.

On the contrary, Stockhausen, like his teacher Messiaen, was a devout Catholic, and *Gesang der Jünglinge* was the last vestige of a far more ambitious project to compose an electronic mass, intended for liturgical use.

What Stockhausen achieves in this short piece, lasting a little under a quarter of an hour, is not only a synthesis between the serial system and electronic composition, but also, and far more significantly, a synthesis between electronically produced and vocal sounds. There are places in *Gesang der Jünglinge* where we can't be sure if we're hearing a human voice or not. The voice has taken on strange, otherworldly qualities, but, equally, the electronic music has been humanised. The machine even praises God. And, as in *Gruppen* and *Carré*, the sounds swirl around the audience's heads, from loudspeaker to loudspeaker.

Early concerts of electronic music were oddly formal events, little different to other concerts in terms of audience etiquette. With no performers to look at, the audience gave its undivided attention to a stage that was bare but for loudspeaker cabinets. At the end, it clapped and sometimes a composer emerged to take a bow. But audiences for contemporary music in general continued to grow more and more specialist. There was no single reason for this. Part of the problem lay with the advent of the long-playing record. The advances in technology that made electronic music a reality, also made private listening a simpler and far more common activity than had previously been possible. But the gulf between the composer and the average concert-goer was also widening.

Varèse once argued that composers were not ahead of their times (how could they be?), but that audiences were behind the times. Probably they were, but the cause of their antagonism to contemporary concert music was clearly more than just a dog-in-the-manger attitude to anything new. Audiences felt betrayed by serialism. They felt that composers had adopted an obscure and aggressively intellectual pose — there's many a program note to bear this theory out — and that this excluded the everyday music lover from any real sense of participation in new music. In fact, the intellectual rigour involved in composing a serial work was not necessarily of a higher order than that required for the writing of a Bach fugue — very often the reverse — and the evidence of many of the works

I have been discussing is that they were far from being the desic-
cated experiences audiences feared. Varèse's music is visceral; Boulez's
Le marteau is dazzlingly colourful, often dramatic; Stockhausen's
Gesang der Jünglinge is the music of deep mystical faith. Above all,
perhaps, there was Cage, the ultimate democrat, whose music didn't
really exist without the imaginative participation of listeners. But
these four were great composers, and I would like to suggest that
most of the damage being done to the composer-audience relationship was by the legion of lesser composers around the world who
now found themselves writing serial music. Serialism did not, of
itself, bestow talent on a composer, but for anyone who was interested, the procedures were not especially hard to master, and they
had the effect of turning a relatively giftless composer, overnight,
into a musical sophisticate. Their pieces may have sounded awful,
but the composers could justify every single note in relation to an
impressive set of charts. Serial composition took place, increasingly,
in university music departments. Here, the activity counted as
research and was written up in mind-numbing technical reports that
frequently found their way into concert programs. Any concert-goer
reading this stuff was likely to end up feeling, at best, angry; at
worst, foolish.

What is particularly sad about the situation I've described
is that all serial composers — and, in time, just about all living
composers — became box-office liabilities. Audiences found it
impossible to separate the wheat from the chaff. Perhaps they were
unwilling; certainly, many of them felt they were being asked to
perform this Solomon-like act on the basis of too little information.
Contemporary music, it seemed to the average listener, required a
special training, so audiences lost interest, taking refuge in a solid
but unrelieved diet of popular classics. If necessary, they would
abandon the concert hall and stay home with their new long-playing
records. The response of many composers was to throw up their
hands and then get on with their work.

Perhaps the most surprising development in 1950s art music
was the late conversion to serialism of Igor Stravinsky. It was a surprise for a number of reasons. Stravinsky was 70 when he wrote his
first serial piece, and he had a reputation for being temperamentally
at odds with twelve-tone music. Besides the evidence of his own

neo-classical style over three decades, there was also his longstanding 'feud' with Schoenberg. In his *Philosophy of Modern Music*, Theodor Adorno had rightly distinguished between the work of the two composers. As was his prerogative, Adorno had come down in favour of Schoenberg, but his line of argument involved fierce criticism of the neo-classical Stravinsky, an attack that made little distinction between admittedly lightweight pieces such as the *Capriccio*, and masterpieces like the *Symphony of Psalms*. Partly as a result of Adorno's polemic, the Schoenberg-Stravinsky debate raged in musical circles, with younger composers feeling compelled to declare which side they were on. By this time, the exiled Schoenberg and Stravinsky were Hollywood neighbours, and the feud began to take on a tabloid-newspaper quality. Like most of what one reads in the tabloids, there was little truth in it. In 1983, the Australian composer Vincent Plush visited Paul Pisk in Los Angeles. Pisk, just turned 90, had been Arnold Schoenberg's secretary and he showed Plush the cafe in Brentwood where, he said, Schoenberg and Stravinsky used to meet for coffee on Saturday mornings.

Whatever the relationship between Stravinsky and Schoenberg, it was the music of Webern that eventually turned Stravinsky into a serialist. Still, it is surely significant that he waited until Schoenberg himself, the founder of serialism and the last survivor of the second Viennese school, was dead, before he allowed his interest in twelve-tone music to become widely known.

In 1951, the year of Schoenberg's death, the premiere of Stravinsky's opera *The Rake's Progress* had marked the culmination of his neo-classical period. *The Rake* is an old-fashioned morality play, with a libretto by W. H. Auden and Chester Kallman, based on William Hogarth's engravings of the taverns and gaming houses, back streets and brothels of 18th-century London. John Gay's *The Beggar's Opera*, whose first performance in 1728 predated Hogarth's images by five years, was a model for Stravinsky's *Rake*, as it had been for Brecht and Weill's *The Threepenny Opera*. But for all the opera's touches of Georgian authenticity, it is Mozart whose influence is stamped all over Stravinsky's piece. The bustling overture and classical mix of harpsichord-accompanied recitatives and *da capo* arias, ensembles and choruses, remind us, at every turn, that Tom Rakewell is the operatic scion of Don Giovanni. The premiere of *The Rake's Progress* was even given at the Fenice theatre in Venice, home to the real life 18th-century Don Juan, Giacomo Casanova.

Five years later, Venice was the scene of another Stravinsky premiere. This time the building that housed it was grander even than the Fenice, the subject of the piece a good deal less worldly than *The Rake's Progress*, and the musical language far removed from neo-classicism. *Canticum sacrum*, performed at St Mark's Cathedral in 1956, was the first of Stravinsky's serial masterpieces. Drawing its structure from the building for which it was designed, *Canticum sacrum* is an appropriately monolithic work, and its serial language bolsters its rather stern nature. Listening to the piece in the context of Stravinsky's earlier music, it seems, at first, to be a completely new direction for the composer. But it wasn't.

Here are the syncopations of *The Rite of Spring*, the austere drama of *Oedipus Rex*, the chiselled clarity of the Mass, the lyricism of *Orpheus* and the Byzantine serenity of the final pages of the *Symphony of Psalms*. These characteristics are now all greatly refined, but they haven't gone away. And neither has the Russian accent of this most distinctive of 20th-century composers. If the serial works of contemporary music's lesser lights often seem an undistinguished and indistinguishable blur of academic dissonance, it was Stravinsky's great achievement to demonstrate that serialism was merely a technique, and that, as with any other technique, a composer of genuine stature and originality could stamp his or her personality all over it.

The decade and a half following World War II saw unprecedented changes in music, but by no means every composer was concerned with the serialism of a Boulez or the chance operations of a Cage. British composers, for instance, were slow to come to musical modernism. There were a few, notably Elisabeth Lutyens, who, even before the war, had readily embraced the music of Webern, but the dominant British figure remained the brilliant and conservative Benjamin Britten. Following the enormous popular and critical success of *Peter Grimes*, Britten embarked on a string of operatic works. Some of them were for chamber forces — *The Rape of Lucretia*, for example, and *The Turn of the Screw* — but others matched *Grimes* in scale and ambition. *Billy Budd*, based on the novella by Herman Melville and to a libretto by E.M. Forster, is arguably the equal of *Grimes* in achievement. Britten's success affected older composers, too. It's surely no coincidence that both William Walton and Michael Tippett should have immersed themselves in their first full-length operas in the years after *Peter Grimes*. In Tippett's opera, *The Midsummer Marriage*, a completely individual imagination had its first proper flowering. And 'flowering' really is the word. The bounding lyricism of Tippett's score had few antecedents, and none at all in the 20th century. You have to go back — as Tippett himself did — to the later Elizabethans, in particular Orlando Gibbons, and to the music of Purcell, to discover its roots. Just as Vaughan Williams's discovery of Tallis, at the beginning of the century, had enabled him to evolve a personal style founded in English music of the past, yet wholly fresh in its outlook, so Gibbons and Purcell provided Tippett with models of intricate polyphony and word setting that had remained dormant for centuries. There was nothing archaic about *The Midsummer Marriage*, but there was nothing modernist about it either.

The German, Hans Werner Henze, was another matter. At the beginning of the 1950s, Henze had been a member — if always a sceptical one — of the Darmstadt push. His second string quartet of 1952 was highly systematised music. But he soon tired of this, heading south to Italy and warmer climes, musically as well as climatically. Sitting in a piazza slurping Chianti held a greater attraction for Henze than doing sums in Darmstadt. With a flourish, he laid his romantic cards on the table in a lengthy song cycle for tenor, guitar and ensemble, to words by the German poet Friedrich Hölderlin. If we consider post-war modernism in Marxist terms — and it's always tempting — Henze's *Kammermusik* of 1958 was tantamount to revisionism on a grand scale. It was also a bid to find an audience that didn't consist of party apparatchiks. It was, if you like, an attempt at social responsibility.

Paradoxically, social responsibility lay behind Elliott Carter's move in the opposite direction. Like his fellow American, Aaron Copland, Carter had initially believed that his music should attempt to reach the widest possible public. His symphony and his early ballets all inhabit an essentially tonal harmonic world in which folk- and jazz-influenced melodic lines are never far away. By the late 1940s, however, Carter was becoming dissatisfied with this music: it wasn't even proving that popular. He began to feel that his duty to society was not to provide audiences with what he thought they would instantly like, but rather to offer them an altogether richer, more complex experience. In 1951, at the age of 43, he spent a Varèse-like period in the Sonora desert, near Tucson, Arizona. Here he composed his first string quartet. It was an ambitious work, lasting nearly three-quarters of an hour, and it made no concessions to anyone, least of all the players:

> I decided for once to write a work very interesting to myself, and to say to hell with the public and the performers too. I wanted to write a work that carried out completely the various ideas I had at that time about the form of music, about texture and harmony — about everything.

The surprise was that the music attracted very real interest. The piece won a prize in Belgium and, in spite of its considerable difficulties, it began to receive more regular performances than Carter's so-called popular music.

In Carter we find one of the great individualists of the late 20th century. He was never a serial composer, any more than he found himself involved with the chance operations of his contemporary and Greenwich Village neighbour, John Cage. Carter, we must remember was born in 1908, the *annus mirabilis* of the second Viennese school. He was befriended by Charles Ives, and grew up in a modernist world, acquiring the works of Joyce and Proust as they were first published. Even if he did not uncover it until the 1950s, his aesthetic was formed long before serialism or chance music existed.

So, Carter's music was modernist, but it was also humanist. The composer often spoke of it in terms of a human drama. In his string quartets, for instance, Carter invested individual instruments, or pairs of instruments, with distinct, anthropomorphic characteristics. Writing of his second quartet, composed in 1959, he described the *dramatis personae* in some detail. The first violin has music that is 'fantastic, ornate, and mercurial', while the second 'has a laconic, orderly character'. The viola 'adds its repertory of expressive motifs' to the whole and the cello is 'impetuous', sometimes managing to escape from the other three players. Carter referred to this work as 'a four-way conversation' and likened each instrument to 'a character in an opera'.

One of the formative influences on Elliott Carter was jazz. His early works, like those of Copland, contained traces of the style, as part of their attempt to appeal to a mass audience, but even after he abandoned such populism, the jazz influence remained a significant factor in his work. Carter's music no longer bore any outward resemblance to jazz, but the extreme rhythmic flexibility that characterises Carter's post-war compositions, derives substantially from the composer's early experiences of swing. Of course, by the late 1940s and early '50s, jazz itself had developed along lines that were markedly less appealing to a mass audience. The experimentalism that characterised the work of avant-garde composers on both sides of the Atlantic had a parallel in jazz. Certainly, the jazz of the 1950s was far removed from its origins in the whorehouses of New Orleans. While composers like Ravel and Stravinsky had turned to ragtime and traditional jazz in search of artistic renewal, now many jazz musicians openly admired the avant-garde music of the concert hall.

After Charlie Parker's death in 1955, his widow paid a visit to Edgard Varèse. Varèse knew of Parker's admiration for his music, because Parker had visited him to ask for composition lessons, but he was surprised to learn how Parker had often followed him around the streets of Greenwich Village, too shy to strike up a conversation. There is no obvious debt to Varèse in Parker's music, but the direction in which he took jazz was hardly less radical than that in which Varèse took his own work. Perhaps, a closer parallel exists between Parker's be-bop style and the music of Webern with its fragmentation of the melodic line; Parker's saxophone and the bent trumpet of his regular collaborator Dizzy Gillespie created glosses and tropes on familiar jazz standards until they bore so little resemblance to the originals they had to be given new names. Scrape off the surface of Parker's 'Hot House', for example, and you will discover the Cole Porter song 'What Is This Thing Called Love?'; buried under 'Bird of Paradise' is Jerome Kern's 'All the Things You Are'. They are musical palimpsests, the new pieces improvised on top of the old. The chord progressions — what jazz musicians call 'changes' — are identical, but the pieces have separate and distinct identities, and nothing of the original melody remains in the new piece. The most famous example of all is Parker's treatment of the Morgan Lewis tune 'How High the Moon', which in Parker's hands became 'Ornithology'.

Parker typically worked with a small combo consisting of his alto saxophone, alone or together with Gillespie or Miles Davis's trumpet, above a rhythm section of guitar, piano, bass and drums. It was a chamber music approach to jazz, allowing for a good deal of intimacy amid the be-bop exuberance. Davis's groundbreaking 'Birth of the Cool' sessions of 1950 consolidated that intimacy in thoughtful, harmonically rich compositions that leave behind the idea of the jazz standard: these were all original compositions. The personnel included saxophonists Gerry Mulligan and Lee Konitz, and on French horn — an unlikely jazz instrument — the young composer Gunther Schuller.

The mood of introspection deepened. The music of pianist and composer Thelonious Monk was unprecedentedly dark and dissonant, its rhythmically dislocated chords articulated with Monk's characteristic stabbing action. Bill Evans cultivated an equally introverted piano style, though with a rather more lyrical sound than Monk's, and it was Evans who teamed up with Miles Davis at the end of the 1950s for one of the most influential recordings ever made. *Kind of Blue* was notable for the speed of its music, which was slow, and the length of its tracks, which were long — just five of them on an album lasting 45 minutes. Equally unusual were the album's somewhat analytical sleeve notes, written by Evans who explained how much of the music on *Kind of Blue* was built on scales — the Dorian mode in the case of the album's opening track, 'So What' — rather than the chord changes that had been the foundation of most earlier jazz. The free floating effect thus achieved was not unlike that of Messiaen's early music, and for precisely the same reason.

All these musicians made appearances on popular radio shows and now, also, on television, but there was little denying that modern jazz was turning into a connoisseur's music. Duke Ellington, for instance, had always gone to lengths to distinguish between his work as a bandleader and as a composer; between pop tunes, like 'Don't Get Around Much Any More' and 'I'm Beginning to See the

Light' and more ambitious, symphonic conceptions like the 50-minute *Black, Brown and Beige* of 1943 or the *Far East Suite* of 20 years later.

With classical music and jazz aimed increasingly at listeners of some refinement, it seems inevitable that a new form of popular music should have emerged. But that rock and roll would turn out to be the most influential and widely heard music in history could hardly have been anticipated.

Rock and roll didn't come from nowhere. Go to the 'jump music' that Fats Waller and Louis Jordan were playing in the 1940s, and you will hear the rhythm of rock in embryo; likewise, the electrification of the blues that had occurred in post-war Chicago was formative in the rock and roll vocal style and also provided the harmonic template of the new music. Phil and Leonard Chess, who ran Chess records in Chicago, had a string of independent hits in the 1950s with rhythm and blues performers such as Little Walter, Muddy Waters and Etta James, and later Chuck Berry and Bo Diddley. But it still wasn't rock and roll. The extra ingredient needed to convert rhythm and blues to rock and roll, was white country music, which is why Sam Phillips's Sun Records studio in Memphis, Tennessee, played such a significant role in early rock. This was the recording home not only of bluesmen such as B. B. King and Howlin' Wolf, but also of the country singer Johnny Cash. Phillips's protégé — shortly to become his legend — successfully fused these elements. In order to understand the impact of Elvis Presley on 1950s America, one has to try to put from one's mind what came after him, musically and politically. Think, instead, of the popular artists of the day: think of Bing Crosby and Rosemary Clooney and Perry Como; think of Frank Sinatra and the Nelson Riddle Orchestra. *Then* listen to Elvis singing 'Mystery Train'.

As with any oral tradition, it's impossible to give a neat or even accurate history of the birth of rock. By the time the first sound recordings of it were made, rock and roll already existed. Bill Haley's 'Rock Around the Clock' can claim to be one of the earliest examples of the style, though the recording was largely ignored at its 1954 release, only to resurface with a vengeance the following year when it was used under the opening credits of *The Blackboard Jungle*. Richard Brooks's film was set in the classroom of an urban high school, its students seething with hatred and hormones. It's no masterpiece, but the scene in which Glenn Ford's students smash his collection of jazz 78s does have a certain symbolism, and it frightened the hell out of middle-class parents.

The incessant up-tempo beat and the high volume of rock and roll frightened them, too, but arguably more threatening still to the way of life of Eisenhower-voting, Donna Reed-watching Americans was the voice of rock and roll. It wasn't so much what the voice was singing — early rock lyrics were pretty undistinguished — it was the way it sounded. Elvis's voice outraged white middle-class parents because he sounded black. In the 1950s, racial segregation was still the norm, particularly in the southern United States. That any white singer should want to sound like an African American was bad enough, but that the children of respectable white parents might want to listen to him was intolerable. Middle America came out fighting. Church leaders pontificated, radio stations were petitioned; but the larger record companies were starting to realise there was money to be made from rock and roll. RCA paid Sam Phillips a handsome sum for Elvis Presley, and within a year he accounted for half the label's popular music profits.

Rock and roll was primarily a *recording* phenomenon. Wherever its stylistic roots were buried, it was the sound recording that nurtured it. As the LP revolutionised classical listening, so the seven-inch, 45-rpm single quickly became the standard currency of rock music — more so, in a way, because whilst the LP of a Beethoven symphony was only a recording, the single of Chuck Berry's 'Roll Over Beethoven' *was* 'Roll Over Beethoven'. The score of a classical piece was the text; with rock music, as with jazz before it, the recording was the text. Other performers might cover the same song, as the Beatles later did with 'Roll Over Beethoven', but the result would only be a new text. These texts were comparatively inexpensive — most teenagers had the 89 cents necessary to buy a single — and they gained added presence from another technological advance: the transistor radio. Soon, just about every beach, park and main street in the USA echoed to the sound of rock and roll.

The power of voices like Elvis Presley's or Little Richard's, and the ubiquity of their recordings, quickly led to a situation where the song itself was no longer of primary importance. What mattered was the *sound*. The 1950s teenager identified with the style of this music as much as its content, and increasingly with the style of the singer, so record labels were soon searching for ways of making their artists sound unique. Before the days of multi-tracking and digital editing, the methods may have been primitive, but they could still be effective. Elvis Presley's recording of 'Heartbreak Hotel', for example, seemed to require a cavernous quality — but how to create this for the microphone? The solution was low-tech and ingenious. Elvis's producer sent him down to the other end of the studio and told him to sing louder.

On 29 October 1957, the *New York Post* published the view that 'rock music is the most brutal, ugly, vicious form of expression . . . sly, lewd — in plain fact, dirty . . . a rancid-smelling aphrodisiac . . . martial music of every delinquent on the face of the earth'. The words were attributed to none other than Frank Sinatra, whose earnings were beginning to take a dip as a result of competition from his rock and roll challengers and whose records themselves had probably been among those trashed by the students in *The Blackboard Jungle*.

If you were not a rock and roll musician you could of course bleat about teenage delinquency, like Sinatra, but a further option was to climb aboard the bandwagon. In 1957, Leonard Bernstein did just that. *West Side Story* obviously wasn't rock and roll, but it aped many of its mannerisms as surely as its on-stage characters affected the attitudes of the juvenile delinquent. Stephen Sondheim's lyrics and Bernstein's brilliant score were immensely successful, and while its Broadway run was hardly popular with the sort of kids depicted on stage, it probably allowed many of their parents to contemplate their changing world. Bernstein's gang members — all of them, deep down, with hearts of gold — were the sanitisation of a genuine social problem. Still, as Tony and Maria, *West Side Story*'s latter-day Romeo and Juliet, sang of the 'Somewhere' to which they would one day escape, it was hard not to become caught up in their sense of hope. Paradoxically, in the 1960s, much of that hope would be sustained by the 'rancid smelling aphrodisiac' of rock music itself. By the same token, the score of *West Side Story* — at the time just a great Broadway show — would offer coming generations of concert-hall composers a powerful model for reuniting the popular and the serious.

The 1950s was a decade of musical extremes, exemplified, one might think, by the simultaneous appearance of *Le marteau sans maître* and 'Rock Around the Clock'. And yet these two pieces of music do share certain qualities, political if not aesthetic, social if not musical. It is true, *Le marteau* represented a relaxation of the total serialism of Boulez's earlier pieces, and that there were, just around the corner, rougher, tougher rock and rollers than Bill Haley, but what the Darmstadt composers desired (a musical zero hour) and what Haley, Elvis, Little Richard and Jerry Lee Lewis demonstrated (a zero hour of another sort) were equally radical. Boulez's distaste for the revival of pre-war neo-classicism in liberated Paris was as great as American teenagers' disappointment at the survival of Bing Crosby. Darmstadt and early rock were both reactions against the attempts of older generations to return to life as it had been before the war, as though the Third Reich, the Holocaust and the massive military and civilian slaughter had been a mere hiccough of history.

Total serialism and three-chord rock and roll were music *in extremis*. Each had zealous young advocates as well as older antagonists. But each, also, was to prove necessary for the future of music, burning off the old growth to make way for the new. These relatively Spartan musics would blossom significantly in the 1960s, but such regeneration was made possible by the post-war generation's insistence on its zero hours.

PROTEST AND REVIVAL

If you were to search for the distinctive sound of the concert hall in the 1960s, it would be hard to go past the voice of the American singer Cathy Berberian. She is most obviously associated with the music of her husband Luciano Berio — even after their separation, an amicable and imaginative divorce settlement meant that Berio continued to compose roughly one piece a year for her — but both Stravinsky and Cage also wrote for Berberian. She sang in many of the first modern performances of Italian baroque opera, and in solo recitals her repertoire ranged 'from Monteverdi to the Beatles'.

Berberian had an astonishing assortment of voices, and arguably her greatest gift was her power of mimicry. Ranging freely across both soprano and alto registers, she could give a passable imitation of Marlene Dietrich, sound like a nimble *coloratura*, or become a Sardinian fish-wife; she could produce a tone of great purity, but also, if called for, lashings of operatic wobble. Berberian was probably the first 'classical' singer regularly to use a microphone. She sometimes used one even in straight concerts to bring an added control and intimacy to her voice. She was also a good actor and not a bad dancer. Composers, especially Berio, drew on all her talents, and in the process opened up many new possibilities in the concert hall and the opera house.

Luciano Berio was born in 1925, the same year as Pierre Boulez. Like Boulez, he became a visitor to the Darmstadt summer school, where his fascination with the possibilities of serialism grew. But Berio was temperamentally very different from his colleague. He had been born into a family of jobbing musicians, and there was always an element of the artisan in Berio's compositions: he never became so involved in his own musical world that he forgot that audiences like to be entertained. In addition to an Italianate refinement and lyricism, his music was also naturally theatrical, and he loved words as much for their sounds as their meanings. Three pieces Berio composed for Cathy Berberian's voice demonstrate these aspects of his music, though the first was not so much written *for* her voice as *with* it.

Visage, of 1961, is a piece of *musique concrète* originally commissioned by Italian radio. It involves no singing as such, but instead Berberian's vocalisations describe an arc of emotional extremes, from hilarity to deep distress. Not only is there no singing in *Visage*, there are no actual words, except, that is, for 'parole' — the Italian for 'words'. Berio subjected Cathy Berberian's recorded voice to much editing and extended it electronically. The result is a sort of music–theatre, one in which theatrical sounds are stripped of their context and made to function in a purely musical manner. At least, that's the theory. But sounds of sexual pleasure, or fear and panic, can never be purely musical; they are bound to evoke some sort of scenario. When the management of Italian radio listened to the piece they had commissioned, they must have imagined a particularly vivid one, because they branded it 'obscene' and refused to broadcast it.

In the same year as *Visage*, Berio completed the ambitious cycle of pieces he called *Epifanie*. Actually, it is two cycles, consisting of seven orchestral pieces interleaved with six vocal settings for Cathy Berberian, each to a text by a different writer. The writers are Proust, Joyce and Brecht, the Spanish poet Antonio Machado, the French structuralist Claude Simon, and Berio's friend and frequent collaborator, the Italian poet Edoardo Sanguineti. The orchestral movements are clearly related to each other in that they share a dense and intricate approach to texture, but Berio handles the vocal movements very differently. The Proust setting, for example, is simple and lyrical, lying low in the singer's mezzo register, from time to time turning into speech; the Joyce is pitched somewhere between *coloratura* and the squealing of an excitable child; the passage from Claude Simon is spoken quickly, in an expressionless monotone; and the Brecht calls for Berberian's most dramatic soprano. Berio originally permitted nine possible orders for the thirteen pieces that make up the entire cycle, but in the composer's own performances, and in the commercial recording he conducted, he preferred the order where the Proust setting comes first and the Brecht last. In 1992, he completely overhauled the work, gave it the English title *Epiphanies*, adjusted the order of two of the orchestral pieces, added a handful of transitional passages, then fixed it once and for all.

There is a good reason for hearing Brecht's words last. Berio selected his texts in consultation with Umberto Eco, and the common theme addressed by his six writers is trees, their beauty and symbolism. Brecht's poem, however, calls into question the politics of the entire piece. The presence of 'An die Nachgeborenen' ('To Future Generations') undermines the reflective, sometimes celebratory nature of the earlier vocal settings. Bluntly, it insists that in a world filled with injustice, singing about trees is immoral. The use of Brecht's poem in this context is itself, of course, a Brechtian device; it poses the question: 'What are we all doing here in the concert hall, when we could be outside improving the world?' Interrogatory moments such as this became something of a Berio trademark in his later works. In *Sinfonia* (1968), a voice from within the orchestra reminds us that music 'can't stop the wars, can't make the old younger or lower the price of bread, can't erase solitude or dull the tread outside the door'. In *Coro* (1977), the passing parade of folk poetry is repeatedly interrupted by a line from Pablo Neruda: 'come and see the blood in the streets'. On their own, these words cultivate a pregnant sense of foreboding. But at the end of the hour-long work, the context is revealed in a longer section from Neruda's poem. Once again, it turns the spotlight on Berio's audience, and on Berio himself, demanding that we abandon the bourgeois concerns of our music and poetry and take a look at the violence around us.

And you will ask: why doesn't his poetry
speak of dreams and leaves
and the great volcanoes of his native land?

Come and see the blood in the streets.
Come and see
the blood in the streets.
Come and see the blood
in the streets!

Perhaps it was qualms such as these that encouraged Berio to turn to folk song; perhaps it was simply the opportunity to provide another musical display cabinet for half a dozen of Cathy Berberian's voices. At any rate, the 1964 piece known simply as *Folk Songs* has become Berio's most frequently performed work, and a significant one in terms of post-war musical aesthetics. In later pieces, particularly the aforementioned *Coro*, Berio would integrate the gestures of folk singing with his own musical style, but in *Folk Songs* he contented himself with making colourful arrangements of songs for Berberian and a small ensemble.

The eleven numbers that comprise *Folk Songs* consist of traditional songs from America, Armenia, France, Sicily, Italy, Sardinia and Azerbaijan, together with two songs actually composed by Berio almost twenty years before. The composer's grasp of the idiom is such that it is not easy for the innocent listener to identify which are his own contributions. Berio has protested that he is no ethnomusicologist, still his arrangements of the traditional material capture the simplicity and rawness of the songs and this is particularly apparent if one compares his versions of two of the 'Songs of the Auvergne' with the celebrated prettifications of the same material by Marie Joseph Canteloube.

The admission of folkloric elements into notated music was not in itself new. One can go back to late mediaeval times and discover them in church music, especially in the so-called 'parody' masses which wove folk melodies into the rich textures of early polyphony. Folk song had also been a vital part of early modernism. Its influence was essential to the music of Bartók and Stravinsky, each of whom not only made arrangements of traditional songs, but also wrote, from time to time, in folk idioms. These tendencies, however, were banished by the Darmstadt composers, in the general post-war clearing of musical decks and for Berio to raise the matter again might have been thought to be in poor taste. Folk-song arrangements were all very well for conservatives like Benjamin Britten or ideological backsliders like Hans Werner Henze, but Berio was a card-carrying member of the avant garde. In fact, in opening Darmstadt's doors to the demotic world of the folk song, Berio disregarded none of its principles concerning the invention of new musical languages; rather, he admitted the richness of traditional musical styles and techniques as a means of extending the expressive range of modernism.

It may seem naive, today, but the modernist search for new musical languages continued to be viewed by composers as a political act. Precisely how avant-garde music related to the oppressed masses was a rather tricky issue — not too many factory workers attended concerts at the Darmstadt summer school — but the composers' commitment was genuine enough. It was surely only a matter of time before consciousnesses were sufficiently raised that modernism would become the musical *lingua franca* of social revolution.

What inspired this climate of political radicalism is difficult to pinpoint, but it affected far more than the music of the concert hall. In the United States, where in the 1950s the Communist Party had collapsed, the union movement had begun to thrive. Along with it came a revival of interest in folk music, but not at all in the sense in which Berio adopted it. For all his political commitment, it was the *music* of folk song that appealed to the Italian composer. In the American folk-song revival, what mattered were the words. In the 1930s and '40s, singer–songwriters like Leadbelly and Woody Guthrie had performed material with a strong social conscience, the latter writing his celebration of democracy, 'This Land is Your Land', in direct response to the coy jingoism of Irving Berlin's 'God Bless America'. In the 1950s, the Weavers became the unofficial voices of organised labour, resurrecting old workers' songs that retained their relevance to dispossessed minorities such as African Americans, and to the millions who spent their waking hours at the conveyor belt of American capitalism. The establishment did its best to discredit them and even had lies told to the House Un-American Activities Committee resulting in the Weavers losing their recording contract with Decca and being banned from network television.

By 1963, when Bob Dylan sang 'The times, they are a-changing', he was still really predicting events, rather than summing them up, but his song was quickly adopted as an anthem by the generation born after World War II. It was a generation that believed in progress in spite of the atom bomb; that believed in freedom of speech in spite of the McCarthy witch-hunt. And in spite of the Berlin Wall, the Cuban missile crisis, and America's involvement in Vietnam, it was a profoundly optimistic generation. All the ills and injustices of the world could be put right, and in 1963, to the accompaniment of Dylan and other political singers like Odetta and the Weavers' Pete Seeger, 200,000 people went to Washington, demanding civil rights for the Negro. The 'juvenile delinquents' of the 1950s had come of age; the rebels without a cause had finally found a few.

In truth, these 'Armies of the Night' were probably not exactly the same kids who had trashed Glenn Ford's record collection in *The Blackboard Jungle*; Dylan's fans tended to be college-educated and politically aware. Probably they even liked jazz. But something of that earlier spirit and energy was at work, and now it was harnessed to a political crusade. If it had frightened parents, back in the 1950s, because it seemed directionless, now, at least, even the most conservative members of the John Birch Society could see where this energy was aimed. It was aimed at them.

At least they no longer had to worry about rock and roll. By 1960, the perceived threat that rock music posed to white, middle-aged, middle-class Americans had apparently been neutralised. Elvis Presley was in the army, Chuck Berry was in gaol, and Buddy Holly was dead. Jerry Lee Lewis was in disgrace, having married his thirteen-year-old cousin — bigamously, as it turned out. And Little Richard had abandoned an Australian tour to announce his retirement at a Sydney press conference. He explained that he had met God, and God didn't like rock and roll. Even before these events, the record company executives who had been quick to capitalise on the enormous popularity of early rock, had also played a significant part in taming it. Buddy Holly is a prime example. At three years, his career was certainly short, but it lasted long enough to undergo some considerable changes. Like Elvis, the Everly

Brothers, and most of the other rock and roll acts whose origins were in country music, Holly had also recorded pop ballads. Increasingly he had been persuaded — perhaps he didn't even need persuading — to trade the coarse energy of rock and roll for catchy pop tunes that could just as easily have been sung by Perry Como. A good example of Holly at his most inoffensive is 'Every Day'. There is no electric guitar on this track; instead, we hear, of all things, a Sugar Plum Fairy celesta. The snarling vocal that characterised a song like 'Rave On' is transformed into the somewhat impish voice of a boy that anyone's mom would be happy to have round for milk and cookies. And the pounding drums of 'Peggy Sue' are nowhere to be heard, replaced by what sounds uncannily like a half-hearted Swedish massage.

The big stars of American pop music in the early 1960s consisted of clean-cut teen idols with unlikely names such as Bobby Vee and Fabian. They sang anodyne ballads in sobbing voices, often accompanied by orchestral strings. The strange thing was that American teenagers didn't seem to mind: they kept on buying the records anyway.

If rock and roll itself seemed to be finished, however, pop music in the United States was by no means devoid of original ideas. Record producer Phil Spector was exceptionally original and full of ideas, not all of them in especially good taste. His first hit, in 1958, had been a maudlin little song he had written and produced for a group called the Teddy Bears. He had taken the title and opening line of the song, 'To Know Him Is To Love Him', from the headstone of his father's grave, while the tune itself was a half-speed version of 'When the Red Red Robin Comes Bob Bob Bobbin' Along'. 'To Know Him Is To Love Him' already had an individual sound, but Phil Spector was destined for grander and louder things. By 1961, as the 21-year-old, millionaire head of his own record label, his stable of performers included a number of all-girl vocal groups such as the Crystals, the Shirelles and the Ronettes. But while the Crystals may be nominally the performers of 'Da Doo Ron Ron', the two-minute song was actually the work of dozens of musicians under the direction of Spector himself. The distinctive production quality that Phil Spector developed on these records, known as the 'wall of sound', involved multi-tracking voices, guitars, pianos, drums and orchestral instruments, cramming the

material into the narrow confines of already-primitive mono technology. The finished product was grandiose and overpowering.

Of course, rock and roll itself was not finished, and neither was
its tough, raw progenitor, rhythm and blues. In Chicago, Leonard
and Phil Chess still put out records by Muddy Waters and Howlin'
Wolf, and they still attracted a cult following in Europe. So that the
next wave of rock and roll should have come from England was not
as strange as it might, at the time, have seemed. Europe had long had
a fascination with American music. Jazz, in particular, had enjoyed
an enormous following there since the 1920s. Paris, Berlin, Prague,
Stockholm, Copenhagen and London had all, at one time or another,
had flourishing jazz scenes, even when American enthusiasm for the
music had dwindled. Now, as American audiences lost interest in
rhythm and blues, it too was kept alive in Europe, especially in the
blues clubs of London. As with jazz, rhythm and blues found a
European audience that was at odds with the music's working class
roots. The blues clubs were patronised by Gauloise-smoking young
intellectuals with hair over their collars, students from art schools
who were doubtless attracted to the music by its seeming exoticism.
Such were the origins of the Rolling Stones, a London-based rhythm
and blues outfit who took their name from an old Muddy Waters
song. Much of their material consisted of authentic-sounding cover
versions of Chicago blues; Mick Jagger successfully aping the vocal
characteristics of the style; Brian Jones's harmonica sounding like the
genuine article; and Keith Richards's heavily syncopated rhythm
guitar giving the music its infectious drive and distinction. Above all,
it was every bit as dangerous as early rock and roll. One of the
Rolling Stones' first hits was a song written for Buddy Holly; but
Holly's version of 'Not Fade Away' seems a tame affair compared with
the Stones' version.

Further north, in Liverpool, the Beatles were not unaffected by
the blues, but they drew their inspiration from a wider stylistic pool,
including black vocal groups from Detroit like the Marvelettes and
Smokey Robinson and the Miracles, Phil Spector's stable of girl
groups, and white, close-harmony ensembles like the Four Seasons.
The Beatles were never merely rock and rollers. Their early material,
reflecting their versatility as entertainers, even included show tunes,
'Till There Was You' from Meredith Willson's *The Music Man*, appear-

ing on their second album. But the Beatles performed primarily their own original material.

Whether or not they knew it — probably they didn't — the songs that John Lennon and Paul McCartney wrote, had a harmonic sophistication that went well beyond the eight-, twelve-, and sixteen-bar formulas of the blues. 'From Me to You', the Beatles' third single, is hardly sophisticated in terms of its lyrics, particularly by comparison with some of the later Lennon and McCartney songs, but musically it has several distinctive touches, which, in its day, gave it considerable novelty and which still have a certain freshness. The move from C major to G minor for the middle eight bars is quite a surprise, and the opening, wordless motif with its modulation from C major to its relative minor, A, is closer to the harmonic language of the English folk tradition than to the music of the Mississippi delta. Race memory? Who knows? Certainly the emergence of the Beatles came hard on the heels of an English folk-song revival that had, in turn, affected the skiffle bands who were the Beatles' immediate precursors. Whatever it was that made the Beatles so distinctive — very likely it was sheer talent — it was noticed by millions of people around the world. Not even Elvis Presley had had this kind of success.

The Beatles' musical progress was as astonishing as their popularity. By the end of 1965, three years after their successful EMI audition, they had recorded 'Yesterday' with McCartney's vocal accompanied only by acoustic guitar and a string quartet, and 'Norwegian Wood', which employed an Indian sitar; they had also experimented several times with the sound of distorted guitars using a fuzz box. The group was spending more and more time in the studio, applying its considerable curiosity to the available technology, and requiring producer George Martin and his engineers to find innovative solutions to an apparently endless stream of ideas for new sounds.

Revolver, the album released in 1966, is full of products of the Beatles' fertile imaginations, most of them involving the ever-expanding gadgetry of the recording studio. 'Tomorrow Never Knows', the album's final track, was the most extreme example of Beatles experimentation up to this point. Instrumentally, the song contains some fine, relentless drumming, doubled on a monotone by the bass guitar, but the song, as released, owes little to conventional rock music or its instruments. It is the outcome of a considerable amount of overdubbing, tape manipulation and electronically altered sounds. Tape loops are a particularly strong feature of the track, repeating the same material over and over, often backwards. John Lennon's lyric advises his listeners to 'Turn off your mind, relax and float down-stream', and, part-way through the three-minute song, Lennon's voice becomes suddenly disembodied, the result of feeding it through the revolving speaker inside a Hammond organ. Clearly, 'Tomorrow Never Knows' was unrepeatable 'live', and in August 1966, the same month *Revolver* was released, the group played its final concert in San Francisco's Candlestick Park. It might be argued that, with *Revolver*, the Beatles abandoned mainstream pop altogether, but, given their fame, it would probably be truer to say they expanded its horizons.

It is axiomatic that the 1960s gave rise to several events so vividly etched on the memories of those who lived through them that they still remember what they were doing at the time. President Kennedy's assassination is the obvious example. Another is the first moon landing. In the case of the latter, everyone was doing the same thing — watching it on television. Most people who remember the '60s also recall where they were the first time they heard *Sgt Pepper's Lonely Hearts Club Band*.

Sgt Pepper appeared in 1967, and was an early example of the 'concept album'. The Beatles' albums had steadily become less like compilations of individual songs, and more like integral statements in which the songs were related to each other, as William Mann was among the first to point out. Mann was the chief music critic of *The Times* newspaper in London, and he had taken to reviewing the Beatles' albums on release, just as he would the premiere of a new work by Berio or Stockhausen. In his review of *Sgt Pepper* he told his readers to expect, 'sooner or later', the pop equivalent of Schumann's *Dichterliebe*.

The idea of the new album was that the Beatles were not 'The Beatles' but the 'Lonely Hearts Club Band' of the title. In this guise, they would introduce themselves and their guests and play a set of songs, musical-hall style. Although, somewhere along the line, the original idea seems to have become scrambled, there remain vestiges of the 'Sgt Pepper' conceit: in the opening song and subsequent introduction of singer 'Billy Shears'; in the oom-pah accompaniment to McCartney's 'When I'm Sixty-Four'; and in Lennon's 'Being for the Benefit of Mr Kite' whose words were taken, almost verbatim, from a Victorian circus poster. It is there, too, on the album's famous cover. Designed by the artist Peter Blake, it shows the four Beatles dressed in brightly coloured military uniforms, clutching musical instruments. These members of Sgt Pepper's band are surrounded by a throng of on-lookers among whom are waxwork dummies of the Beatles themselves. The rest of the crowd consists of effigies of Beatle heroes, including Karl Marx and Carl Gustav Jung, Aldous Huxley and Dylan Thomas, Oscar Wilde and Edgar Allan Poe. The handful of women among the 70-odd faces are pin-ups and sex symbols like Mae West and Marilyn Monroe (though, strangely, Shirley Temple makes three appearances). One of the more surprising figures on the cover — top left, between Lenny Bruce and W. C. Fields — is Karlheinz Stockhausen.

Sgt Pepper's Lonely Hearts Club Band has what is probably the most famous record cover in history, yet its really significant feature was not the photography on the front, but the words on the rear. Today we take such documentation for granted, but *Sgt Pepper* was the first pop album to publish its song lyrics in this manner, and the implication is obvious: the Beatles expected their new record to be listened to with the same kind of attention commonly given to classical music. In 1963, their first album, *Please Please Me*, had been recorded in a little under ten hours; *Sgt Pepper* took 129 days. The Beatles now required a correspondingly greater investment of time and effort from their listeners.

Ultimately, what distinguishes the work of the Beatles is what distinguishes most good composers: a musical idiolect. Stravinsky is a good example of this. In his pre-World War I ballets, in the so-called 'Russian' pieces like *The Soldier's Tale* and *Les noces*, in his neo-classical works, even in the serial miniatures he was composing as late as 1966, the composer's personality emerges. The outward trappings of the music may vary greatly, but Stravinsky's distinctive voice is always clearly audible. So it was with the Beatles: from the classic pop of 'She Loves You', to the self-conscious avant-garde of 'Revolution 9', to the burlesque good humour of 'You Know My Name', we are unmistakably hearing the Beatles.

This musical 'voice-print' became more important than ever in the pop music of the 1960s. The definition of pop broadened on a weekly basis, rock and roll being but one of the shaping forces behind it. Were the Beach Boys rock and roll? Were the Byrds? And what about Jimi Hendrix? His music was as rooted in the blues as any straightforward rock and roll, but there was nothing straight-forward about his guitar playing. A blistering noise issued forth from Hendrix's Stratocaster, his technique characterised by a lyrical flexi-bility, the swing of modern jazz, and an improvisational brilliance unmatched at the time and seldom rivalled since.

In 1968, the Belfast-born Van Morrison released a record that sold poorly. There were no hit singles from it, and the album itself failed to reach the top 200. Yet it has remained in the catalogue ever since, and it continues to feature in those lists of 'Greatest Rock Albums of All Time' that pop magazines insist upon running. The album was *Astral Weeks*, and the strange thing about it, given its status as one of the 'Greatest Rock Albums of All Time', is that it isn't rock and roll at all. There is no electric guitar on *Astral Weeks*, no electric bass, no keyboards and no heavy drums. Morrison's album was far removed from the joyous noise of Jimi Hendrix, but it was even further from the commercial world of sugar-coated pop ballads. On *Astral Weeks*, Morrison worked exclusively with jazz musicians, including Connie Kay of the Modern Jazz Quartet, recording the album in two days. Prominent in the instrumental sound of the album is flute and acoustic bass. Later there was some overdubbing: punchy brass on to one song, discreet strings and even a harpsi-chord on another. The musical arrangements suited the words of Morrison's songs, which were certainly not about the things rock and roll was supposed to be about. Celtic mysticism, Eastern philos-ophy and religion, and classic literature were all influences on Van Morrison's song-writing and so was a nostalgic yearning for his Belfast youth. Morrison may have been only 22 at the time, but he was always old.

Astral Weeks sums up the state of popular music a decade and a bit after the emergence of rock and roll. There is a degree of sophis-tication in its lyrics, music and production, that would scarcely have seemed credible to Bill Haley when he recorded 'Rock Around the Clock'. Part of *Astral Weeks'* sophistication is that it was a collection of songs and always intended as such: if not, perhaps, the modern *Dichterliebe* William Mann had predicted, it nevertheless functioned like a song cycle. And it sold like a classical album, too: its success was neither instant nor evanescent: *Astral Weeks* will sell as many copies this year as it did in 1968 and has every year in between.

To appreciate the richness that was in popular music by the late 1960s, you only have to consider some of the other artists releasing major albums in the same year as Morrison's *Astral Weeks*: Bob Dylan's *John Wesley Harding*, the Beatles' 'white' album, and Simon & Garfunkel's *Bookends* all came out that year; Marvin Gaye's *In the Groove*, the Byrds' *Sweetheart of the Rodeo*, Frank Zappa's *Lumpy Gravy*, and the Band's *Music from Big Pink* give some further indication of the variety; Deep Purple's first album appeared, and so did Joni Mitchell's; the Doors released *Waiting for the Sun*, and the Grateful Dead put out *Anthem of the Sun*. The year's hit singles included José Feliciano's ecstatic version of the Doors' 'Light My Fire', Hendrix's cover of Dylan's 'All Along the Watchtower', and the virginal voice of Welsh teenager Mary Hopkin in a pallid little torch-song called 'Those Were the Days'. Not all of this music was influential, but it demonstrates the stylistic range that had become current by 1968.

Avant-garde concert-hall composers had scarcely been known for their diversity of style. The first book of *Structures*, Boulez's two-piano work of 1951, shared with John Cage's *Music of Changes*, composed the same year, a spiky, atonal language. There seems nothing strange about this until one recalls that the aesthetics, aims and techniques of these two composers were so radically at odds. It is not impossible that 1951 may have been the last moment in history that you could use the term 'modern music' and reasonably expect people to know what you meant by it. By the early 1960s, much had changed, including Boulez and Cage who could hardly be confused with each other any longer.

Boulez had latched on to an urbane concert style, full of poise and even wit. As he broke free of the self-imposed shackles of total serialism, his musical structures became ever more labyrinthine. His third piano sonata, for example, involved its performer in the constant selection of musical moments. All the materials are precisely notated, but the order in which they appear is left to the pianist who must choose from a number of possibilities. Boulez has compared the score to the map of a town. The town's landmarks are fixed, as are its streets, but with the aid of a map, the traveller can move around them in many different ways. Certain streets will offer the possibility of detours down side roads; others will lead you somewhere specific but by a circuitous route; a few may prove to be dead ends. The sonata was prompted by Stéphane Mallarmé's poem 'Un coup de dés' ('A Throw of the Dice'), whose layout on the page Boulez's piece resembles. In *Pli selon pli* ('Fold upon fold'), an hour-long musical portrait of Mallarmé, Boulez applied some of the same techniques to his orchestral writing. There are moments in the score where the conductor is responsible for the precise ordering of events, just as the pianist is in the third sonata.

This technique was further expanded in *Eclat* (1965), for a small orchestra of just fifteen players, the reduced size facilitating a greater degree of flexibility. The players in *Eclat* are dominated by a solo pianist, shadowed by two instrumental groups. One of these is made up of two woodwinds, two brass and two stringed instruments, all capable of sustaining notes; the other group consists of a glittering array of eight instruments that are either plucked or struck — including harp, guitar, mandolin, cimbalom and various tuned percussion. Their sounds, like those of the piano, begin to die the instant they are born. As with the third sonata and *Pli selon pli*, all the music in *Eclat* is fully notated, but the instrumentalists' points of entry are left up to the conductor. So the piece begins with a cadenza from the soloist, gently underpinned by sustained notes from the wind and strings. The other players sit there, poised to play. They are waiting for the conductor's cues to fire off their individual responses, each player's entry being determined by the length of time the previous sounds are taking to die. Boulez described the experience of conducting *Eclat* as like improvising on the ensemble, and now he set about expanding the work in terms of its length and the size of its ensemble, calling the new version *Eclat/Multiples*.

What really impresses about *Eclat*, in its original and expanded forms, is the remarkable refinement of sonority. Each sound in the piece is evidently placed with great care and precision, whether by Boulez the composer or Boulez the conductor. It is obvious that this music's creator has worked closely with performers and their instruments and that he knows their capabilities. In spite of Boulez's ambivalent attitude to the past, *Eclat* and *Eclat/Multiples* demonstrate his close connection to the traditions of the concert hall. Over the coming decades, his music would show more and more the debts to his composer forebears Webern and Berg, Stravinsky and Debussy, even Wagner.

There is no parallel here with Cage's development. To speak of style in John Cage's music is simply to be irrelevant: how his music *sounded* was entirely beside the point. Cage had become more determined than ever to rid his pieces of all ties to his ego, and in the process had abdicated responsibility for the content of his music. This doesn't mean that, in a performance of Cage, anything goes. Quite the opposite: the performers in Cage's music do not improvise — that would involve acts of will on their part, and Cage was no more interested in his players' wills than he was in his own. Chance operations such as consulting the *I Ching* require that composer and performer alike surrender their wills; only through the most rigorously disciplined approach to these operations can the ego be overcome. This is the true meaning of the term 'aleatoric' in music. It comes from the Latin *alea* ('dice'), and it refers to the element of sheer chance that this implies.

If Boulez and Cage's respective ideologies now rendered their own work utterly distinct, the general broadening of musical styles in the 1960s was also affected by new blood. From the mid 1950s on, many new composers emerged — the last wave of modernists, if you like — and they brought with them the same kind of open-minded and inclusive attitudes that characterised Luciano Berio's music. Even previously hard-line modernist composers now broadened their gazes significantly. In Europe, Beatle-hero Karlheinz Stockhausen had become a particularly unpredictable musical voice.

Virtually every piece Stockhausen composed was a brand new event, and from quite early in his career he began to cultivate an attitude of perpetual renewal. Once a particular permutation of instruments had been employed in a piece, it was never to be used again: each new work would have a new ensemble. This attitude was also beginning to effect the style of Stockhausen's music. If we discount Cage from this discussion, because he wasn't interested in composing in the conventional sense, it might be argued that

Stockhausen was the first composer to have no style of his own. What interested him was content. If the content were right, the outward trappings of style would look after themselves.

A piece that preoccupied Stockhausen for much of the 1960s was *Momente* ('Moments'), first completed in 1962, expanded in 1965, and expanded again in 1969. The title relates to the composer's increasing conviction that music, like life, was a series of moments, and that the only connections between them are ones we make for ourselves. It is possible to trace Stockhausen's attitude back to his encounter with the pitch constellations of Messiaen's *Mode de valeurs et d'intensités*, but equally we can find the origins of 'moment form' in a work like Debussy's *Jeux*, which moves from one idea to another with scarcely a backward glance, or to the independent and seemingly unrelated blocks of sound in the music of Varèse. Stockhausen's *Momente* also emphasised 'vernacular' sounds such as driving rhythms and chanting, rather than conventionally operatic singing, and in this the composer moved ever closer to the idea of music as a celebratory event, a form of ritual. From the stage, the soprano calls to the other singers and players and they make their way down through the audience aisles. Clapping, stamping, hissing and shouting — sounds familiar to the composer from audiences at some of his concerts — all form part of the musical fabric of *Momente*, so that in a performance before an aggressive or exuberantly appreciative public, it can sometimes be hard to separate the music from the response. And this was precisely Stockhausen's aim. The pounding drum rhythms at the opening of the final version of *Momente* also alert us to a sudden narrowing of the gap between what was happening in the concert hall and the music of the pop charts. Stockhausen's inspiration, on this occasion, was from West Africa, but then so, in a roundabout way, was Bo Diddley's.

Stockhausen and Boulez were not alone in shrugging off the strictures of total serialism, but there were many more composers for whom it had never really been an issue. One was Iannis Xenakis. Born to Greek parents living in Romania, Xenakis had fought in the Greek resistance during the war and been badly wounded. After the war, he fled to Paris and, in his absence, was sentenced to death by the military government in Athens. Like Boulez and Stockhausen, he joined Messiaen's harmony class. Xenakis may not have been much good at harmony, but his teacher recognised in him a real talent for sound and structure — the latter hardly surprising, since Xenakis, on arrival in Paris, had become an assistant to the great modernist architect Le Corbusier. Putting this training to good use, Xenakis began to create music in which slabs of searingly intense sound moved across each other with all the force and inevitability of shifting continental plates. The effect was frankly dramatic: it is no coincidence that some of Xenakis's works have had titles suggestive of the theatre of ancient Greece. Most of his earliest pieces, however, get their names from mathematics. Xenakis's music was never serially derived, but still less was it the product of aural intuition. Since he was dealing with masses of notes, moving together, he employed statistical procedures to generate them, turning to the theories of probability which governed the behaviour of large scale phenomena. It is not that pitch is unimportant in this music, but it is only of relative importance; the traditional functions of harmony are replaced by the changing textures, their densities and volumes. It follows, then, that to play a wrong note in a piece by Xenakis is not as great a sin as it would be to play the right note too quietly, or too loudly, or without the appropriate tone colour.

Györgi Ligeti was another composer who was fascinated by texture. Like Xenakis, he had fled political oppression, arriving in Germany in 1956, after the Soviet invasion of his native Hungary and the subsequent imposition of martial law. In the orchestral works *Apparitions* and *Atmosphères*, Ligeti explored a very personal approach to texture. Although both pieces are short — about nine minutes each — they employ large forces: in the case of *Atmosphères*, quadruple woodwind, six horns, four each of trumpets and trombones and strings to match. The brevity of the music and the large scale of the orchestra invite comparisons with the early orchestral pieces of Webern, but Ligeti's musical imagination could hardly have been further removed from Webern's. Ligeti's scores did not lack precision; on the contrary, the existence of 56 individual string parts in *Atmospheres* is ample demonstration of the detail in the piece. But the nature of this detail creates an overall impression of vagueness. Ligeti called his technique 'micropolyphony'. In *Atmosphères*, for instance, each of the 28 violins plays a slightly different version of the same material. Each player has a precisely notated part that is unique, but the listener hears the 28-violin aggregate of this: a dense mass of sound. Ten years after *Atmosphères*, Ligeti composed a piece for women's voices and small orchestra whose title, *Clocks and Clouds*, beautifully describes this technique. The instrumentalists play with clock-like precision; the listener experiences slowly shifting clouds of sonority.

In Poland, Krzysztof Penderecki and Witold Lutoslawski were thinking along rather similar lines. Penderecki's *Threnody to the Victims of Hiroshima*, composed in 1960, is for strings alone, but like Ligeti, the composer allocates each player an individual part — 52 of them, this time. Where Ligeti's string writing was conventionally notated, however, Penderecki makes use of graphics to indicate matters such as pitch and duration. Pitch tends to be relative — as high as possible, at the start of the piece — and for much of *Threnody*, duration is measured in seconds rather than in crotchets and quavers. The work's dedication 'to the victims of Hiroshima' was added only after the first performance, and does not seem to have been in Penderecki's mind at all when he was composing the piece. But effects such as knocking on the wood of the instruments and bowing on the 'wrong' side of the bridge, together with the sheer violence of the music, certainly conjure apocalyptic visions of a world splintering apart.

Lutoslawski's music, generally more debonair than Penderecki's, was hardly less innovative in its deployment of orchestral forces. In *Venetian Games* of 1961, the first piece in which Lutoslawski really displayed his own highly original voice, he used a technique he called 'aleatoric counterpoint', even though it wasn't really aleatoric at all. The players' individual parts are fully notated, but for long stretches they are not synchronised with each other, so the music has a dense and elaborate texture. Presumably, these random relationships between the different lines were what Lutoslawski meant by 'aleatoric', yet the composer retained a very strict control over the harmonic shape of *Venetian Games*, limiting the pitches allocated to his players so that only certain combinations of notes could occur. Although there is a playful exuberance to much of the piece, the appearance of the word 'games' in the title should not mislead us. Lutoslawski was to become one of the most serious-minded and respected composers of the late 20th century and, with this work, he unveiled the compositional method he would use until his death in 1994.

The fact that most of the really invigorating developments in European music of the early 1960s came from an Italian, a Greek, a Hungarian and two Poles is significant, and the significance is that they were not Austrian, German or French. The classical tradition, insofar as a tradition existed any more, had emigrated from the major European metropolises. It had taken firm root, now, not only in the rest of Europe and the United States, but in most of the rest of the world.

From the mid 1960s, Peter Sculthorpe began to occupy a position in Australian musical life similar to the one Aaron Copland held in the United States, though, initially at least, with certain complications. In 1965, Sculthorpe's orchestral piece, *Sun Music*, was premiered by the Sydney Symphony Orchestra at the Commonwealth Arts Festival in London. It was well received and the London critics, for once almost excessively generous, ventured the opinion that the composer might come to represent the voice of Australia. Neville Cardus in the *Guardian* predicted that Sculthorpe would 'lay the foundations of an original and characteristic Australian music'. Back home, the press was less kind, the *Australian* informing its readers that *Sun Music* had been 'a flop', attracting only lukewarm applause from a sparse audience. The contrasting views are not actually contradictory — perhaps the hall wasn't full, perhaps the audience wasn't impressed — but it was symptomatic of the cultural insecurity of 1960s Australia that its press should have reported on these aspects of Sculthorpe's premiere, rather than the positive response of the critics who had actually heard the piece.

If the Australian press's cringing reaction to *Sun Music* was not altogether surprising, the positive response of the British press was, at least in one respect. Many of the sounds and some of the notation of *Sun Music* closely resemble the work of Penderecki. Sculthorpe later insisted that when he composed his piece he was unaware of *Threnody to the Victims of Hiroshima*; but the London critics would certainly have known it, so their suggestion that *Sun Music* was somehow distinctively Australian reads a little oddly. And yet whether the high, wailing violins of Sculthorpe's work originated in Sydney or Warsaw, their aptness as a sonic depiction of a flat, red

Australian outback under a glaring sun can hardly be questioned. Sculthorpe composed three more orchestral works before the end of the 1960s, eventually giving them all the title *Sun Music*, but he wasn't standing still. He felt he needed to say something in his music about Australia, yet, at the time, he considered it would be insensitive to deal with Aboriginal material, so he turned to Indonesia, Australia's nearest Asian neighbour, where he discovered musical traditions of enormous richness. In *Sun Music III*, writing in a consciously oriental style, Sculthorpe took the melodic shapes and periodic rhythms of the Balinese *gamelan*, and in *Sun Music II* (the last of the four to be composed) he adapted the rhythmic structures of the *ketjak*, the Balinese 'monkey dance'. Sculthorpe's reticence about employing Aboriginal materials did not last, but for the time being he expanded his exploration of Asia to include what he described as the 'greatest music of the human race' — *gagaku*, the court music of Japan.

In 1968, Sculthorpe first met the Japanese composer Toru Takemitsu and the two became firm friends, recognising each other as kindred spirits. They shared a degree of ambivalence concerning the traditions of Western music; both composers lived (to use E. M. Forster's words about the poet Cavafy) 'at a slight angle to the universe'. The piece that properly launched Takemitsu in the West was the extraordinary *November Steps* for orchestra and two soloists playing the traditional Japanese instruments the *shakuhachi* and the *biwa* — the former an end-blown bamboo flute, the latter a kind of banjo. As we might predict, the first thing that strikes us on hearing this music is its sonorities, but it is not only the Japanese instruments that sound so fresh: in *November Steps*, Takemitsu proves himself a master orchestrator, unleashing unexpected combinations of instruments on his listeners so that there are moments in this piece when one wonders if one is truly hearing an orchestra at all. In their new context, the *shakuhachi* and the *biwa* themselves conjure sounds that might almost be electronic in origin. Given that so many Western composers had already been drawn to the traditional musics of the East, it should not surprise us that Japan now produced one of the century's most genuinely poetic — and, in *November Steps*, genuinely dramatic — musical minds.

At the end of the decade, Japan itself became a focal point for

new music, as Xenakis, Berio, Kagel, Stockhausen and more con-
verged on Osaka for Expo '70. It was Stockhausen who stole the
show with months of performances of his work in the German pavil-
ion. Some of these pieces were the most intuitive that Stockhausen
had yet composed, and they required their performers to be every
bit as intuitive as their creator. In *Plus-Minus* of 1963, Stockhausen
had begun to think in terms of the transformations within a piece —
the additions and subtractions — as separate from the musical
material. What had begun as an exercise for his students, evolved
into a series of works that explored these processes more fully, while
leaving the nature of the material to look after itself. In some pieces,
the performers use their knowledge of Stockhausen's earlier music to
generate the raw material for their transformations; in others, short-
wave radio receivers were employed to 'import' sounds into the
performance (a strategy also adopted by Cage, from the 1950s on).
Several new experiments in this direction occurred at Osaka, as did
performances of pieces for which the players were provided only
with short texts, of a more or less instructive nature, as the basis for
Stockhausen's most intuitive music yet.

The other important Stockhausen work at Expo '70 was
Stimmung for six voices, composed in 1968. The title means 'tuning',
and Stockhausen intended it in several senses. The most obvious is
the standard musical sense of being in tune: *Stimmung* is sung to
a single chord of B flat, and the composer sanctions — indeed
requests — that, from time to time, one or more of the voices go flat
or sharp, and then come back into tune. The second sense in which
the title functions is that of the six singers 'tuning in' to each other:
the work lasts for anything between an hour and 90 minutes, and is
performed without a conductor, so that the individual singers must
know the piece and each other thoroughly in order to perform it.
Ninety minutes of B flat might sound like a lot, but this relates to the
third meaning of *Stimmung*: a tuning into eternity. The spiritual
quality this suggests is reinforced throughout the work by the calling
out of names of divinities from many of the world's religions: Hindu,
Christian, Judaic, Australian Aboriginal, and Aztec; and it was
among the Aztecs — at any rate, among the ruins of their ancient
civilisation — that Stockhausen first began to imagine *Stimmung*.

When he returned to the house in which his wife and young

children were staying on Long Island Sound, he was able to compose only by singing to himself very quietly, so as not to disturb his sleeping progeny. He found himself producing harmonics — overtones — by means of altering the shape of his mouth to form different vowels; in this way the sound world of *Stimmung* evolved. The piece is very much of its time: its intensity, its spirituality, its moments of humour, above all its dream-like nature: all these qualities were typical of the 'summer of love' whose spirit was still in the American air as Stockhausen composed the piece in the first months of 1968.

It would be difficult to imagine a more contrasting piece to *Stimmung* than the one composed by Peter Maxwell Davies the following year. *Eight Songs for a Mad King*, almost single handedly, reinvented the genre of small scale music-theatre, that had begun with Schoenberg and Stravinsky. The king in question was George III of England, whose madness we now know to have been the result of physical rather than mental illness. Historical accuracy, however, is of little concern in Maxwell Davies's piece, because its subject is madness itself. The composer has even suggested that the male singer we see on stage wearing a night-shirt and a crown, may not be King George at all, but merely one who believes himself to be King George. Maxwell Davies composed the piece in 1969 for his ensemble, the Pierrot Players, which, as its name suggests, consisted of the five instruments required to perform Schoenberg's *Pierrot lunaire*. To these he added a percussionist. In *Eight Songs for a Mad King* the players also have dramatic roles. The percussionist is the king's gaoler, leading him off-stage at the end of the work, beating a large bass drum with a cat-o'-nine-tails. The flute, clarinet, violin and cello play inside giant bird cages; they represent the bullfinches to whom George attempted to teach Handel's *Messiah*; the bars of their cages also stand for the bars of hospital beds in a psychiatric ward. The sung text is by the Australian poet and novelist Randolph Stow, and woven into it are quotations from the king himself, many of them taken from Fanny Burney's diary. So the text presents both the historical George and a fictitious one.

In terms of its vocal demands, the role of King George goes beyond anything Berio had imagined for Cathy Berberian, though, like Berio, Maxwell Davies had a specific singer in mind. Roy Hart not only had a range of over four octaves, but also the ability to sing chords, and the composer exploited Hart's abilities to produce 'the sounds made by human beings under extreme duress, physical and mental'. The vocal line ranges from cracked, throaty noises to shrieks, from a 'knifelike' falsetto to dog-like ululations, and from 'strangled high wheezing harmonics' to an 'in-style' baroque trill which suddenly transforms into a florid vocal display directed by the composer to be performed 'like a horse'.

The grab-bag of styles that constitutes *Eight Songs for a Mad King* has the effect of jarring our sensibilities, amplifying and illuminating the stream of insanity coming from the king. Occasionally — as with the authentic quotations from George III — the musical quotes serve to locate the piece historically, but these are frequently distorted, underlining the king's deranged state of mind. At the beginning of the seventh song, for example, the king readies himself for a rendition of one of his favourite bits of Handel, as a bar-room piano smooches its way through the introduction to 'Comfort ye, my people'. What follows is called a 'Country Dance', but in reality it's a foxtrot which plays as the king cups his hands into a makeshift megaphone, shouting about 'sin'. At the climax of this, the cycle's penultimate song, he reaches into the violinist's cage, snatching the instrument from the player's hands and smashing it to pieces. This is a ritualised giving-in to his own insanity. Once he has admitted it, he can proceed soberly to announce his own death, and recite his obituary until the percussionist/gaoler leads him howling from the stage.

Perhaps the contrast between the serenity of Stockhausen's *Stimmung* and the hyperactive unpleasantness of *Eight Songs for a Mad King* is simply one of political climate. In between, in the middle of 1968, came the assassinations of Martin Luther King and Robert Kennedy, dealing twin blows to the civil rights movement and radical American politics in general. Violent riots and police brutality followed at the Democratic convention in Chicago, and Richard Nixon was narrowly elected president. In Czechoslovakia, Alexander Dubček's 'Prague spring' was brought to an abrupt end when Soviet tanks rolled into the city one night. Student riots in Paris, the so-called *événements*, seemed hugely idealistic at the time, but — after they had been quelled — seemed hugely pointless in that they had only succeeded in confirming the views of those they had sought to dislodge from power.

One result of the *événements* was the politicisation of Hans Werner Henze. It was not that he had previously been apolitical, but suddenly his composing seemed more like pamphleteering. Every new work was a manifesto; this was music as agitprop. Given the urgency of his political message, the quality of the music itself varied alarmingly. One of the better works, his ambitious cantata, *The Raft of the 'Medusa'*, was dedicated to Che Guevara. It was based on Géricault's famous painting, now hanging in the Louvre, depicting dying sailors on a raft which their officers had cut loose in the Atlantic ocean after the frigate, the *Medusa*, was holed when it ran aground on a reef. In December 1968, the Hamburg premiere of Henze's piece was abandoned without a note being heard. Members of the large chorus had objected to a red flag on the stage and in the near riot that ensued, the police were called and the librettist arrested. Undeterred, Henze released a public statement in which he announced that in future he would devote himself to revolutionary works, and for a London concert he was scheduled to conduct with the English Chamber Orchestra two months later, he hastily assembled a twenty-minute rant entitled *Essay on Pigs*. The text concerned the recent assassination attempt on the German student leader Rudi Dutschke, and the voice was that of Roy Hart, for whom Maxwell Davies was then writing his *Eight Songs*. By now, Henze the Revolutionary, was unstoppable and as the music poured out of him its quality lurched from work to work. Two music-theatre pieces demonstrate the varying standards. *El cimarrón* (1970), the story of a runaway Cuban slave, is uneven, but retains its power, largely thanks to the restricted scale of its performance: one singer and three instruments. But *The Tedious Way to the Place of Natascha Ungeheuer*, composed the following year, was an ill-disciplined collage of trite music and triter politics. Different instrumental groups role-played the class struggle. A brass quintet in police helmets stood for the authorities; a '*Pierrot*' ensemble, dressed in hospital smocks, represented the sick bourgeoisie — and note that this was not only the ensemble associated with Schoenberg's *Pierrot lunaire* but, by now, also the basic line-up of virtually every new-music ensemble in the world. The implication was clear: avant-garde art music was part of the problem. Meanwhile, the student underground was symbolised in the piece by a rock group.

Politics and collage came together far more subtly in a work first performed in 1968, perhaps the quintessential work of the 1960s concert hall. It was composed by Luciano Berio for the Swingle Singers and the New York Philharmonic and its generic title, *Sinfonia*, disguises its very nature: this is anything but abstract music. But the title is perfectly appropriate, too, for this is a piece about the symphony, about its history and the social conventions that have grown up around it. The dedication of the work to the Philharmonic's conductor Leonard Bernstein is also appropriate, because this is generous, inclusive music, that reunites the old and the new, the serious and the popular, in a manner the 20th century badly needed. Bernstein himself somehow represented that quest. The third movement is headed *In ruhig fliessender Bewegung* ('with a quietly flowing motion'), which is the same legend appearing at the top of the scherzo in Mahler's *Resurrection* symphony. Berio takes this scherzo and makes it the undercurrent of his own piece; he has described it as running through his music like a river, sometimes flowing strongly at the surface, sometimes disappearing underground. On top of the Mahler, Berio superimposes a great deal of information, literary and musical. The text comes, very largely, from Samuel Beckett's characteristically bleak and ironic fiction, *The Unnamable*, but there are also words of Berio's own. The non-Mahlerian music mainly consists of quotations from other pieces and some of these are sparked by comments in the text. For example, when one of the voices mentions 'the play of waves', we hear a couple of seconds from Debussy's *La mer.* Other musical objects in Berio's piece are taken from Bach, Beethoven, Berlioz, Brahms, Berg, Schoenberg, Webern, Stockhausen and Berio himself. Many of these quotations are fleeting, even obscure; others are instantly recognisable, as when the 'Dance of the Earth' from Stravinsky's *The Rite of Spring* begins to tunnel its way out of the dense weft of sound that Berio has created.

As the movement rushes ahead, urged on by cries of 'Keep going!', while other voices shout 'Stop!', one of the singers notices the people in the audience and begins to speculate on the reasons for their presence. Are they even here willingly? At this point, as though to reassure the listeners, one of the waltzes from Strauss's *Der Rosenkavalier* suddenly erupts into life, crashes through a few bars of Ravel's *La valse*, and emerges, unscathed, on the other side.

The third movement of *Sinfonia* is Berio simultaneously celebrating the symphony and launching a critique of it. Why are those people sitting there, giving us their attention? Are they, perhaps, feeling trapped, socially paralysed? What is the point of all this? And what good could possibly come of it? However much we may wish it, there is no music that can 'make tulips grow' or 'alter the flow of ocean currents'; although a voice tells us that 'we must believe it's true', we know perfectly well that it isn't. But Berio's final message is more equivocal. As long as the music plays, perhaps there is hope — even, as he puts it, of 'resurrection'. As Mahler's scherzo gently unravels and the speaker personally thanks the conductor for his work, we know we'll be back in the concert hall next time for some temporary solace.

BACK TO BASICS

An old man, sleeping rough in London, sings a verse of a hymn. And he means it, too. He may be dirty and homeless, but, in the words of the hymn, he believes that 'Jesus' Blood' has never failed him yet. This was recorded in 1971 by the film maker Alan Power, who was shooting a documentary about vagrancy, and he played it to his friend, the British composer Gavin Bryars. Bryars was moved by what he described as 'the tramp's humanity and simple faith', and he wrote a modest chordal accompaniment to fit with the old man's voice endlessly repeating the same verse on a tape loop. Bryars orchestrated the accompaniment so as to introduce the instruments a few at a time. First the tramp sings alone, then he is joined by a string quintet, then by a guitar and double bass, then woodwind, then brass. All this takes about 25 minutes, while the old man's voice remains completely unchanged.

Or does it? Literally, of course, it does; but as we are drawn in to the rather hypnotic experience of Bryars's piece, the tramp's voice seems to be subtly altering the phrasing of the song. It is an aural illusion; it's like staring at one of those densely patterned pages until you suddenly see the 3-D rabbit. And it's a standard effect of music that, for better or for worse, has become known as 'minimalist'.

Minimalism was a reaction against modernism, against the work of composers who packed their music with information. It had no interest in making statements; it was not music about ideas, but about sound pure and simple — particularly simple. It aimed to take the art back to its basics. Minimalist music employs a tiny amount of material and, typically, repeats it over a long period of time. The material may gradually evolve into something else, or, as with Gavin Bryars's *Jesus' Blood never failed me yet*, may only seem to evolve, the transformation taking place in our minds. The term, borrowed, like so many before it, from the visual arts, seems to have been first applied to music by the critic Michael Nyman, who went on to become the composer Michael Nyman. Tracing the origins of minimalism is problematic, and it might be argued that certain pieces of baroque music work in a broadly minimalist manner: the last movement of Bach's third *Brandenburg* concerto would be an example. Then there is the first movement of Beethoven's *Pastoral* symphony whose development section repeats the same figure 72 times. But these are moments in larger works, and they contain a good deal more harmonic variety than is generally the case with minimalist music of the 20th century. In fact, the roots of modern minimalism are not in the classical tradition at all. Minimalism was an American invention, and seems to have been inspired, in part, by the examples of other American musics, all of which had their own origins in the vernacular.

Jazz, blues, gospel, rock and roll: the popular musics of the last hundred years have gained international currency. They quickly came to dominate Western culture; they provided the soundtrack of 20th-century life. More than ubiquitous, they were unavoidable. And they all originated in the United States of America. The generations growing up there after World War II identified with this music to an unprecedented degree, and perhaps inevitably young composers in American colleges began to question the style of the music they were being taught to write. Not only did it seem to lack the energy and spontaneity of jazz and rock, it found only small audiences, usually drawn from those same colleges. Steve Reich had a perfectly conventional musical education first at the Juilliard School in New York and then at Mills College in Oakland, California, but by night he was listening to jazz musicians like John Coltrane. Jazz improvisation was supposed to be beneath the dignity of a serious composition student in the early 1960s, but Steve Reich has described the awakening in him of the subversive notion that perhaps Coltrane had more to offer than the strict serialism Reich was being taught.

> This interest in jazz continued, although my playing of it trailed off as a drummer — I sort of swept that under the rug at Juilliard, after all, composers don't play jazz drums. But when I was through with Mills [in 1963], there was on the one hand the image of people who were writing what was called in those days 'paper music' — very black with notes, totally beyond the ability of the composer to play, one doubted whether in fact he heard it in his or her head — and there was John Coltrane picking up his saxophone and the music just came out.

Reich reasoned that the music of the post-war European avant garde was all very well for Europeans — it had, after all, grown out of their traditions, however much composers like Boulez and Stockhausen liked to believe they had made a clean break with the past — but for Americans, raised on Chuck Berry and Bill Haley, it would no longer do.

Even if jazz was the catalyst for Steve Reich to find his own voice as a composer, he was never really interested in its mannerisms, as many Europeans had been in the 1920s and '30s. As an American, there was another tradition Reich could tap into. It was not much more than half a century old, but the pioneers of American experimentalism offered an attractive alternative to European 'paper music'. Henry Cowell, Ruth Crawford Seeger, Edgard Varèse, John Cage and the instrument inventor and sometime hobo, Harry Partch, were among the composers in this rather broad church. Stylistically different from each other, they shared a kind of rugged radicalism, each in his or her own way, creating a musical language from the ground up. Like many an American pioneer before him, Reich the New Yorker packed his bags and went west to California. Not only was San Francisco further away from Europe, it seemed, in the mid 1960s, to be a centre of artistic freedom. Two of the newest members of the experimentalist tradition were Reich's new Californian neighbours, La Monte Young and Terry Riley.

The work of La Monte Young, in particular, clearly shows the connection between minimalism and experimentalism. In 1960, Young was very much the conceptual artist. In *Piano Piece No. 1 for David Tudor*, he instructs the pianist to bring a bale of hay and a bucket of water on to the stage for the piano to eat and drink. There are two methods of continuing the piece. One is for the pianist to feed the piano by pouring the contents of the bucket and pitch-forking the hay into the instrument. The other is simply to leave them next to the piano, the piece being over when the piano has either eaten or elected not to. In *Piano Piece No. 1 for Terry Riley*, Young instructs the player to put the flat side of the instrument flush against a wall and then push as hard as possible. If the piano goes through the wall, the composer advises, the pianist should keep pushing in the same direction, regardless of new obstacles. This piece is over when the player is too exhausted to push any more.

It would be stretching things to describe La Monte Young's pieces as music, though conceivably some interesting sounds might result from performances of either of them. I suppose the technical term for these events is what people in the 1960s were pleased to call 'happenings'. What they show us, above all, is Young's intense dissatisfaction with the world of art music, and his application of humour as a solution. But amusing as these works may be (unless, of course, you're the owner of the piano, or the wall), Young wasn't exactly joking. His conceptual events used humour to make a serious point, and that point, I think, is partly to do with the way that the composition and performance of new music had seemed to Young to have become highly specialised activities. Doubtless he would have argued that listening to it was an equally specialised task. Young's response to the problem of playing and understanding contemporary scores, was to produce works that could be per-formed by anybody and required no understanding at all.

In *Composition 1960 #7*, La Monte Young actually wrote some notes. Two of them, to be precise: a B and an F sharp in the middle of the keyboard, giving an interval of a perfect fifth which the performer is instructed to hold 'for a long time'. On this occasion, Young wasn't being 'conceptual' — or, at least, not just conceptual — he genuinely liked the open fifth and its gradual decay. His next pieces all took unisons, octaves or fifths, and prolonged them using electronics and tapes. Alvin Lucier was another composer attracted to the simplicity of drones. Assuming one was in the mood — and, in San Francisco in the 1960s, most people were — these simple drones produced a contemplative effect. Several of Young and Lucier's drone pieces had their first hearings at the San Francisco Tape Music Centre, founded by the like-minded Pauline Oliveros, whose own music at the time was becoming more specifically linked to the practice of meditation and increasingly came to involve mantra-like chanting.

In 1964, Terry Riley took the next step with a piece that's usually considered to be the first major work of musical minimalism. He called it, simply, *In C*, and as that title spells out, the piece is harmonically completely static: it starts out in the key of C and remains that way for the next hour or so. The instruments are unspecified, anyone can play, and the participants are invited to join in as they feel like it, holding on to a pattern of notes until it seems time to move to the next pattern. In the spirit of John Cage, this is music without an aim. It is an antidote to the aesthetic of a composer like Pierre Boulez; this is not music you have to pay much attention to, it doesn't require its audience to work or even think. With most Western art music, composers are keen to cover their tracks; they function rather like conjurers, wanting their audience to experience the illusion, and not to worry too much about how it was achieved. Of course one can analyse a Bach fugue, say, in order to reveal its mechanics, but that isn't where the music lies. Terry Riley's *In C* is a bit like the Pompidou Centre in Paris, which has all its plumbing on the outside. The composer disguises nothing. The music operates entirely at the surface; the process by which one melodic pattern gradually changes into another is not simply the mechanism that drives the music, but the music itself.

In 1969, Alvin Lucier came up with a piece whose basic material was a description of the process by which the piece itself would develop. In *I am sitting in a room*, Lucier reads a text into a tape-recorder, and then he plays it back, recording it on a second tape-recorder, and so on, until the original recording has disappeared, replaced by the ambient rhythms of the room itself. The description of the activity is the material of the music, and the activity described is the process by which the music develops; the longer the process continues, the less distinct the description of the activity becomes. *I am sitting in a room* is its own program note, analysis, and even review, and as Alvin Lucier's voice becomes less distinct with every re-recording, the last thing we recognise is the composer's characteristic stammer, now detached from its owner like the Cheshire cat's grin.

Process as music greatly interested the young Steve Reich, and one of his earliest pieces, like Gavin Bryars's *Jesus' Blood*, began with a voice on a tape loop. Reich recorded an African–American preacher called Brother Walter alerting shoppers in San Francisco's Union Square to the impending apocalypse. The piece begins with a single phrase from Brother Walter's sermon — 'it's gonna rain'. Reich made two tape loops of the phrase and ran them, in unison, on two tape machines. Perhaps the machines were not operating at quite the same speed, or perhaps one loop was imperceptibly longer than the other: whatever the reason, the loops gradually became out of phase with each other. Reich discovered that the more loops you used, the more the preacher's voice took on an abstract quality; eventually the sense of the words was completely lost, replaced by a gradually transforming succession of rhythms and textures.

The effect of *It's Gonna Rain* and much other early minimalism, is trance-inducing. These pieces are, in a sense, anti-intellectual. They are concerned with sensation alone. There is no equivalent in early minimalist music of Boulez's rigorous dialogue with the grammar, structure and deep meaning of a poet's text, such as happens in *Le marteau sans maître* and *Pli selon pli*; and neither were minimalist composers concerned with the intricate cross relations between musical styles that characterise much of Luciano Berio's music of the 1960s and '70s. Still, if minimalism, virtually by definition, was not particularly 'interesting' in itself, the *idea* of minimalism certainly was.

As it developed in sophistication, minimalism began to draw on still other influences that lay outside the concert hall. Just as Debussy and, later, Messiaen, Boulez, Britten and Sculthorpe had been attracted, in their very different ways, to the Indonesian *gamelan*, Steve Reich began to investigate African drumming. In 1970, he even made a field trip to Ghana, to study the music. The experience wasn't especially revelatory for Reich — he was drawn to Africa in the first place because he had heard recordings and noticed they contained some of the same patterns that appeared in his own music — but it confirmed him in his creative inclinations, and the result, in 1971, was a large scale piece entitled *Drumming* composed for his own ensemble, Steve Reich and Musicians.

Like Riley's *In C* and much other music of the period, *Drumming* is an open-ended affair in which the players' slowly evolving rhythmic patterns continue for as long as feels right on the night; in live performance *Drumming* can last well over an hour. The process Reich perfected in this piece was really very simple, but its effect is mesmeric. *Drumming* begins with a single bongo stroke followed by a silence; the action is then repeated. Although we can't hear it, the bongo marks the ninth beat of a twelve-beat bar, so the silence, in fact, contains eleven rests. Bit by bit, these rests are substituted for further bongo strokes, until the texture of the music begins to fill out (later the process will be reversed). The tempo is constant, but as more beats are added, and the silence is increasingly subdivided, the listener has the illusion (that word again) of the music running ahead ever faster. The rhythmic cell that generates the entire piece, is an eight-note one, spread across the twelve available beats. But the players don't start their rhythms on the same beat of the bar so their patterns overlap, filling in each other's rests until the drum strokes run on continuously. From time to time, other drummers join in and drop out (something Reich must have observed in Ghana); there are also moments at which they move towards rhythmic unison. This is achieved by individual players getting ahead of the beat and, at first, the result is a sonic blur. But when the process is completed and the mist has cleared, the drummers are revealed playing the pattern as one. It's a 'live' version of what happens to the out-of-phase tape loops in *It's Gonna Rain*. The following sections of *Drumming* employ tuned percussion and women's voices (impersonating marimbas), and later a piccolo, aided by whistling, to fill out the sound of the glockenspiels. The bongos themselves had been tuned, but now the keyboard percussion and voices make the pitches clearer and, almost by default, Reich finds himself dealing with fragments of melody. *Drumming* was a turning point in the composer's career. After it, he abandoned the use of phasing procedures, made greater use of the technique of evolving rhythmic lines, and began to extend both his melodies and his harmonic palette. The works he composed throughout the 1970s, such as *Music for Mallet Instruments, Voices and Organ* (1973), *Music for 18 Musicians* (1976) and *Music for a Large Ensemble* (1979), are a very long way from La Monte Young's one-chord *Composition 1960 #7*. Critics continued to pin the label on him, but it should have been clear to anyone who heard these new pieces that Steve Reich had outgrown minimalism.

Where Reich had travelled to Ghana to find 'confirmation' of his ideas, Philip Glass's exposure to the music of the Indian subcontinent was more of an accident. In 1965, Glass was in the middle of studies with Nadia Boulanger in Paris. A year or two with Boulanger had become a rite of passage for American composers since Aaron Copland and Virgil Thomson had studied with her 40 years before. Like any student trying to make ends meet, Glass took a part-time job, and he was lucky enough to find one that required a musical skill. He was hired to work on a film for which the sitar player Ravi Shankar was composing some of the music. The music was to be played by European musicians, and Glass was required to notate it for them. Shankar sang the individual lines and Glass wrote them down. Being a Westerner, Glass found places in the score to insert bar lines, but when the music was performed, Shankar's tabla player, Alla Rakha, immediately spotted the appearance of unasked-for rhythmic stresses. Glass moved the bar lines, and the stresses moved with them. Finally, the bar lines were eliminated, the stresses disappeared and Glass, suddenly, was on the road to his own distinctive brand of minimalism.

Back in New York City and supporting himself by driving a cab, Glass found a small but enthusiastic audience for his music. Prominent among them were visual artists, film makers and theatre people; few if any of them were subscribers to the Philharmonic or the Met. In 1971, the year of Reich's *Drumming*, Glass began work on his own extended ensemble work, *Music in 12 Parts*. At nearly four hours, it was three times longer than Reich's piece, but it resembled it in being a catalogue of all Glass's musical concerns to date — a sort of minimalist *Art of Fugue* — and it paved the way for his next, even bigger project, the opera *Einstein on the Beach* of 1976.

Glass's collaboration with the stage director Robert Wilson was a watershed for minimalism. *Einstein on the Beach* is in no sense a conventional opera, except that it involves staged spectacle. There is no plot; nothing really happens during the four hours it takes to perform. The opera provides visual and dramatic equivalents of the music itself, in that the audience is invited to experience the entire work in the present tense. This, I suppose, might be said to be the rationale of minimalist art, and in music it can be traced back, through John Cage's work in the 1940s and '50s, to Erik Satie. No argument is being advanced, the listener is not required to engage with the music (what is there to engage with?); we are asked only to listen and, in the case of *Einstein on the Beach*, to look. The repetitions of phrases, the simple harmonies, the Mozartian Alberti basses — ostinato arpeggios that in the Classical period had supported themes, but in Glass's music are left alone to be themselves: all these features encourage a kind of rapt contemplation, rather than active thought.

Contemplation of a quieter sort characterised the music of two other composers in the 1970s, one of them in what was still the Soviet Union, the other in Australia. In each case, the element of exact repetition associated with Reich and Glass was tempered, but the musical materials were still extremely limited. In 1977, the Estonian, Arvo Pärt, in writing his brief *Cantus in Memory of Benjamin Britten*, took a descending melodic minor scale and had it played at different speeds in different octaves by the members of a string orchestra. Although these are the only notes in the piece, the effect is surprisingly rich. It is like a gentle peal of bells, and Pärt spoke of this style as 'tintinnabulation'. Three years before, Anne Boyd, like many of her Australian colleagues, was looking north to Indonesia. Her piano piece, *Angklung* (1974) has only four notes — B flat, A flat, E flat and F flat — though as with Pärt's *Cantus*, they turn up in more than one octave. This, in itself, is a function of Boyd's source material for the piece, the *gamelan angklung* of Bali and Java, the bamboo rattles of which each produce a single pitch with octave doublings. Although the pitch material is truly minimal, and the piece itself never raises its voice above a hushed *pianissimo*, there is an element of unpredictability about *Angklung*. The little flourishes are continually rearranged — like hearing wind chimes in an intermittent breeze — and the repeated notes that emerge from each flourish vary in number. You can, I think, listen to this piece in two quite different frames of mind. The first is the one the composer herself intended: a state of intense inner peace, 'concerned with the tuning of ourselves with others and with the natural world of which we are part'. But I find Anne Boyd's music just a bit too interesting for that. The response that *Angklung* draws from me is one of sitting on the edge of my seat in expectation of the next change in the pattern, and of always being wrong in my predictions.

If some of the impulses that sparked minimalist music came from observing the greater spontaneity of pop and the more instant communication between pop musicians and their audiences, it didn't take long before the influence was working in the opposite direction. In 1972, a 20-year-old English guitarist called Mike Oldfield produced an album that was closer to a complete musical work than anything before it in pop music, and from its first moments, the stamp of minimalism was obvious. *Tubular Bells* was the product of many solitary months in a recording studio, the composer Oldfield playing all the instrumental lines on a range of instruments. Arguably, the first five minutes contain the most original and distinguished music of the whole piece, because here Oldfield wasn't trying to do too much. As the piece continues, new instruments and new themes are added, gradually weakening the structure, because there's no really pertinent reason why one thing follows another. It's as though Oldfield has grown impatient with his minimalist creation and elected to make something happen. Whatever its shortcomings, though, *Tubular Bells* remains a landmark, and not least because it's a rare example of a pop album without songs.

At various stages in its history, the classical tradition had been enriched by the popular music of the day. I'm thinking of all those late-medieval masses constructed over popular tunes, of Haydn's fondness for gypsy music, of Mozart's for Turkish percussion and Schubert's for the Hungarian tunes that he heard in the cafes of 19th-century Vienna. But the widespread fascination that early 20th-century composers demonstrated for every kind of popular music was without precedent. An ascetically pure figure like Webern was very much the exception; and even Webern, in his quartet Op. 22, was drawn to use the tenor saxophone. But in the years following

World War II the distinction between popular music and art music became a chasm, as record companies pursued commercial success on the pop charts and concert-hall composers retreated into universities. The importance of Luciano Berio — a composer of undoubted stature — re-embracing elements of popular culture cannot be over-estimated. And now, perhaps for the first time in history, the influence was no longer one-way. Mike Oldfield's attraction to minimalism was further evidence of a new era in which the gulf between art music and popular music was being bridged. The young Frank Zappa had corresponded with his hero Edgard Varèse, and Karlheinz Stockhausen — already iconised on the cover of the Beatles' *Sgt Pepper* — had begun to attract progressive rock musicians to his lectures. For European bands such as Can and Tangerine Dream, and for the San Francisco-based Grateful Dead, it was Stockhausen's electronic music that held the greatest appeal, and the Deutsche Grammophon recordings of his work were selling surprisingly well.

Stockhausen himself continued to expand his range with every new piece, and following his intuitive works of the late 1960s, the music now took on a more dynamic character. Perhaps the composer wasn't immune to the heavy rock of his hairy acolytes, but, with Stockhausen, outside influences were always filtered through his own idiosyncratic imagination. The orchestral work *Trans*, indeed, came to him in a dream. Stockhausen saw a stage on which two rows of string players, one raised up behind the other as in a school photograph, faced out into the auditorium, playing 'like robots', motionless but for their synchronised bowing arms; wind, brass and percussion players were placed behind the strings and consequently out of view. At irregular intervals, a giant weaver's shuttle rocketed across in front of the musicians as though the stage were some massive loom. The whole scene was bathed in a misty, violet-red glow, resembling, it must be said, nothing so much as a late-'60s rock concert, the psychedelic lighting filtered though a haze of marijuana smoke. Stockhausen certainly wasn't the first composer to dream a piece of music — Stravinsky maintained he had dreamt his Octet of 1923 — but it was typical of Stockhausen to set about making his dream come literally true.

On 16 October 1971, at the Donaueschingen Festival in Germany, the curtain slowly went up on Stockhausen's violet-coloured dream and the audience let out its spontaneous gasp of astonishment. Forty string players in evening dress sat facing the audience behind a gauze curtain, their bows moving up and down in unanimous slow motion, the recorded sound of a weaving loom synchronising their playing with the wind and percussion behind them. Stockhausen stipulated that performances of *Trans* should take place in a theatre, not a concert hall, and the theatrical elements of the piece don't end with its staging. A series of dream-like interruptions occurs — Stockhausen called them 'strange musical events' — beginning with a military drummer marching in from the wings prompting one of the viola players to turn, suddenly, into a gypsy violinist. A little later, a theatre attendant brings on a music stand with a lamp. The stand is placed in front of one of the cellists and the lamp turned on, the cellist immediately launching into a big romantic solo which stops and starts as the lamp goes off and on. The concert master, seated in the middle of the front row of strings, becomes stuck on a high harmonic, repeating it over and over until he becomes the focus of attention for all the other players who stare at him in horror. A piccolo trumpeter, apparently floating high above the strings, blows a fanfare, coughs and wheezes, then promptly vanishes.

What are these interruptions about? Presumably they were part of the composer's original dream, and so perhaps require no further justification: after all, if we've already accepted robotic string players, violet lighting and a weaver's shuttle, why would a floating trumpet player cause us to raise our eyebrows? I suppose it might be significant that both drummer and trumpeter play martial music, but we're entering psychoanalytic territory here. Stockhausen himself wrote that the turning on and off of the cellist's lamp was a joke against orchestral players who can only play when they can see the music, and there's little doubt that, at some level, the composer intended all these interruptions humorously. Stockhausen had long been concerned with humour, from the raucous laughter that forms part of the soprano's repertoire of sounds in *Momente*, to occurrences in other works that can best be construed as jokes: in *Stimmung* the six close-harmonising singers pause in the middle of the hour-long piece to pronounce the word 'barbershop', then they continue as before; in *Mantra*, another hour-long work for two pianos with electronically modified sound, the performers suddenly call to each other over their instruments; in *Atmen gibt das Leben* . . . ('Breathing Gives Life') — Stockhausen's choral opera of 1974 — one of the singers develops the hiccoughs. It seems to me these moments emphasise the humanity of Stockhausen's music, and the fact that (except in the electronic pieces) human beings are producing the sounds that reach our ears. Because the performers are *only* human, they are not perfect, and Stockhausen builds the potential imperfections into his scores. With *Stimmung*, for example, the composer knew that precise intonation over an hour and more would be hard to maintain, so in the instructions at the front of the score he encourages his singers to have occasional lapses of intonation, before coming back into tune (remember *Stimmung* means 'tuning in'). Likewise, these singers have to breathe, and the composer allows them to do so at will, asking them to begin singing again at the point where they would have been had they not stopped to breathe; and since these pauses for breath form punctuation marks in the music, it follows that the capacity of the singers' lungs becomes a factor in the shape of the performance. I think the moments of overt humour in Stockhausen's music are extensions of this concern with humanity and its frailties. They don't detract from the seriousness of the overall work; on the contrary, they tend to underline it.

Trans was composed very quickly, the composer not stopping to revise or question his decisions, but ploughing on, nineteen or twenty hours a day for two months. Stockhausen had become convinced that music came to him from some higher being. Like Stravinsky with *The Rite of Spring*, Stockhausen felt himself to be a vessel through which music passed.

In the latter half of 1977, he began work on the most ambitious project of his life, indeed the most ambitious musical project of the 20th century. It would occupy him, he announced, until well into the next millennium. *Licht* ('Light') was the operatic cycle to out-Wagner Wagner. When complete, it would comprise not four, but seven operas, each one named for a day of the week. The first of them, *Donnerstag*, or 'Thursday', premiered at La Scala in Milan in 1981, and further operas would continue to appear at the rate of one every three or so years. The works themselves were no more conventionally operatic than Glass's *Einstein on the Beach*, though there are some clear differences between the intentions of Stockhausen and his American colleague. The operas that comprise *Licht* do have plots — arcane, esoteric plots that hinge on the power struggle between Lucifer and the Archangel Michael — but they frequently give rise to musical types that seldom turn up in the opera house. *Samstag* ('Saturday'), for instance, contains a half-hour piano solo (*Klavierstück XIII*) which, like virtually every section of every one of Stockhausen's operas, can be extracted from its dramatic context and played independently. Many of these works, like the piano piece from *Samstag*, are solo works, with or without accompaniment, the accompaniment often being on tape. In between opera premieres, Stockhausen, his trumpeter and saxophonist sons, pianist daughter, clarinettist wife, and flute-playing girlfriend, now set off on concert tours performing these extracts, like an avant-garde Family von Trapp. Yet none of these public activities seemed to staunch the flow of new music from the prolific composer.

Apart from in his youth, Pierre Boulez was never prolific, and as his conducting duties expanded in the 1960s, he composed less and less. By 1971, he was chief conductor of the BBC Symphony Orchestra in London and of the New York Philharmonic, and his own music was being neglected. At the end of 1973, however, his colleague and friend, the Italian composer Bruno Maderna died, and the event prompted a major new score from Boulez whose world premiere he conducted in London eighteen months later. *Rituel: in memoriam Bruno Maderna* was a new departure for Boulez.

In his original program note for the piece, Boulez described *Rituel* in terms of a funeral rite for his late colleague, versets and responses from an imaginary priest and congregation. The orchestra is divided into eight groups. At the rear of the platform is the largest of these, a chorus of fourteen brass instruments, together with racks of gongs and tam-tams (seven of each). In *Rituel*, the brass players always follow the conductor, but the two percussionists who play along with them strike their gongs independently. The other seven groups range in size from a single oboe, to two clarinets, to three flutes, and so on, up to a string sextet, and a wind septet. Sometimes these groups join in with the conducted brass music, but they can also function quite independently of the conductor and the other groups. In this role, each group has its own time-keeper in the form of a percussion player. *Rituel*, then, opens with a quiet chord from the brass, muted and mysterious, and decorated by gongs, followed by a slow melodic line from the solo oboe, together with its time-keeping drummer. There were several facets of *Rituel* that were new for Boulez, and one of them was the relative simplicity of its melodic lines. Equally, there was no piece before *Rituel* (though several have come since) in which Boulez made his structure so instantly clear. It's partly to do with the spatial distribution of the players on the platform and with the timing and nature of their musical utterances — in other words, with the ritual elements of *Rituel* — but it also relates to the memorability of the pulses, melodic lines and chords which makes it comparatively easy to follow the slow progress of the piece.

Finally, and this, I think, is unique in Boulez's output as a composer, there is a veiled quotation running throughout this work, a reference to another 20th-century piece, equally ritualistic and created, like *Rituel*, in homage to a dead colleague. The figure recurs throughout Boulez's score as a point of punctuation; it is a long-held chord, immediately followed by a staccato repetition. It crops up too in Stravinsky's *Symphonies of Wind Instruments*, composed more than half a century earlier in memory of Debussy, and Boulez's use of it in his 'ceremony of extinction' for Bruno Maderna was perfectly deliberate.

It may be that the appearance of pulses in *Rituel* also results from the influence of another composer. Although, this time, surely not a conscious influence, the music of the English composer Harrison Birtwistle had by 1975, firmly insinuated itself in Boulez's consciousness and, as a conductor, Boulez was an important champion of Birtwistle's work.

In the history of 20th-century music, Harrison Birtwistle may come to occupy his own private pigeon hole; his work has few antecedents. In the late 1950s, Birtwistle had been part of the so-called Manchester school of composers that included Peter Maxwell Davies and Alexander Goehr. They were students together at the Royal Northern College of Music, but Birtwistle was never much of a talker and, doubtless intimidated by his more articulate colleagues, he spent his student days practising the clarinet; any music he may have written was stashed away in a drawer. Unlike

Maxwell Davies and Goehr, Birtwistle was not attracted to the advanced serial methods advocated by the Darmstadt composers, and at the time virtually insisted upon by Boulez. His music was utterly personal and his techniques largely intuitive. Birtwistle's pieces don't seem to have been composed so much as dug up out of the earth.

In calling his 1971 orchestral work *An Imaginary Landscape*, Birtwistle was naming one of his primary creative obsessions. His pieces tend to be like landscapes in a number of ways. With Birtwistle, there is often the sense of entering a piece of music. Once inside, the listener discovers a distinctive sound world, full of dark sonorities and rough edges (the composer has said that if he were a sculptor, you would be able to see the chisel marks in his work). Like a landscape, too, Birtwistle's music is concerned with foreground, middle ground and background; an idea might make its first appearance in the distance, then, without warning, turn up prominently in the foreground. With many of his pieces, and particularly those from the 1970s, we seem to be slowly journeying through this landscape in the company of the composer, a latter-day Virgil, who directs our gaze but leaves us to make sense of what we see.

In 1972, Birtwistle unearthed a new and particularly sombre piece called *The Triumph of Time*. It takes its title from an allegorical engraving by the 16th-century Flemish artist Pieter Bruegel the Elder depicting the figures of Time riding on a cart, followed by Death slumped on an emaciated horse, and Pride, blowing his own trumpet, astride an elephant. They are making an apparently slow procession through a landscape in which all before them flourishes, while everything in their wake is devastation. Ahead of them are the trappings of wealth and success, but behind them houses burn, a gale blows and a boat is lost at sea. Birtwistle had composed the music before he saw Bruegel's engraving, but the music and the image illustrate each other perfectly. The lopsided tread of harp, low strings and horns sets the grim processional in motion, and soon we hear the first of two fixed musical objects, an ornate but mournful melody on the cor anglais. This will return again, unchanged, and so will the second object, a three-note figure, rising, then falling, played by an amplified soprano saxophone.

These figures function as signposts in Birtwistle's musical landscape, they help the listeners to locate themselves in the piece, but they also have a ritualistic function. For Birtwistle, music seems to be a kind of ritual, and ritual tends to be repetitive. As audience members, it is impossible for us to know the significance of Birtwistle's rituals — perhaps the composer himself does not know — so listening to one of his pieces is a little like being a tourist who arrives at a temple or some other sacred sight, where the locals are performing activities that capture our attention but never give up their secrets. The more we watch, the more we find connections between the activities. We may even imagine we have discovered some rationale behind them, but whatever significance we attach to what we see, it is unlikely it will be the same significance felt by an initiate. Occasionally, in Birtwistle's pieces, players will get up and move to a different part of the stage to play a certain figure or sequence of figures. The action has the effect of drawing our attention to the music in a quite different manner, and underlining its significance — whatever that significance may be. It is a dramatic device, of course, but it's not a drama we can explain. To use the title of Birtwistle's chamber orchestra piece of 1984, this is *Secret Theatre*.

Someone else much concerned with the dramatic potential of purely instrumental music was the Scottish composer Thea Musgrave. In a series of concertos written from the late 1960s onwards, Musgrave allocated dramatic actions to members of her orchestra. Often, this was no more than asking individual players to stand in order to declaim their solos, rather like members of a 1940s big band. But in the Horn Concerto of 1971, written for Barry Tuckwell, Musgrave has the soloist interact with the orchestral horns in a very striking manner. The concerto began to take shape in the composer's mind when she received a postcard from the soloist who was holidaying in Mexico. The postcard showed a number of stone statues grouped around a central statue. At the climax of her Horn Concerto, then, Musgrave has the horn players in the orchestra move out into the auditorium so that they surround the other performers and the audience. While the conductor continues to control the orchestra, the horn players now take their cues from the soloist, setting up a sequence of calling figures that float above the rest of the music and around the auditorium.

A different attitude to musical drama occurs in the work of

Elliott Carter. Carter had often spoken of his string quartets as human dramas, and of the individual players having roles. In 1975 he composed his first vocal work in nearly 30 years: a setting for soprano and nine instruments of six poems by Elizabeth Bishop, entitled *A Mirror on Which to Dwell*. Carter's return to text-setting surprised many people. But, even in the chamber and orchestral works he had written in the 1950s and '60s, he had never abandoned his literary interests. In the Double Concerto for Harpsichord and Piano with Two Chamber Orchestras (1961), two contrasting literary texts provided inspiration. The stark and appalling lines about chaos from Lucretius's *De rerum natura* and an ironic passage on the same topic in Pope's *Dunciad*, helped Carter to discover the idiosyncratic formal plan — one might almost call it a scenario — for his concerto. They also suggested a solution to the problem of handling the very different characters of the work's two solo instruments. The relationship between the Concerto for Orchestra of 1969 and St John Perse's poem, 'Winds', is particularly strong. Although the text itself is still absent from the piece, it is inextricably woven into the fabric of Carter's multi-faceted score, and a knowledge of it serves as what Boulez once called 'a source of irrigation' for the music. The poem provided Carter not only with the windy sound world of the Concerto's opening and closing pages, but also the exceptionally complex, four-in-one movement structure of the whole.

A Symphony of Three Orchestras, composed in 1976, was the result of its composer's long-term fascination with Hart Crane's poem, *The Bridge*, which dated back to his student days at Harvard, when he had intended to employ the text in a large scale choral work. This mooted cantata came to nothing, the composer rejecting the text, he said, because the poem was so pessimistic he did not wish to be depressed for the length of time it would take to compose the piece. But the text remained important to Carter, and one section of it surfaced again in the scenario of his 1936 ballet, *Pocahontas*. When he finally composed *A Symphony of Three Orchestras* he did so in the space of six months, which, for Carter, was very quick indeed.

The opening lines of *The Bridge* inspired both the form and, in a sense, the content of *A Symphony of Three Orchestras*; the introductory bars of the piece, with their misty, stratospheric strings, squawking flutes and clarinets, and high, wheeling solo trumpet, evoke Crane's opening lines, describing a grey dawn over Brooklyn Bridge:

> How many dawns, chill from his rippling rest
> The seagull's wings shall dip and pivot him,
> Shedding white rings of tumult, building high
> Over the chained bay waters Liberty.

Carter acknowledged the link between poem and music in his program note for the piece, saying that 'although *A Symphony of Three Orchestras* is not in any sense an attempt to express the poem of Hart Crane in music, many of the musical ideas were suggested by it and other works of his'. The use of illustrative devices in Carter's work was by no means unusual, but in being so specifically programmatic, the introduction to *A Symphony* was rare for Carter. In the Elizabeth Bishop songs of *A Mirror on Which to Dwell*, however, and in two more vocal works that now followed on their heels, Carter dealt in musical literalism to a surprising degree.

The pieces were *Syringa* (1978), which takes a specially written text by John Ashbery and juxtaposes it with words in ancient Greek about the Orpheus myth, and *In Sleep, in Thunder* (1981), a setting of six poems by the composer's late friend, Robert Lowell. Together with *A Mirror on Which to Dwell* they form a triptych that might almost be a musical autobiography of the composer. It's not just that the music sometimes illustrates the text, as when the guitar impersonates Orpheus's lute in *Syringa*, but that the text seems to refer to Carter's music, rather in the manner that Stefan George's words about 'the air from another planet' had given specific meaning to Schoenberg's break with tonality in his second string quartet.

The third song in *A Mirror on Which to Dwell* sets Elizabeth Bishop's poem, 'Sandpiper'. It seems pretty clear that Bishop intended the bird in the title as an image of herself, and it may be coincidence but Carter allocates a solo role to the oboe, the instrument he had played as a student. In Bishop's poem, the sandpiper runs along the edge of the ocean, pecking away, 'preoccupied,/ looking for something, something, something', and Carter's piping oboe impersonates it. Bishop describes the 'finical' bird 'in a state of controlled panic', but she also uses a broader brush to show us the 'interrupting water' of the Atlantic. 'The world is a mist,' she tells us. 'And then the world is/minute and vast and clear.' These are all appropriate images for Carter's style and for the way his music operates in time and space.

The ebb and flow of tempo and texture in his works is extremely flexible, and in this song we view the activity through the experience of the sandpiper/oboe, or if you like the poet/composer. The oboe pecks away in a constant fast tempo, but the other instruments create slower moving sheets of sound, like the ocean's 'interrupting water'. When the tempo of the other players increases, the sandpiper/oboe 'runs, he runs straight through it', stubbornly refusing to be distracted, maintaining his tempo all the while.

Elliott Carter once said that music should be as complex as the best poetry or philosophy, and his own works certainly illustrate this statement. In Carter's pieces we find the antithesis of minimalism, because while La Monte Young, Alvin Lucier, Pauline Oliveros and the later minimalists expected their audiences to open their ears but disengage their brains, Carter requires our full attention. His music may have an attractive and colourful surface, certainly a very active one, but there are also details, correspondences and cross-references to be picked up if we're quick enough. Carter's critics have accused him of over-complexity, but the composer's response was always that the world is a complex place and that his music attempted to deal with that, rather than reducing the human experience to a few simple patterns. For that reason alone, Carter's audience was never likely to be as large as Philip Glass's. But how often do poets and philosophers turn up on bestseller lists?

Another composer branded complex by the polemicists of postmodernism was Brian Ferneyhough. Although born in England, Ferneyhough has not lived there since the 1960s, preferring Europe and, later, California. On paper, Ferneyhough's music is unprecedentedly complex. His performers are often confronted by six or seven different pieces of data in order to produce a single sound. Ferneyhough is liable to give his string players information about the position of the bow on the string, the angle at which it should be held, and the amount of pressure to be applied. Dynamics shift in a seemingly arbitrary manner; tempo is almost never constant, it is always speeding up and slowing down; and pitch is similarly fluid, slipping and sliding about in the cracks between the notes of the chromatic scale. Above all, rhythm is complicated to the point at which it can be regarded merely as the means of placing sounds in time. But this is on paper. These issues are for the performer. What does the listener hear?

Oddly enough, Ferneyhough's music is not particularly complex for the listener. I will go further and suggest that, as with minimalism, this is also music that takes us back to basics, back to the very act of projecting sounds in time and space, back to the edges of eloquence. Aesthetically, however, it is the reverse of minimalism: there are no neat, reassuring phrases to latch on to, no gradually mutating patterns to follow; instead, Ferneyhough is concerned with the primordial struggle to give shape to sound. In his flute solo *Cassandra's Dream Song* (1970), the performer becomes the Trojan prophet, doomed never to be believed, as she tries to make the elders of Argos heed her warnings. Like all Ferneyhough's pieces, *Cassandra's Dream Song* is visceral music, verging on pain. The urgency of the performance is seemingly at odds with the precise detail on the page, and yet it is the physical struggle to realise all this detail that gives the performance its dramatic impact. The inherent paradox of Ferneyhough's music is that the amount of information in the score makes it almost impossible for the performer to achieve total accuracy: each performance is a new struggle and the results will always be, in a sense, provisional. For Ferneyhough, the act of composing is also like this, and here is another paradox. For all their apparent precision, the scores themselves are only makeshift, and by way of demonstrating this, in the mid 1970s Ferneyhough composed the same work twice. At first glance, the score of *Funérailles* (1978), for seven strings and harp, looks like a piece in two movements. But it isn't. It is the same basic material, treated differently: two distinct outcomes for the one piece. Ferneyhough insists that the pieces should not be performed separately, but also that they should not be played back to back. Something else — another piece, or an interval — should come between them in order to emphasise their separate identities.

The critics of this music — and there are many of them — tend to focus on the visual complexity of the scores. But the fact is that

Ferneyhough is as concerned with the physicality of sound as Erik Satie or any of the early minimalists. The patent difference is that Ferneyhough's music also makes demands on us: it disturbs our mental equilibrium; it forces us to confront it head on. In this sense, it belongs to the same modernist tradition as Schoenberg's *Erwartung* and Stravinsky's *The Rite of Spring*.

By the 1970s, that tradition was under threat. More than this, a composer's right to make such demands on an audience was up for debate, and it was essentially a political debate. There were strong individual voices, particularly in the United States, who were pre-pared to argue, in words and music, against what they took to be the modernist hegemony of composers like Boulez, Carter and Ferney-hough. And they were strong, in part, because they pulled big audiences. Modern music, they argued, did not have to be unpopu-lar. And anyway, what was so modern about composing in an atonal musical language whose roots lay in pre-World War I German expressionism? As a new generation of composers re-embraced tonality in their scores, many older modernists began to recant. The Americans George Rochberg and Leon Kirchner, who both turned 60 at the end of the decade, had moved away from their post-Schoenberg styles in works that included passages you could analyse and increasingly hear as tonal; a decade younger, the Australian Richard Meale abandoned his very personal exploration of the Boulezian aesthetic and, in his orchestral piece *Viridian* (1979), com-menced an equally personal exploration of a language rather closer to Debussy. Who were the radicals now?

If all acts of composition could be viewed in a political light, perhaps the time had finally arrived for the concert hall to become the crucible for political change that Nono, Henze and others had always believed possible. But, after the failures of the 1960s, com-posers of a revolutionary mien were rather thin on the ground. While Nono maintained his modernist belief that the materials and lan-guage of music must change alongside society itself, Henze continued to engage with the texts and music of revolutionary societies such as Cuba. More successful than either of these Europeans, however, at least from the point of getting his political message across, was the American, Frederic Rzewski. As a virtuoso pianist, Rzewski had given some of the most committed performances of now-classic works of the post-war avant-garde: Stockhausen's piano pieces, Boulez's second sonata and the like. But by the 1970s, Rzewski, whose own music owed little to these European models, had more obviously political causes to fight.

In September 1971, there was a revolt among the inmates at Attica prison in up-state New York, brutally put down by the National Guard who shot dead a number of the protesters. Rzewski used a letter written by Sam Melville, one of the murdered inmates, as the basis of his 1972 piece, *Coming Together*. Melville speaks in his letter of his time in prison, and of a growing sense of freedom, security and 'a greater coming together', as a loud, fast, bluesy, bass riff almost drowns him out.

Rzewski's piano piece, *Winnsboro Cotton Mill Blues* grew out of watching Martin Ritt's 1979 movie *Norma Rae*, which concerns the unionisation of the textiles industry in Alabama. A feature of Ritt's film is the constant din of the machinery. It dominates the sound-track and Rzewski incorporated it into his piece, so that the music seems to take on the Romantically tinged realism of a Zola novel. In Rzewski's work, in *Coming Together* and *Winnsboro Cotton Mill Blues*, the repetitiveness of minimalist technique merges with political protest: it is not only the musical figures that are being repeated, but the message; and the message is squarely aimed at the bourgeois concert-goer. But, though they may be political tracts, these pieces are also powerful music, and Rzewski's is an original voice. *Winnsboro Cotton Mill Blues* fuses the technical virtuosity of keyboard composers from Liszt to Boulez with the noisy machine-driven world of Mosolov, Antheil and Varèse; it also brings the vernacular music of the blues into the concert hall. The sounds are complex, but direct; repetitious, yet goal-driven; they alternate between searing dissonance and common chords. Although Rzewski never intended it, *Winnsboro Cotton Mill Blues* sums up a great deal about the first eight decades of 20th-century music, and proposes a stylistic and philosophical template for the last two.

THE ME
GENERATION

The 20th century has been characterised by change — technological, political and social. In particular, the speed at which most of these changes have occurred has been breathtaking. All previous centuries had witnessed developments in musical style, but none the frequency and radicalness of the changes that have occurred in the last hundred years. By the early 1980s a stylistic shift had overtaken the music of many of the world's best known composers that could scarcely have been predicted fifteen years earlier.

American minimalism was certainly responsible for some of it. Even composers who never became minimalists were affected by the new simplicity that typified this music: simplicity of harmony and in some cases melody, and a return to regular pulses and recognisable rhythmic patterns.

On the face of it, one of the least likely composers to undergo these changes, and one of the most interesting examples of the phenomenon, was György Ligeti, the 1960s pioneer of micropolyphony and hero of the avant-garde. That the creator of *San Francisco Polyphony* — Ligeti's dense, detailed orchestral work of 1974 —

might, four years later, produce the infectiously syncopated cha-conne for harpsichord called *Hungarian Rock*, gives some idea of the scale of the transformation.

What had changed in Ligeti's music? In a word, it was the pres-ence of vernacular elements in his pieces. He had in no sense reverted to tonality, as others had — pressed to describe his new style, Ligeti called it 'non-atonal' — but he seemed to have picked over the detritus of music's past and gathered up what took his fancy. So we encounter tonally related objects in his works — inter-vals like thirds, and fifths and sixths — but they do not function in a tonal manner. Melody had always been an important element in Ligeti's music, it was just that in his orchestral pieces of the 1960s and early 1970s, there were so many independent melodic strands occurring simultaneously that they tended to vaporise into a thick cloud of sound. The same was true of his use of rhythm. What we discover, then, in Ligeti's music of the 1980s, is not so much a simplification of these elements, as a clarification. The composer's interest in the music of sub-Saharan Africa, for example, had encouraged him to fix his rhythmic patterns so that the repetitions could now be perceived. In spite of its title, *Hungarian Rock* is a perfect example of this African influence, and the harpsichord, with its plucked strings, might almost be a giant Ugandan thumb piano. The South African-born Kevin Volans often composed for the harpsi-chord in a comparable manner and to similar effect.

Two works intervened between the orchestral piece *San Francisco Polyphony* and *Hungarian Rock*. One was a set of three pieces for two pianos, the central movement of which was given the significant title of *Selbstporträt mit Reich und Riley* ('Self portrait with Reich and Riley'). It was like an admission of the influence minimal-ism had had on the composer. Ligeti's other major piece of the mid 1970s was his first opera, *Le grand macabre*. Adapted from *The Ballad of the Grand Macabre* by the Belgian playwright Michel de Ghelderode, Ligeti's opera is set in the mythical Breughelland, a state that is corrupt, through and through, where it has been announced that the world will end tonight, and where two lovers (originally, Spermando and Clitoria, though their names were later altered to Amando and Amanda) are searching for a quiet place to consum-mate their barely controllable sexual appetites. *Le grand macabre* opens, like Monteverdi's *Orfeo*, with a toccata — though here it is played, not by brass instruments, but car horns — and the opera closes with another baroque device, a passacaglia. This is a repeated ground bass, and over it the two lovers sing fragments of rapturous melody. *Le grand macabre* was a turning point for Ligeti.

Operas often change composers. The business of making the sung dialogue and dramatic development comprehensible can result in the simplification of a composer's language. Because of this general tendency, it was not at all clear from *Le grand macabre* that Ligeti had changed as radically as he in fact had. And the harpsichord solo *Hungarian Rock* was a five-minute party piece, so surely one couldn't read too much into that. In fact, the real clue to Ligeti's stylistic shift had come in that two-piano piece *Selbstporträt*, not only because of its acknowledgement of American minimalism, but also because of its bracketed subtitle: in full, the piece is called *Selbstporträt mit Reich und Riley (und Chopin ist auch dabei)* ('and Chopin is close by, too'). This reference to an important 19th-century composer takes on greater significance in the light of Ligeti's first work of the 1980s: a Horn Trio, subtitled 'Hommage à Brahms'.

Unlike many other composers of the period, Ligeti was not being stylistically archaic in these works — the music never actually sounded like Chopin or Brahms — but the subtitles do suggest that he was starting to aim at a greater emotional content in his music, and in the Horn Trio he found it. Ligeti borrowed the instrumentation of horn, violin and piano from Brahms's trio of 1865, but there are no overt references to the piece itself (although, the opening of Ligeti's work, with the violin playing a double-stopped major third, does fleetingly recall the beginning of Brahms's clarinet quintet). There is one other debt to Brahms's trio, beyond the choice of instruments. Brahms's first movement is slow and it is followed by a scherzo; Ligeti does the same, only he replaces the conventional scherzo with one of those wind-up, perpetual motion devices typical of his music from the late 1960s. The third and fourth sections of Brahms's trio are a slow movement, headed *Mesto* ('sad'), and an exuberant, galloping finale. Ligeti reverses this order: he writes an out-of-step march rather than a gallop and places it third, ending with a slow movement of infinite sadness. Like the finale of the opera, this is a passacaglia. It is marked *Lamento*, and it comprises seven of the most authentically tragic minutes in late 20th-century music. Simple, step-like figures of four, five or three notes droop slowly downwards, like tears zig-zagging down a grieving face. The sense of great loss is palpable and it increases as the movement makes its way, inexorably towards a shattering climax. The coda of Ligeti's lament is hollow, desolate; grief is an exhausting business.

News spread quickly about what Ligeti had done in his Horn Trio and a great deal of nonsense was spoken about the piece, largely by those who had not yet heard it. Some modernists talked of Ligeti's backsliding; others, who thought of themselves as post-modernist, acclaimed the trio as evidence of its composer's con-version. Of course, they were all wrong. In his Horn Trio, Ligeti was being himself, no more, no less. The music had all the high seriousness that modernists liked to believe was exclusively theirs, and the piece was, moreover, a complete original: no charge of backsliding could be upheld, unless, that is, it was deemed inap-propriate for modernist music to pack such a profound emotional punch. And those qualities of originality and emotion mark out Ligeti's piece as very different from the clever playfulness that typi-fied a lot of postmodernist art. The truth was that just as Ligeti had been one of the most compelling and ingenious musical creators of the 1960s, so he was set to become equally significant to the 1980s and '90s.

Ligeti's next project was to be a piano concerto, but in sketch-ing ideas for it, he was side-tracked into writing a series of solo *Etudes*. In spite of their generic title, these pieces were not a further nod in the direction of Chopin, but rather something quite new. Ligeti had become enthralled by the music of Conlon Nancarrow, an American-born composer resident in Mexico City since 1940 after his involvement in the Spanish civil war brought him into political disfavour in his homeland. In the 1940s, Nancarrow had taken to composing for the mechanical player piano. He created the piano rolls himself, punching the holes into the long sheets of paper that would activate the hammers of the instrument. The process allowed Nancarrow to generate music that was, in most cases, impossible for a mere human to play, partly because it tended to be so dense with notes that eight or nine arms would have been necessary to reach them all, and partly because most of the pieces involved the overlaying of multiple pulses, metres and rhythms, such that a second or third brain might also have come in useful.

The rhythmic complexity wasn't, of itself, so startlingly new. In America alone, Charles Ives, Ruth Crawford Seeger and later Elliott Carter had all explored the simultaneous use of several different tempos, and Ligeti's own music of the 1960s and '70s is a blur of intricate cross-rhythms. The difference was that Nancarrow habitually called upon the gestures of jazz. The Studies for Player Piano of Nancarrow resemble the hectic, free improvisations of pianist Cecil Taylor, in their willingness to pile jazz riff on top of jazz riff. James Tenney described the first and last movements of Nancarrow's Study #3 as 'surreal . . . as if Jimmy Yancy, Fats Waller, James P. Johnson and Art Tatum were all ecstatically jamming together in heaven'.

Because of the absence of early recordings, and because recordings would have been the only way to hear this music, Ligeti did not encounter Nancarrow's Studies until the middle of 1980, and then it was by accident. The rhythmic complexity of the Studies immediately appealed to him and helped to clarify his thinking, but the presence of sounds from vernacular music — common chords and jazz rhythms — was probably just as important, and the influence of the 70-year-old Nancarrow on the 60-year-old Ligeti can be heard very clearly in the first book of *Etudes*. From the point of view of style, it is there most obviously in the feverish motion of the first piece, *Désordres* ('Disorderliness'), its title hinting at the composer's growing interest in chaos theory. But in some of the *études* that follow — for instance the fifth one, called *Arc-en-ciel* ('Rainbow') — the style changes, though the techniques, much simplified, remain. For the most part *Arc-en-ciel* consists of slow-moving semiquavers, the top line — I suppose I might as well come right out and call it the melody — grouping these beats into threes and twos to produce a gentle, Stravinsky-like syncopation. In its tonal ambiguity, the harmony recalls late Scriabin.

Ligeti's shift of style brings into focus an apparent crisis in contemporary music. Put simply, it was becoming harder to know what was modern. Terms such as 'avant-garde', which had once seemed so appropriate, were now meaningless. Was Ligeti moving in a conservative direction in his Horn Trio and his *Etudes*? Or was this a radical new thrust? Perhaps 1970s minimalism had been radical. Its simple forms were certainly a breath of fresh air after some of the extreme complexity in music since World War II, but to composers like Pierre Boulez and Elliott Carter, minimalism was little more than a set of easy solutions. As Boulez said, the human brain was surely capable of doing a bit more work than this.

In 1985, the musicologist Peter Franklin described the works of Brian Ferneyhough as 'orthodox avant-garde conservatism'. What he meant, presumably, was that in seeking to maintain a line of musical enquiry that began with the second Viennese school and continued, in the 1950s, with Boulez, Stockhausen and Nono, Ferneyhough was avoiding or ignoring the 'unorthdox rearguard radicalism' of, say, the American minimalists. But what Franklin achieves with his statement is little more than a demonstration of the impotence of political labels in the late 20th century. This, we must remember, was an era of doublespeak, of Ronald Reagan and of Margaret Thatcher, an ultra-right-wing leader who described her policies as 'radical'.

Ligeti's 1960s investigations of sonority and texture were in any case not yet over. If he himself no longer had much interest in the area, there were others who did. One of them was a former pupil of Ferneyhough, the Finnish composer Kaija Saariaho. Saariaho's work, rather like some of her teacher's, seems to exist at the edges of music. In a succession of pieces from the mid 1980s, she explored the very nature of sound, often with the assistance of computers. In 1985, the same year Ligeti published his first book of *Etudes*, Saariaho began work on a piece for nine instruments and live electronics. *Lichtbogen* ('Arcs of Light') recalls in its title the fifth of Ligeti's new pieces, *Arc-en-ciel*, but in its concern with texture it seems to continue the Hungarian composer's earlier work. The starting point for *Lichtbogen* was Saariaho's computer analysis of a cello's harmonics. The composer went into a recording studio with a cellist who produced for her a range of different bow pressures. When a bow is drawn across a cello string we hear a tone, but we also hear a certain amount of noise: the noise of horse-hair scraping gut or metal. The more pressure the cellist applies, the louder the tone becomes, but, equally, the more noise is generated. This subtly shifting spectrum of sound between tone and noise not only governed the sound world of

Lichtbogen, it also determined its structure: everything that happens in the piece relates to it. The dominant instrument of the work, however, is not the cello, but a solo flute, whose relative breathiness offers another version of the tone-noise spectrum. The first sound we hear is that of pure breath coming through the instrument, gradually forming itself into a tone. Saariaho seems to conjure *Lichtbogen* from the very basic materials of music, the instruments continually struggling towards eloquence before finally sinking back once more into silence.

Lichtbogen was a commission from the French Ministry of Culture and, by the mid 1980s, Kaija Saariaho was living and working in Paris where she had attached herself to the Institute for Musical and Acoustical Research, or, to give it its French acronym, IRCAM. With generous funding from the French government, Pierre Boulez had set up the institute in 1977, staffing it with scientists and musicians. Beyond its remit as a laboratory for pure research, IRCAM also had a practical function. Boulez recognised that the problem with so much electronic music was that it was created by technicians who composed, rather than by composers who had learned to work with the new technology. Part of his vision for IRCAM was that composers might come there to work with experts in the area. After all, if composers could write orchestral pieces without being able to play all the instruments, why should they be able to work their own gear when it came to creating music with electronic sounds?

One of those who worked at IRCAM in its early days was the Englishman Jonathan Harvey. As a student, Harvey had been greatly encouraged by Benjamin Britten and this is reflected in his output as a composer, an important part of which consists of works for church choirs. But Harvey was also drawn to modernism, writing one of the earliest (and one of the best) monographs on the work of Stockhausen. It was Stockhausen's *Gesang der Jünglinge* that, in a way, provided the model for Harvey's first work at IRCAM, because not only does it have, like the Stockhausen, a religious intent, it also makes use of a boy's voice — in this case, Harvey's son who was a chorister at Winchester Cathedral. The title of the piece was *Mortuos plango, vivos voco*. These words are part of the Latin inscription on the great tenor bell of the cathedral: 'I weep for the dead, I call to the living . . .' Armed with recordings of the bell and of his son intoning its inscription, Harvey headed for IRCAM where he composed what still strikes me as one of the few totally successful pieces of computer music.

The reasons for its success stem from Harvey's resourcefulness in dealing with his simple materials. There was, and still is, a tendency for composers of electronic music to feel that a piece is over only when they had pushed every available button and twiddled every knob. But *Mortuos plango* is exceptionally disciplined. Everything in the piece emerges from the computer analysis of the boy's voice and the bell, and from their subsequent manipulation in which the boy becomes the bell, and the bell, the boy. As in *Lichtbogen*, the structure of the piece also derives from these analyses: all the musical details, large and small, from the timing of events to the voicing of chords. The result is a fabulous intensity. More striking still, I suppose, is that, for a piece composed with a computer and existing only on tape, *Mortuos plango* is a curiously humane work. In taking traditional musical objects and exploring them with the latest technology, Jonathan Harvey's piece forms an unlikely bridge between the English provincialism of Benjamin Britten on the one hand and the cosmopolitan modernism of Boulez on the other.

Boulez's own compositions continued to progress in fits and starts, interrupted by conducting engagements and by his duties as director of IRCAM. His own creative project at the institute was *Répons* (literally, 'Response', but in the liturgical sense), for a large ensemble of woodwind, brass and strings, with six answering soloists playing two pianos, harp, cimbalom, vibraphone and xylophone (doubling glockenspiel). The main ensemble is on a stage at the centre of the auditorium with the audience surrounding it; the soloists are placed around the perimeter walls, surrounding the audience. The distinction between the two groups of players is further underlined by the nature of the music they are given. The large ensemble has music that is rhythmically very regular — at times it seems almost deliberately banal — but the soloists, when they finally enter, do so with flamboyant flourishes. The relationship between the ensembles of *Répons* and the one Boulez had earlier employed in *Eclat/Multiples* seems obvious. Both pieces have a large group of instruments that can sustain their notes, and a smaller number of soloists whose notes begin to die away immediately after their attack. But, courtesy of IRCAM, there is a third component to *Répons*. As the introductory bars, played by the main ensemble, reach their conclusion, the soloists all make their entries. Before their sounds can die away, they have been picked up and carried on by a computer that also begins to transform them. It is as though the music has suddenly entered a new dimension.

Répons was first heard as a twenty-minute torso in 1981. It was performed again the following year by which time it had grown to 30 minutes. By 1984, although still unfinished, it lasted three-quarters of an hour. Boulez has said that he believes the piece ultimately needs to be twice as long as that, but for the time being it remains a work in progress. Among Boulez's pieces, *Répons* is not alone in its state of incompletion. Most of his works have undergone revision, some quite belatedly: the cantata *Le visage nuptial*, first composed in 1946 and 1947, was substantially revised in 1957, and did not find its final form until 1988. The third piano sonata remains incomplete, as does the orchestration of *Notations*, the twelve piano miniatures of 1945 which Boulez began to transform for large orchestra in 1977. *Eclat/Multiples* (already a reworking of *Eclat*) lies unfinished, and so does *Livre pour cordes*. This work began life as a string quartet in 1949, and was published in 1960, minus its fourth movement. In 1968, Boulez took parts 1a and 1b and recomposed them for string orchestra, intending to do the same for the rest of the piece. But when, 21 years later, he finally returned to the work, it was to recompose those same sections yet again.

I must say I find this attitude rather invigorating, especially coming from one who is generally acknowledged to be such a formative influence on late 20th-century music. The fact that Boulez's catalogue contains so many pieces that remain in a state of flux is not only evidence of high standards and a continually enquiring mind, but it also demonstrates this composer's scepticism about the concept of 'the work'. However great we believe a piece of music to be, there has come the moment in its construction when its composer has decided that enough is enough: whether it be Beethoven and the *Missa solemnis* or Wagner and *The Ring*, composers reach the point when they conclude: 'That will just have to do.' As Auden wrote, a poem is never finished, only abandoned. In keeping so many of his pieces open-ended, Boulez draws our attention to the arbitrariness of this moment of abandonment. There are always other possibilities, as Ferneyhough acknowledged when he wrote his two different versions of *Funérailles*, and as Cage reaffirmed every day of his life. The late 20th century has tended to be rather dogmatic in its thinking; we want to know what is important, and we want to know now; we like completion, closure. Boulez's perspective is refreshing precisely because he remains flexible in his approach, always seeing new possibilities.

I suppose there is also a danger inherent in such openmindedness. Boulez's Italian contemporary, Franco Donatoni, was so open-minded during the early stages of his career — even in the middle of it — that he seemed to change course with the frequency of a dodgem car. Bartók was an early influence; then, in the early 1950s, Donatoni came under the sway of Boulez and the other Darmstadt composers. By the beginning of the 1960s, he had traded the systematic precision of Boulez for the chance operations of John Cage, and by the middle of that decade he had fallen silent — perhaps a logical consequence of following Cage's path.

Donatoni was 50 before he began to write his own very distinctive brand of music. His pieces now tended to be short, often in two movements that explored related material in contrasting ways: a sort of stunted variation form. The starting point for a new piece was frequently some fragment thrown up by the previous work, so we can observe a chain reaction in Donatoni's music of the 1970s and '80s. And yet he was still not immune from influence. In an ensemble piece of 1984, intended as a 60th birthday offering for Boulez, Donatoni opted for the 'sincerest form of flattery'. *Cadeau* ('Gift') shows that he had heard and already absorbed Boulez's *Répons* of three years earlier. Scored for eleven instruments, *Cadeau* is another of Donatoni's bipartite structures, but for once there is no real break between the two movements. On the contrary, these movements overlap one another, and they are movements in more than one sense, because each explores a characteristic type of motion: these are movements about movement. Wind and brass instruments begin the piece with a standard Donatoni ploy. Small groups of notes — we might think of them as cells — begin to proliferate in a manner that is perfectly audible and easy to follow. The tempo is quick, the rhythms are jerky and accented, and the overall texture, typical of this composer, is rather busy. The wind players sit on one side of the stage; on the other, as yet silent, are three percussionists and a harp. Their glittering entry to the piece is a moment of pure theatre that cannot help but recall the first appearance of the percussive soloists in Boulez's *Répons*. As in *Répons*, these new sonorities come complete with new material, heralding the second part of the piece. Now, instead of the forward motion of the wind and brass writing, the music twists and swirls. Before long these opposite musical types begin to attract each other; we hear them pulling together, and pulling apart. Like most of his mature pieces, Donatoni's *Cadeau* is all over in about ten minutes, but by its end everything has changed; two apparently irreconcilable musical types have been made to coexist, a hybrid has been born, and some element of this new material will now be used to generate the next piece.

Franco Donatoni's susceptibility to influence caused him more changes of stylistic direction than any other major figure in the second half of the 20th century, save perhaps for Stockhausen who from the late 1950s had made a point of starting every new piece afresh. But by the 1980s, for a composer to have at least one major change of direction had become the norm. The catalyst for Ligeti had been writing an opera, and this also prompted Richard Meale's stylistic U-turn.

The first evidence that Meale had left behind him the modernism of his early career came in *Viridian* for orchestra and the second string quartet (1980).The opera that prompted the change had been in the composer's mind for some years before, though it would not be heard until 1986. Patrick White's novel *Voss*, published in 1957, had often been held up as the ideal subject for an Australian opera, and Meale was by no means the first composer to contemplate it. The fictional Johann Ulrich Voss, loosely based on the 19th-century explorer Ludwig Leichhardt, is a man of great determination, driven by his passions, and drawn to explore the interior of the continent. Before he departs on his expedition, he meets a Sydney woman, Laura Trevelyan, and in a sense it is their relationship that is the novel's real subject and Voss's own interior that he ends up exploring. The fact that, for most of the novel, they are separated by half a continent — Laura in her garden, Voss in his desert, direct communication an impossibility — might have been thought a problem for Meale and his librettist David Malouf. But they soon realised that this was the very stuff of opera. Opera permits and even encourages the simultaneous presentation of contrasting ideas and characters.

Patrick White had hoped for a musical setting of his novel that would be as stark and unforgiving as Voss himself and the landscape he explores, but Meale felt differently. In particular, Laura, he reasoned, was 'a diatonic lady', by virtue of her nature and her place in 19th-century Sydney society. To have offered her the leaping, fractured vocal lines of a Boulez or a Maxwell Davies — or of Ligeti's mythical figures in *Le grand macabre* — would have been to distort her character. Voss, too, is given conventionally singable lines, although he occasionally lapses into gruff speech, a device that accentuates his blunt and forthright nature and his outsider status. In the opera's pivotal scene, immediately prior to the explorer's departure, Laura and Voss are alone in her garden at night, the social gulf between them almost as great as the physical one that is about to open up. The frank lyricism of this music and its rich, lush treatment recall *Viridian*, Meale's orchestral exploration of the textures and colours of Australia's rainforests. But where *Viridian* was often dense and intertwined (like a rainforest), Laura's garden is more orderly.

After *Voss*, in his first symphony and third string quartet, Meale shifted further away from the modernism of his earlier music. On the surface, this sounded very like a retrogressive move: critics commented that the symphony was Brucknerian, while the quartet seemed to return to the language of Dvořák, if not Mendelssohn. But Meale's lyrical impulse, now so much to the fore, had always been present in his music: the harmonic language of *Viridian* may contrast with that of his orchestral *Nocturnes* (1967), but the gestures have quite a bit in common, and although the orchestration is quite different, there is a warmth about the sound of both pieces, a delight in sonority. In Meale's music of the 1980s, we hear an awareness of musical history — perhaps 'gratitude' is not too strong a term — that was also present in the work of Takemitsu, Lutoslawski and even Boulez. It manifested itself in a rhythmic simplification, a more obviously functional approach to harmony, and great attention to the quality of sound — this last attribute having been an ever-present feature of all these composers' music. Meale's motivation for exploring such common and familiar materials seems to have been entirely personal, the decision of a composer in late middle age who, like Ligeti, was becoming more himself. With some of Meale's more politically minded colleagues, however, there was a degree of fanaticism involved in this return to tonality. It was almost a form of 'pay back' for the years in which modernist attitudes had seemed to dominate concerts and music broadcasting, as well as the academies in which these composers had studied. But already there was another sort of composer who was more broad-minded, and also aware of the self-inflicted harm that might result from dogmatism of any kind.

The American composer, John Adams, is a good example of this. Ten years younger than Steve Reich and Philip Glass, both of whom were important early influences, Adams did not exhibit the same degree of antipathy towards modernism that they had, certainly not to the music itself: he even conducted some accomplished performances of Schoenberg. Minimalism had happened, the revolution against modernism was surely over and there was no longer the same need to build barricades. Adams and his generation could get on with finding their voices in the 1980s, believing the good fight to have been fought and won. His music was made possible by minimalism, but it was also partly a reaction to it. His first opera also seemed like a reaction to the politics of the previous generation.

Even before he was driven from office by the political scandal of Watergate in 1973, the conservative Richard Nixon had been a figure of hate among most artists in the 1960s and '70s. To make Nixon the central character of an opera would have been controversial enough, but to attempt a reappraisal of his years in office was surely symbolic. *Nixon in China* did both. Its librettist, Alice Goodman, maintained that she had no interest in writing a satirical piece, which would have been the only option ten years before when the president's foreign-policy achievements were inevitably overshadowed by his socially divisive internal policies and by the corruption in his administration.

Nixon in China had its premiere in 1987, eighteen months after Meale's *Voss*, and Adams's subject was as American as Meale's was Australian. Both operas had flawed, even tragic heroes, but where the fictional tragedy of Voss was played out on stage, Nixon's fall from grace was not alluded to. Still, audience members must surely have had Watergate at the backs of their minds as they watched the opera. How could they not? Richard and Pat Nixon, Chou En-lai and Kissinger, Mao Zedong and Madame Mao were such recent history. Operatic treatments of history and politics were nothing new, but these people had made their way from the small screen of television news to the opera stage in record time; four of them were still alive. Around the time of *Nixon in China*, and especially after it, similar transformations were overtaking other figures from modern American history. There was already Anthony Davis's opera *X: the life and times of Malcolm X*, first staged in 1985; other topical operas included John Moran's multimedia *The Manson Family* (1990), Ezra Laderman's *Marilyn* (1995), and Michael Daugherty's *Jackie O* (1997). John Adams's own second opera was *The Death of Klinghoffer*, concerning the 1985 hijacking of the ocean liner *Achille Lauro* and the killing of the wheelchair-bound passenger, Leon Klinghoffer. Malcolm X, Marilyn Monroe, Jacqueline Kennedy-Onassis and, of course, Leon Klinghoffer were all dead when they were turned into operas, and the murderer Charles Manson, though alive, was hardly in a position to attend the work his crimes had inspired. But at the time of *Nixon's* premiere, there was much speculation about whether the real-life former president would turn up to see himself on stage. He didn't, but the possibility served to underline how recent were the events Adams was representing, and the fact that Adams believed opera might have the same immediate relevance for his audience as Mozart and Verdi's operas had had for theirs.

The music of *Nixon in China* bears many of the trademarks of 1970s minimalism, especially the work of Philip Glass. There is the modality of its harmonic language and the use of scales and swirling arpeggios. The latter often create a sense of frantic activity, while the music is restrained from genuine progress by the refusal of harmonic development. The spectacular arrival on stage of the president's aircraft, *The Spirit of '76*, is one of these moments. By the time we see it, the plane is taxi-ing to a halt, but the noise of the jet engines is still intense. Adams portrays this with harmony that swings slowly back and forth between two big chords a tritone apart; it is going nowhere. But the surface of the music surges with energy, just like the engines. If the sound of this music is familiar enough, Adams's use of it is new, partly because in *Nixon* it is suddenly an illustrative device and partly because of the brash, full-blown romanticism of its scoring. Indeed the grandiloquence of the scoring might itself be thought of as illustrative, given the great moment that Adams and Goodman patently attached to Nixon's arrival in Beijing. Even the vocal lines, with their typical minimalist repetitions, now take on another dimension. These are politicians in the age of the sound bite, and what do such figures do but utter short, catchy, self-important statements, and repeat them until the message is driven home? 'News' may have 'a kind of mystery', as Adams's Nixon insists, but it tends to be a stage-managed mystery.

The minimalism that had initially impressed Adams and that we hear him working with, inflating and finally transcending in *Nixon in China*, was already behind Steve Reich by the 1980s. In *Different Trains* (1988), Reich created what he referred to as a musical documentary. The trains of the title included those the composer had travelled on as a small child during World War II, as he shuttled back and forth between his estranged parents on the east and west coasts of the United States. But Reich was also concerned with the trains that, as a Jew, he might have been riding on in Europe during this period. The real subject of *Different Trains* was the Holocaust. Reich recorded an interview with his elderly governess reminiscing about their journeys together nearly 50 years before, and with a retired Pullman porter who had worked on those same trains. He also collected recordings of three Holocaust survivors, roughly his own age and now living in the United States, speaking of their experiences.

Although the use of taped speech was a throwback to Reich's earlier pieces like *It's Gonna Rain*, this time his treatment of the voices was different. He took fragments of speech and notated their melodic patterns. With the aid of a sampling keyboard and computer, he could adjust the pitch of the voices, where necessary, so the spoken notes were 'in tune', before transferring them back to tape. Besides train whistles and air-raid sirens (which Reich treated exactly like the voices), the other sounds in the piece were provided by the Kronos String Quartet. In fact there are four quartets in the piece — in a live performance, three of them are on tape — and the melodic material they play is derived, like everything else in *Different Trains*, from the fragments of recorded speech. We hear the governess or the porter or one of the Holocaust survivors speak, and then a member of the quartet picks up the rhythm and melodic inflection; the opposite can also occur, when the melodic pattern is established before we encounter the spoken phrase on which it was based. In some ways, the most affecting moments of *Different Trains* are those when no words are heard and one is left with the musical echoes of speech, prolonged by the strings, the private, often painful, recollections having been transformed into an abstract memorial.

It is significant that Reich returned to text-driven music in the late 1980s; significant, too, that he did it in New York City where rap, the street poetry of young African Americans, was the predominant sound of popular music. *Different Trains* was a far cry from Run DMC, but as with rap, the music came from the sounds and rhythms of the words rather more than from their meanings, which is why Reich's piece has that element of abstraction. The influence of rap on Steve Reich had a certain logic to it. With rap, young black Americans reclaimed the high-tech rhythms of the disco; they took the music back on to the streets, in much the same way that the punk bands of the mid 1970s had returned rock and roll to the garage and minimalist composers had rescued art music from the clutches of the modernists. In 1995, Reich emphasised the connection between rap and his own music in *City Life*, a musical study of New York employing the same sampling techniques as *Different Trains*, and a larger band of instruments whose range was extended by sounds of the city, such as slamming car doors, police sirens and pile drivers.

Patterns of speech had figured in the work of many American composers since the 1960s when sound-text artists such as Charles Amirkhanian, Robert Ashley, and Charles Dodge had first begun to experiment with the spoken word live in concert, in the theatre, or on tape. The specifically American tradition of sound text can be traced back even further to the music of Harry Partch whose recitations to the accompaniment of bands of self-invented instruments are a corner of American composition whose full ramifications are still emerging. In the 1970s and early 1980s, two composer-performers, Meredith Monk and Laurie Anderson, brought these experiments to a new level of sophistication, and, for Anderson in particular, the close observations of life typical of Partch's texts would be an inspiration.

Like the concerts Partch gave, Anderson's multimedia performances offered a critique of contemporary America. She called her magnum opus *United States*, and her next work *Home of the Brave* (its title coming from the final phrase of 'The Star-Spangled Banner'). Anderson's work dealt with the alienation of the modern American, and was sometimes political, but she was hardly the female Bruce Springsteen this might suggest. Where Springsteen was passionate and concerned, Anderson was detached, ironic and amused. We listen to her pieces and feel we are eavesdropping on the speaker. Generally, the speaker is Anderson herself, but her texts are often assembled from conversations she has overheard, particularly those where she has heard only one side. 'O Superman' (1981) is a good example of this, taking a telephone answer machine and a mother's message left on it as the starting point for the piece. Anderson had always employed technology, but as a composer she was never in awe of the machine. A feature of her concerts in the 1980s was a violin that functioned like a primitive sampler. The bow was strung with a length of magnetic tape bearing musical information, usually a voice. The violin itself, instead of strings and a bridge, had a tape head. When the bow was drawn across the head, it played all or some of what was on the tape, at whatever speed the bow was moving. Such a homespun cannibalisation of available technology is typical of Anderson's work, it shows her taking control of the machine, and this is significant because the technology with which she worked was always as much a target for her scepticism as the world that had developed it. In 'O Superman', which appeared on Anderson's first album, *Big Science*, the detached voice on the machine becomes the voice of the machine itself, warning us (but very sweetly): 'Here come the planes'.

An odd thing happened with 'O Superman'. Laurie Anderson was an experimental artist working in New York's downtown area, performing for the loft-dwelling cognoscenti. She made a thousand copies of 'O Superman' on seven-inch vinyl, and it sold out. Warner Bros took it on, and the record reached No. 2 in the British pop charts. It was not unlike the *Tubular Bells* phenomenon of a decade before; the difference was that whereas Mike Oldfield had come from a background in pop, Anderson had emerged from the visual arts and experimental music. The British charts have never been a guide to anything beyond evanescent fame, but both Oldfield and Anderson's successes proved that the low-art/high-art distinction that had seemed such a fixture in 20th-century music, was far from absolute. In the 1980s, Steve Reich and Philip Glass both performed at rock venues and, substantially, to rock audiences. The composer as a figure in an ivory tower was an increasingly outmoded image.

John Cage had never been interested in ivory towers. His philosophy was always an inclusive one: artistic activities, for him, were a part of everyday life and everyday experience. Cage had long been attracted to the speaking voice and the words that it spoke, although he was less concerned with the intention behind the words. In order to strip them of intention and release new possibilities of meaning, Cage worked with what he called 'mesostics'. These are like acrostics where the first letter of each line of a text, read vertically, produces a word or words. Unlike an acrostic, however, mesostics run down the middle of the page. At first, Cage used them simply to inspire his own poetry, but later his preferred method was to take his mesostic — it could be a word or a phrase or somebody's name — and apply it to an existing text. In *62 Mesostics Re Merce Cunningham* (1971), Cage used the name of the dancer Cunningham, his partner and frequent collaborator, and applied it to Cunningham's own writings. The technique was to take the first letter of the name and look for its first appearance in the text. Cage capitalised the letter and also took a small portion of the original context from the writings, then he moved on to look for the next appearance of the next letter from the name, and so on. The result is a collage of words that exists as a poem, as a visual-art work and also, should anyone be interested, as a score for interpretation in performance.

By the end of the 1970s, Cage was employing mesostics more and more, and to larger and larger texts, most notably James Joyce's *Finnegans Wake*. He now called the process 'writing through' and his first extended work was 'Writing Through *Finnegans Wake*', undertaken using the mesostic 'James Joyce'. Cage began at the end of the novel and worked his way to the front, a not unreasonable decision, given Joyce's book is circular (its final words turn out to be the start

of the novel's truncated first sentence). 'Writing through' was something to which Cage returned several more times during the 1970s
and '80s, including, significantly, 'Writing Through Thoreau's "On the
Duty of Civil Disobedience"' (1985). These all resulted in purely
literary works, but Cage's second writing through *Finnegans Wake*
produced an hour-long radiophonic piece, published as a score entitled ___ , *a* ___ *circus on* ___ (1979). It was a set of instructions for
turning any book into a piece of music, and Cage's realisation of it
was *Roaratorio, an Irish Circus on 'Finnegans Wake'* (1979). Beginning
by 'Writing for a Second Time Through *Finnegans Wake*', Cage went
on to list all the references to sound in Joyce's novel, and all the references to places. There were a lot of both. The next stage was to make
recordings of the sounds mentioned, and to visit (or have friends
visit) the places in order to record them too. Next, Cage recorded
himself intoning the words, and then overdubbed the other sounds
so that they occurred at the moments at which the original text mentioned them, or would have mentioned them had it remained intact.

Joyce's *Finnegans Wake* was never exactly narrative driven, and
by the time Cage had finished with it, it was more fragmentary then
ever, but in *Roaratorio* we find Cage in a cheerfully illustrative mood.
It may not, perhaps, be the 'classic BBC adaptation' of Joyce, but
then, given the nature of the original novel, it's perhaps not too far
removed from that.

All his mature life, Cage was more interested in listening than
composing in the conventional sense. Many of his pieces provide
little more than the opportunity for an audience to listen to the
sounds around them. You might argue that 4'33" was one of the first
pieces of ambient music, but this was not what the flourishing
New-Age record companies of the 1980s meant by the term. In order
to be in any way successful as music, 4'33" required active listening,
but the so-called ambient music that oozed out of many an '80s
sound system was intended to provide little more than a temporary,
womb-like haven for the busy yuppy. There is something profoundly
depressing about this 'life-style' music, designed to be heard but *not*
listened to, like a painting that is meant not to be looked at. This was
not ambient music in that it was necessarily drawn from ambient
sounds, it was music that established an ambience — mood-setting
sound, controlling and manipulative in the way that Cage never was.

The ambient industry was made possible, very largely, by the advent of compact-disc technology, which allowed this stuff to go on uninterrupted for 75 minutes at a time. This, and the disc's supposed indestructibility, were its principal advantages. The extra playing time was also a great benefit for a style of piece not unrelated to ambient music, but infinitely richer in substance and certainly not created with an eye on the cash register. I am thinking here of a range of works composed, especially in the 1980s, that were often too long to fit conveniently on the old LP format, and that were also predominantly quiet and almost immobile so that the surface scratches of vinyl would have reduced their impact. The final pieces of Morton Feldman and Luigi Nono, although very different in other respects, tended towards extreme length and introspection. Feldman's piano solo *For Bunita Marcus* (1985) is a good example, consisting of very simple musical events that evolve quietly, slowly, apparently aimlessly, over 70 minutes. In fact this evolution is anything but aimless: when a chord appears after ten minutes of single notes, its significance is hard to miss. Nono's music was much more concerned than Feldman's with timbre, with the colour of sounds. In this he harked back to the second Viennese school and its conception of *Klangfarbenmelodie* — a theme comprised of tone colours — and the harmonic stasis of the music would not have surprised Schoenberg, who had done something very similar in *Farben*, the third of his Five Orchestral Pieces (1909). But there's no doubt that Schoenberg would have been amazed at the length of Nono's pieces. His string quartet of 1980, *Fragmente — Stille, an Diotima* draws its wispy fragments out over a very still 40 minutes, while the piece Nono produced in 1989, the year before his death, lasts the same amount of time and contains even less material. This was *La lontananza nostalgica utopia futura*, a 'Madrigal for several "travellers" with Gidon Kremer, solo violin, 8 magnetic tapes, and 8 to 10 music stands'.

The last pieces of Feldman and Nono require patience and concentration, and they are very personal statements. Equally, they are immensely generous. The fact that these works often contain the dedicatee's name in the title — Bunita Marcus, Gidon Kremer — is only part of that generosity. A quotation from Hölderlin in Nono's quartet mentions a 'secret world'. It is a secret the composer is prepared to share with anyone who will make the effort.

The 1980s is sometimes spoken of as the 'me generation', a reference to the validating of individual greed by the fashionable politics of Reaganomics and Thatcherism — appropriately ugly terms, I always feel. But, musically speaking, the expression 'me generation' might be thought to connote something rather more positive. It suggests a decade when composers withdrew into themselves, and, like Thoreau, explored 'home cosmology'. Ligeti, Boulez, Feldman and Nono were all more themselves than ever before (Cage, of course, was always Cage). Saariaho, Donatoni and Meale dealt with personal obsessions. Adams, Reich and Anderson looked into their own backyards. This self-scrutiny, as Thoreau had hinted, resulted in each composer becoming a more intense communicator.

But if this suggests a kind of coming together at the end of the 1980s, a meeting of musical minds, it is only in the sense that — as in the wider world — many of the rigid dogmas of earlier decades appeared finally to have been overthrown. In feeling free to be themselves, composers were often pursuing very different aesthetics. As the Cold War began to fizzle, two composers, one American, one Russian, summed up this trend. About all they had in common was their individuality.

Pauline Oliveros, an important figure on San Francisco's experimental music scene in the early 1960s, had only ever had a small, if dedicated following. Galina Ustvolskaya, a former pupil of Shostakovich, was virtually unknown outside the Soviet Union, and hardly known inside it because her music broke so many of the rules. One of the great benefits of the CD revolution was that music by composers like this began to find listeners. As with Feldman and Nono's later works, Oliveros's music might have been made for CD: such is its length, such its quiet strength, it seems to demand the most private of audiences. Paradoxically, the recording was almost anathema to Ustvolskaya's work, which, more than most music, cried out for the dramatic immediacy of live performance.

Oliveros called her musical style 'deep listening', and it had evolved from her chant-like pieces of the 1960s. Drones still played an important part and so did improvisation, to the extent that the composer herself was the foremost performer of her music — another advantage of the CD. *The Roots of the Moment* (1987) is a perfectly typical example of her work. It is for piano accordion in just intonation, played by Oliveros in an interactive electronic environment. The accordion is hooked up to two digital delay processors that can redistribute its sound in time and space, so that although it is really a solo work, played in real time, the effect is of many accordions in one room, or even of a room that is one big accordion. The result, to use another of the composer's descriptions of her work, is a 'sonic meditation'. This is music that makes no bold statements; it is avowedly non-rhetorical. But its strength of personality is too great for us to be able to write it off as mere doodlings.

Where Oliveros's music is instantly welcoming, Ustvolskaya's is more likely to be violently confronting. Her titles tell us nothing — Composition I, Composition II, Sonata No. 6, and so on — and she has resisted invitations to discuss her work or to provide program notes. But she did once stipulate that she preferred her pieces to be played in churches, and not by women.

Ustvolskaya's music is as uncompromising as the composer herself. It is made up of blocks of sound, usually very loud or very quiet, often punctuated by long, precisely measured silences (one thinks of the plays of Beckett and Pinter). That there is a spiritual dimension to her music seems clear, but it is not the comforting brand of spirituality one tends to encounter in the music of Arvo Pärt. The sounds and the silences of Ustvolskaya's pieces offer a view of eternity as something implacable. It will no more bend to our wishes than her music will. It is up to us to come to terms with it. The extent of our willingness to attempt this will be a measure of the success of Ustvolskaya's music, but it will also say a good deal about us. This music — like all genuine art — needs imaginative collaborators. No art does all the work for us, and Ustvolskaya's does less than most. Oliveros offers us the sonic equivalent of a blank, albeit beautifully textured, canvas, and she encourages us to make our own designs on it. Ustvolskaya's designs are bold and stark and brook no opposition. Grasping her music is like grasping a cactus: its beauty is better appreciated from a slight distance.

A NEW WORLD ORDER?

n 1973, Susan Sontag wrote an article about photography for the *New York Review of Books*. In it, she questioned the primacy of the photograph in contemporary life, dismissing the maxim that the camera never lies. Sontag was talking principally about photojournalism, and she suggested that for us to examine a photograph and accept it as a record of the truth, was the very opposite of understanding the world. 'All possibility of understanding is rooted in the ability to say no,' she wrote. 'The "reality" of the world is not in its images, but in its functions. Functioning takes place in time, and must be explained in time.'

Music is a functioning art. It explains itself in time. So can it bring us closer to 'the "reality" of the world'? The poet George Seferis wanted poetry to be 'strong enough to help'. In a world that offers us daily lies — from our newspapers, our televisions and radios, our politicians — we might ask: is music strong enough to help? I think it is, and how it helps is really the subject of this final chapter of *Illegal Harmonies*.

The very 'illegality' of certain harmonies is, of course, itself a way of saying no, and so bringing us closer to Sontag's idea of understanding. With Berio in his *Sinfonia* we may doubt that artists can 'stop the wars . . . make the old younger or lower the price of bread', but they can affect and even change the way we experience art (and life). At some level, all art is about other art, music about other music. And music that specifically courts illegality, that disrupts protocol, that turns convention on its head — a *Rite of Spring*, a *4'33"*, an *In C* — this music is saying no to all the music that has gone before. In saying no, it does not invalidate earlier music (how could it?), but it forces us to examine our responses, to consider all music anew and perhaps better understand it.

Shortly before his death in 1992, John Cage discussed the fact that in the 20th century musical styles had proliferated to the point at which it was no longer possible to speak of a mainstream. There is a connection here with the argument advanced by Francis Fukuyama and others that, by the 1990s, history itself — at least, the notion of history as progress — was over. Cage proposed that while Western music had once been a river, flowing through the baroque period, Classicism, early and late Romanticism, it had begun, at the start of this century, to branch off in many directions. By the last decade, Cage suggested, the river had become a delta, with all that that implied: a multiplicity of streams, dividing and subdividing, sometimes rejoining each other, one or two of them flowing back on themselves.

But this range of styles apart, I suspect that, in their broad concerns, composers at the end of the 20th century and into the 21st are not so very different from earlier composers. We might divide today's art music into six basic areas within which any number of stylistic approaches flourish side by side. There is music with a strong awareness of the past; music that looks to cultures outside the Western tradition; music in the theatre; music that embraces popular culture; music that depends upon a symbiotic relationship with technology; and music in the service of spiritual belief. There is nothing new about any of these categories: they would fit the composers of the 18th century just as well. And, clearly, the pigeonholes are not mutually exclusive. While I can't bring to mind a single piece of the last ten years that fails to fit at least one of the categories, there are plenty that fit several at once.

Composers of earlier centuries often returned to antiquated styles and stratagems, particularly when composing religious works: in his Mass in B minor, Bach employed the techniques of Palestrina; in his C minor Mass, Mozart evoked Handel. It is really just a matter of degree. If the 20th century has been unusually preoccupied with the past, perhaps this is a function of having more of the past available to us, musical and otherwise. It is a curious paradox that a century whose technological advances have permitted unprecedented general access to the music of the past seems also to have alienated listeners from the music of their own time. But it may also be that, because our composers have so frequently forced us to contemplate the nature of the art itself, we have turned to the past in order to place the music of our century in a historical context, and because composers are a part of society, they have felt a consequent need to engage with old music more regularly than before.

The absorption of elements from outside the Western tradition is not a 20th-century phenomenon, either. Haydn and Mozart did it; so did Schubert; so did Brahms. At the end of the 19th century, French composers saw the music of the Orient — real or imagined — as part of the means of escaping the Teutonic shibboleth. Two things happened during the 20th century to expand this area of endeavour beyond a casual affair with exotica. Once again, the sound recording made it possible for Western composers to come into close proximity with Japanese *gagaku* or the pan pipes of Central African pygmies or Tuvan throat singing, without having to go further than the local record store. More significantly, Western music itself emigrated, and composers in Asia, Africa, South America and Australasia brought to it their own influences.

Popular music and art music have always had a close relationship, but after World War II it became an uneasy one. This did not last long: composers would have been foolish to spurn popular influences in this of all centuries. Since the 1960s, the reappearance of pop-derived sounds and styles has rejuvenated the classical tradition and given it some of its most significant works (like Berio's *Sinfonia*) as well as some of its most embarrassing ones (Bernstein's *Mass*).

Technological development in music might seem to be a purely 20th-century phenomenon, until one applies the term more broadly. On the one hand there is what we might think of as compositional technology: the invention of the fugue, for instance, was a techno-logical advance that offered composers new formal possibilities they were able to interpret in a range of styles. On the other hand, there is instrumental technology: Mozart's close involvement in the devel-opment of the clarinet is similar to Boulez's vision of IRCAM as a centre where scientists would work alongside composers, coming up with technological solutions for their creative needs.

The theatre has been important to Western art music since the beginning of the 17th century. It is where Monteverdi, Mozart and Wagner made their greatest musical inventions, and in the early part of the 20th century it was a similar catalyst for Debussy, Schoenberg, Stravinsky, Bartók and Berg.

Established religion has provided the most consistent support for composers in history. Beginning with the School of Notre Dame in the late 1100s, we can trace eight almost uninterrupted centuries of musical patronage by the church, ending only with its discovery of the tambourine. Increasingly, in the 20th century, composers were left to figure out their own spirituality. In the *Symphony of Psalms*, *Canticum sacrum*, *Threni*, and a host of other works, Stravinsky con-tinued to evoke the Russian church of his youth. Schoenberg wres-tled with the Jewish faith in his two most ambitious projects, the oratorio *Die Jacobsleiter* and the opera *Moses und Aron*. Significantly he failed to complete either work. In the last two decades of the century, however, overt spirituality — some would say religiosity — has once more become a feature of many composers' music.

The relationship between composers and the past was a particu-larly fruitful one in the last years of the 20th century. In the case of Judith Weir, it has rarely been a question of engaging with the art music of the past, but with its folk music and folk tales. Often these have come from Weir's native Scotland, but in her search for suitable source materials for her beguiling music she has cast the net far wider. In *The Consolations of Scholarship* (1985), she turned to the ear-liest form of Chinese play, from the 13th-century Yuan dynasty. These plays are rather simple, addressing the audience directly and often entering the realms of magic realism. Even had she wanted to, Weir could not have plundered the material for specific musical or declam-atory effects: we simply do not know how these plays sounded. What attracted Weir to sources such as these was their uncluttered nature.

Unlike more literary texts, these ancient folk tales left a lot of room for the composer's own imagination. The result is a sort of imagined folk music, not too dissimilar from Stravinsky's practices or, in a more abstract sense, the music of Harrison Birtwistle in whose company we seem, unaccountably, to be entering a musical prehistory.

An awareness of the history and traditions of Western art music has been a more common preoccupation for contemporary composers, and inevitably a more conscious, not to say self-conscious matter. Nobody can write a string quartet in which a soprano voice appears, as Brian Ferneyhough did in his Fourth String Quartet (1989–90) without deliberately making reference to Schoenberg's second quartet of 1908, in which its composer first abandoned the use of the key signature and his soprano sang about it. The vital significance of that earlier work to the 20th century forces any similarly scored piece into a knowing dialogue with it, a polemical relationship. A further step along this path comes when a composer invokes an earlier piece or musical style by quoting it.

Roger Smalley began his Cello Concerto in 1985, but about seven minutes into the piece he ran up against a brick wall and stopped composing. Smalley was born in England. His early works were heavily influenced by Maxwell Davies, but at the end of the 1960s he became a student and colleague of Stockhausen. This, in turn, led him to form his own improvisation group. After moving to Western Australia in the mid 1970s, his music changed again. In other words, style has always been an issue for this composer. Smalley had put aside his Cello Concerto at the point where he knew something momentous needed to happen, but didn't know what. In 1996, eleven years later, he picked it up again and carried on. He had realised that what the piece needed at this turning point — unlikely as it might seem — was a few bars of Schumann. Smalley chose a brief passage from midway through the second of Schumann's *Humoreske* for piano. It was appropriate because, in Schumann's piece, the passage had also marked a turning point, coming as a sudden, still oasis, after a passage of rather athletic activity. Spotting the reference in Smalley's concerto, however, is not as simple as you might think, because the composer not only elaborates the original texture, but he also has the cello soloist play an 'inner voice' that Schumann had written into his score on an extra middle stave.

Schumann does not let us hear this melodic line, only the accompanying chords. In his Cello Concerto, however, Roger Smalley allows this secret voice to speak and to guide him towards the conclusion of his own piece.

The Cello Concerto was by no means the first time Smalley had been attracted to the 19th-century keyboard repertoire. An accomplished pianist, Smalley began drawing on the music of Chopin soon after setting aside the concerto. In 1988 he started to compose his *Variations on a Theme of Chopin* — the theme being the Mazurka in B flat minor Op. 24, No. 4 — and a steady trickle of Chopin-related works followed. That Schumann should have provided the key to the Cello Concerto was, then, not so surprising, and Smalley's recent tendency to work with neo-tonal harmonies (perhaps, with Ligeti, one should call these harmonies 'non-atonal') is undoubtedly related to his experience of 19th-century music.

In *The Schubert Blues* (1996), Elena Kats-Chernin took the famous theme from the song 'Der Tod und das Mädchen' ('Death and the Maiden'), already used for a set of variations in the slow movement of Schubert's D minor string quartet. Kats-Chernin was born in Uzbekistan but, like Smalley, emigrated to Australia. As with Smalley's variations, *The Schubert Blues* is for solo piano, but Kats-Chernin approaches her 19th-century material in a very different manner, neither exactly quoting it, nor, in any conventional sense, varying it. Schubert's soft, mysterious chords in the middle of the keyboard are exploded in Kats-Chernin's version. Now they appear, with savage insistence, in the extreme top and bottom registers of the instrument. If the composer was thinking at all about the text of the original song, her version of death is anything but the seductive figure that Schubert had in mind. It is typical of this composer's resourcefulness that no sooner was *The Schubert Blues* complete, but the piece became the starting point for another work. In *Langsam* (1997), for soprano and small ensemble, the vocal part is derived from another Schubert song, 'Du bist die Ruh', but the instruments elaborate the music of *The Schubert Blues*. Clearly, Kats-Chernin's attitude to appropriation applies to her own work as much as that of other composers.

The fact that Smalley and Kats-Chernin both live in a country other than that of their birth is not, perhaps, just coincidence. Throughout the century, it has been common for composers to emigrate: Bartók, Schoenberg and Stravinsky all ended their days in the United States; so did Rahkmaninov, Weill, and Varèse. Not all of these composers left their homelands as willingly as Smalley and Kats-Chernin, but each was affected by his new surroundings, the expatriate experience granting him a new perspective on his music and the traditions behind it. By the early 1990s, three more recent immigrants had begun to earn strong reputations in their adoptive America. This time they did not come from Europe: Tan Dun was born in China, Chinary Ung in Cambodia, and Reza Vali in Iran.

Of the three, it is probably Vali's music that shows its composer's country of origin most immediately, and this is because his compositional starting point is almost always Persian folk song. Many of his works are arrangements of this source material, but they are ingenious arrangements and they project not just the tunes but the spirit of the original music. The examples of Bartók and Stravinsky, and more recently Berio, are all important precursors of Vali's work.

With Chinary Ung and Tan Dun, it is not usually a matter of arranging or even quoting from the indigenous musics of their birthplaces; it is more to do with an aesthetic sense: they bring to the Western concert hall a new kind of viewpoint. In Tan Dun's case, this is frequently a theatrical perspective, because, although his best known music is for orchestra, the composer views this European institution in dramatic and ritualistic terms. Of course, orchestral concerts have always been dramatic and ritualistic, but Western audiences accept the conventions of the concert so readily that it takes a creative mind from outside the tradition to point them out to us. Tan Dun's *Orchestral Theatre I* was composed in 1990, four years after he arrived in New York, and one year after he witnessed, from afar, the violent suppression of the Chinese democracy movement in Beijing's Tiananmen Square. Although the orchestra looks fairly conventional on stage, its sound is coloured by the presence of eleven *xun* — Chinese ocarinas — that have prominent roles in the piece, one of them as a soloist. Stranger still, to the average concert-goer, is that the orchestral musicians are not restricted to their instrumental duties, they must also make ritual vocalisations. *Orchestral Theatre I* challenges our concept of the symphony orchestra, but *Orchestral Theatre II* (1995) forces us to re-evaluate the whole business of concert-going, because this work requires the vocal participation of the audience. The blurring of boundaries in Tan Dun's music has extended to a piece for the Kronos String Quartet entitled *Ghost Opera* (1994). The members of the quartet are joined by a fifth performer who plays the traditional Chinese lute, the *pipa*. All five also play percussion instruments and speak/sing texts. These are taken from two sources: a Chinese folk song and Prospero's 'cloud-capped towers' speech in Act IV of Shakespeare's *The Tempest*.

A theatrical orchestra; an operatic string quartet: to some extent, Tan Dun's dramatisation of the concert platform found its opposite in Liza Lim's opera *The Oresteia* (1992–93). 'Opera' is a lacklustre label for this work, Lim and her collaborator, the director Barrie Kosky, preferring to describe it as 'memory theatre'. Although Lim and Kosky are Australian, both the co-creators of *The Oresteia* have increasingly been conscious of their cultural heritages, respectively Asian and European Jewish. The ancient Greek playwright, Aeschylus, clearly intended his *Oresteia* trilogy as theatre, and in Lim and Kosky's one-hour version, so it remains — extremely physical theatre, at that. But the narrative thrust of the original has gone, as has almost all of the text. In its structure, then, it more closely resembles the logic of music: we no longer have any precise idea why certain characters behave as they do: we are not even sure who some of the characters are: six different singers play the part of Cassandra. In terms of its overturning of stage conventions, *The Oresteia* is a long way from *Nixon in China*, but it is reasonably close to Robert Wilson's work with Philip Glass, particularly the non-linear structure of *Einstein on the Beach*.

Twenty years after *Einstein*, Wilson forged another collaboration with a composer, Lou Reed, a former member of the rock band the Velvet Underground. *Time Rocker*, based on H. G. Wells's novel *The Time Machine*, was staged in Hamburg in 1996. Reed's involvement as composer of a full-length 'opera' (albeit one whose 'orchestra' consisted of two guitars, bass and drums) was symptomatic of the narrowing of the aesthetic and ideological gulf between musical styles that had really begun in the 1960s, when rock musicians began attending lectures by Stockhausen, Berio arranged songs by the Beatles, and the Beatles signed the young British composer John Tavener to their record label, Apple.

The postmodernist refusal of new musical materials led many composers to commence a dialogue with popular culture. This often resulted in consciously polemical works, such as those by Michael Daugherty which embraced the culture of American television, particularly cartoons, and the musical gestures associated with them. The inspiration for Daugherty's *Metropolis* symphony was the 50th anniversary of the *Superman* comics: individual movements have titles such as 'Lex' and 'Krypton'. The 40-minute symphony opens strikingly with a quartet of referee's whistles, before moving into garishly scored 'pursuit' music. The orchestral fabric is percussion-heavy and spiced with synthesiser; the thematic and harmonic ideas owe a debt to popular music in general, and to Hollywood film and TV scores in particular; the rhythms, like those in Bernstein's *West Side Story*, are shot through with Latin-American dance. To the unreconstructed modernist the piece is a provocation, and that, of course, is half of its point. What is interesting — even, perhaps, contradictory — is that Daugherty's world of comics and television is translated here into an extravagant panoply of orchestral sound, when computer technology might have been a more natural medium for the subject. But that is also part of the point: the dragging of popular culture into the concert hall, the hijacking (or reclaiming) of the orchestra as a vehicle for entertainment is as much behind Daugherty's work as an infatuation with the figures of Clark Kent and Lois Lane.

Neil Rolnick is another American composer who has drawn on popular music. Unlike Daugherty, his preferred medium is indeed the computer, and he adopts a rather different attitude to his source material. In *A Robert Johnson Sampler* (1989), Rolnick took the rhythmic patterns and melodic gestures of the great 1930s blues guitarist and deconstructed them in much the same way that Jonathan Harvey had broken down the sounds of the cathedral bell and boy soprano in his earlier *Mortuos plango, vivos voco*. For Rolnick and Harvey, the possibilities offered by the computer analysis and manipulation of found musical objects were similarly attractive; the difference was aesthetic. Where Harvey took rather static musical objects — a tolling bell, an intoning voice — and activated them, Rolnick takes dynamic riffs and makes them monolithic; Harvey discovered the soul of the bell, but Rolnick removes the soul from Johnson's slide guitar and contemplates the structure of the patterns it plays.

By the mid-1980s, contemplations of a conspicuously soulful variety had become a recurrent feature of musical composition, especially that coming from countries within the Soviet Union or its sphere of political influence. The Estonian Arvo Pärt composed specifically religious works of great simplicity. Depending upon your attitude, these pieces are either consistent in their message or too similar to each other to be of more than passing interest. But the Tartar composer, Sofia Gubaidulina, is a more complex case. Her pieces often appear to have a spiritual quality even when they lay no claim to a specific extra-musical — or extra-terrestrial — agenda. They are generally slow moving works that find connections between some of the more interior explorations of sound in the later works of Nono and the crystalline forms of Webern, though without the latter's commitment to compression.

It was not long before attempts at musical transcendence were almost an international norm. The Englishman John Tavener, who had joined the Russian Orthodox church in the 1970s, now devoted himself to 'sacred' works, and to the creation of icons in sound. In Australia, Nigel Butterley's Anglican background tended to lend even his most overtly spiritual pieces an undercurrent of scepticism, but there was nothing in the least sceptical about *From Sorrowing Earth* (1991), his orchestral lament for the planet. In Finland, Einojuhani Rautavaara continued a sequence of pieces begun in the late 1970s whose subject was angels: *Angel of Light*, his seventh symphony of 1993 was a typically generous exploration of a slow moving modal/tonal language that could be traced almost directly back to his fellow countryman Sibelius.

But among 20th-century composers for whom religion has been a central issue, without a doubt the most significant (from a musical point of view) was Messiaen. He hardly composed a work that did not, on some level, reflect his Catholicism. From the early 1940s, his music also grew out of his fascination with birdsong, a spontaneous outpouring that Messiaen considered the purest form of divine praise. The composer recorded the songs of birds not only, as one might expect, on tape, but also in musical notation, and the titles of his pieces describe how systematically he employed this raw material: *Le merle noir* ('The Blackbird'; 1951); *Réveil des oiseaux* ('Dawn Chorus';

1953), *Oiseaux exotiques* ('Exotic Birds'; 1956), the seven-volume work for solo piano, *Catalogue d'oiseaux* ('Catalogue of Birds'; 1956–58), *La fauvette des jardins* ('The Garden Warbler'; 1970); *Petites esquisses d'oiseaux* ('Bird Sketches'; 1985); *Un vitrail et des oiseaux* ('A Stained-Glass Window and Some Birds'; 1986). When, for reasons of geography, Messiaen was unable to hear certain birds in the wild, he worked from recordings. In this way, the birds of New Zealand appear in *Couleurs de la cité céleste* (1963), and Australian birds in *La Transfiguration de Notre Seigneur Jésus-Christ* (1970). In 1988, however, Messiaen visited Australia and was taken into the bush at Tidbinbilla, near Canberra, where one of the great meetings of 20th-century music occurred. Messiaen, who for 40 years had imitated birdsong in his music, came face to face with the avian world's own pre-eminent impersonator, the lyrebird. The bird must have put on quite a show, because in his last major work, the eleven-movement, hour-long orchestral piece, *Eclairs sur l'au-delà* . . . ('Illuminations of the Beyond'; 1987–91), Messiaen devoted an entire movement to its performance. In 'L'oiseau-lyre et la Ville-fiancée', the composer equates the fabulous plumage of the bird with the Bride-City of the Apocalypse, heading the movement with a quotation from the Book of Revelation: 'And I saw the Holy City coming down out of heaven, beautiful as a bride adorned for her husband.' What marks out Messiaen's music from most of the other 'spiritual' composers of the late 20th-century, was an abiding commitment to his own style of modernism, almost as though anything less than continuing this quest would be like abandoning his faith.

Something similar (although minus the Catholicism) has been a prevailing attitude of David Lumsdaine, and for him too birdsong — particularly the sounds of the Australian bush — was a formative and long lasting influence. Although one can find the songs of birds in his orchestral works — *Mandala 5* (1989), for example, has currawongs and magpies — Lumsdaine was always less interested than Messiaen in having instruments impersonate their voices. Lumsdaine's primary vehicle for his birdsong pieces has been the tape recording, and we can perhaps conclude from this that he has been less interested in the symbolism of these creatures than in exploring the sonic land-scapes they inhabit. In a series of three soundscape pieces begun in the 1980s and reaching their final forms in 1995, Lumsdaine took many hours of recordings and edited them down into self-contained habitat studies. He was faithful to the specific locations where the original recordings had been made, and he allowed the sequences to follow their natural diurnal patterns, so that in each case one hears a one-hour condensation of a day (or more) in a particular place at a particular time of year. The act of 'composing' these cycles of natural sounds involved virtually no over-dubbing, it was more a matter of selecting the parts of the recordings that most accurately represented the habitats Lumsdaine had visited, and also those sequences that best demonstrated the contrapuntal — one might almost say conversational — relationships that occur between the various species of bird life found at these locations. The paradox inherent in David Lumsdaine's soundscapes is that while we are made aware of a sort of prelapsarian, *pre-human* music — an avian *Ursonate* — we also encounter the complex relationships and simultaneities characteristic of the modernist aesthetic to which Lumsdaine still adheres. If modernism is in crisis, no one has told Lumsdaine.

The notion that music is in crisis has, of course, been fashionable for most of the 20th century. It is possible to look back over the last ten decades and view the directions composers have taken as a series of crises leading to new possibilities. The crisis of tonality led to atonality; the crisis of atonality led to serialism. The crisis of late Romanticism, inflating horribly into expressionism, reached a new crisis which led to neo-classicism. In turn there was the violent rejection of neo-classicism by composers of the 1950s avant garde, followed by a crisis of the avant garde itself which opened the way to minimalism: modernism challenged by postmodernism. It is, as I say, not an unreasonable view, but it is obviously simplistic, because none of these styles and techniques was hermetic, and the crises mentioned were never actually terminal: it was not as if one style ceased and another took its place. Late Romanticism, for example, flourished right up to the 1940s in the hands of composers as different as Rahkmaninov and Richard Strauss; expressionism was still going strong in the 1960s, thanks to Peter Maxwell Davies; and Stravinsky did not cease writing neo-classical music just because Boulez told him to.

The century's last musical crisis, however, was not caused by composers or even by audiences. Throughout the century, the always evolving technology of sound was a vital, transforming factor in music. The tape-recorder, sine-wave oscillator, ring modulator and synthesiser allowed composers to think differently; wax, shellac, vinyl and now the CD captured, popularised, and promoted music, and they gave its listeners the opportunity to form a close acquaintance with a wide range of sounds. So it is somewhat paradoxical that it has been the recording industry itself that has put music on the horns of its latest dilemma. From the industry's point of view, the new crisis is economic, a crisis of capitalism; from everybody else's point of view, it is to do with falling standards, rising prices, lack of choice and poor service. Major companies will go bust as a result of this crisis, and when they do we should lose no sleep over their fate, because they will have brought it upon themselves.

In the 1980s, the big companies were taken by surprise at the scale of acceptance of CD technology, but for some reason they failed to appreciate that they would not be able to sell recordings of standard repertoire at this rate for ever. By the mid 1990s, most people had already converted to the new format, and replaced their scratched LPs of Beethoven symphonies, Tchaikovsky concertos, Puccini operas and what-not with shiny plastic and metal discs of the same. Suddenly, the bottom dropped out of the market. In order to sell anything at all, the companies had to come up with new products and imaginative ways of marketing them. The result was fatuous advertising campaigns to persuade us that this tenor or that string quartet or this composer was the answer to our prayers: in some cases, literally so, since one of the stranger aspects of this unsightly grab for our cash was to make a simultaneous pitch for our souls: John Tavener, Arvo Pärt and the 13th-century Abbess Hildegard of Bingen were all offered to record buyers as simple paths to redemption. Every other CD on the market had the word 'heaven' or 'spirit' or 'angel' in its title. One particular year, it was nearly impossible to attend a dinner party without having to listen to Gregorian chant over the polenta and sundried tomatoes.

Possibly the most bizarre example of the buy-a-CD-and-go-straight-to-heaven phenomenon was the sudden popularity of a sixteen-year-old symphony by a Polish composer, previously unknown outside contemporary music circles. Henryk Górecki had composed his third symphony back in 1976. It was nearly an hour long, and had three movements, all of them slow, all of them featuring a solo soprano. The symphony had already received more performances than the average new work, and there had been three recordings of it, on relatively small labels. In 1992 a new recording was released. Along with it came a carefully prepared advertising campaign, and Górecki's piece suddenly began to sell.

Three factors helped. One was the uncomplicated immediacy of the music itself. Another was the preparation of a CD single, containing music from the symphony's middle movement. It had a simple, affecting and memorable tune, it was short enough to get air play (even on radio stations that would never normally play such stuff), and the text had a story behind it. This was a four-line prayer, apparently inscribed by an eighteen-year-old girl on the wall of a prison cell in the basement of the Gestapo's headquarters in Zakopane. How eminently marketable!

Next came a film by Tony Palmer, in which the whole of the symphony was played over harrowing images of Nazi concentration camps. Palmer's film was very powerful — it could hardly have been otherwise — but in terms of Górecki's music, it was misleading. The only portion of the sung text in the symphony that has anything to do with the Holocaust is that prayer in the second movement: four lines out of a total of 42 (in the English translation). But people who saw the film now thought they knew what the symphony was 'about'. At the very least, they knew that it was terribly sad. In the popular press, journalists had begun to write about the phenomenon that was Górecki's piece: the 'Symphony of Sorrowful Songs' as it was invariably dubbed. They wrote about how this music filled a gaping need in the late 20th century, starved as it was of spiritual fulfilment.

There can be little doubt that a lot of people in the 1990s did feel and continue to feel spiritually adrift. Why else would they fall for every New-Age con that comes along? Why would they be trying so hard to communicate with dolphins? Why would they go about hugging trees? Górecki's symphony was not a con, but the selling of it and the claims made for it were beginning to make it seem like one. By early 1993, the disc of *Symphony of Sorrowful Songs* had become the recording every fashion-conscious owner of a CD player had to have. Not only was it the best-selling classical disc in most Western countries, in Britain it had reached the top ten of the pop charts. By the end of 1996, it had sold nearly a million copies, worldwide.

The trouble with becoming fashionable is that, sooner or later, you go out of fashion. Within two years of the CD's release, record companies were hailing this or that composer as 'the next Górecki'. It sounds like those pop labels of the 1960s and '70s boasting that they had discovered 'the next Elvis', 'the next Beatles', 'the next Bob Dylan' — claims that in every case ensured the swift failure of these new hopefuls — but that is how record companies were now attempting to market their composers: like pop music. The problem is that most art music simply does not function like pop music. It is not designed in the same way as pop, it benefits from close attention and long acquaintance. The best art music — the best art — requires us to form a relationship with it over a number of years, perhaps a lifetime. I wonder how many of those million copies of Górecki's third symphony were actually listened to. All the way through. More than once.

It is easy to grow despondent when looking at the way the marketing methods of the recording industry have affected listening habits. But, for those with ears to hear beyond the hype, the existence of recordings has made more music available to more people than ever before. And smaller companies, particularly, have brought a great range of new and unfamiliar music before us. If we can find the recordings in the first place, and are willing to invest the time to listen, we are able as never before to get to know and come to terms with even the most complex and challenging pieces.

In 1997, the chief music critic of Britain's *Observer* newspaper described Pierre Boulez's piece . . . *explosante–fixe* . . . as 'lovely'. And so it is. Yet the word does come as a shock. We think of this composer's youthful pronouncements regarding the worthlessness of colleagues who failed to see the need for serialism, the vanity of audiences who applauded the music of Tchaikovsky, the elegance of bombs as a solution to the dreariness of the modern opera house, and we wonder how 'lovely' his music could be. Something, surely, must have changed for this judgment to be true. Was it Boulez? Was it us? Probably a bit of both. Certainly, Boulez's music now had a surface that spoke more directly, particularly as regarded rhythm.

There is also a gorgeous sensuality about the sound world of . . . *explosante–fixe* . . ., although this was not so new: the gong-enveloped alto flute at the close of *Le marteau sans maître* and the glittering ebullience of *Eclat* were hardly dour and academic. But in the later years of the century, there was also a growing sophistication about the general listener, and a greater curiosity, which made the record industry's self-inflicted crisis all the more incongruous. The cynicism of mass marketing and the patently absurd claims made on behalf of the least challenging music were an insulting and potentially destructive response to the consumer's willingness to explore.

One way in which this sophistication manifested itself was in a reassessment of some of the century's unjustly neglected musical figures, composers of real worth who had either never been fashionable — the symphonists Robert Simpson, Douglas Lilburn and Vagn Holmboe — or who had gone out of fashion with the postmodernist backlash against serialism — composers such as Luigi Dallapiccola, Roberto Gerhard and Elisabeth Lutyens. But there was also what we might think of as a growing sophistication on the part of many composers. Four violin concertos of the early 1990s are evidence of the continued mellowing of former modernists, and of burgeoning complexity in the thinking of a one-time postmodernist.

In György Ligeti's Violin Concerto (1990–92), the exceptional rhythmic mutability of his works from the 1980s was matched by a similarly fluid approach to harmony, and especially to tuning. In the second movement, the soloist presents a simple, folk-like melodic fragment that never really develops but is rather held up to a series of distorting mirrors. The fragment is passed between instruments that are tuned according to a range of different coordinates: a violin and a viola in the orchestra are tuned, respectively, to the natural harmonics of the double bass's G and A strings; the horns play on their natural harmonics; finally, the oboe, clarinet and bassoon players trade their instruments for ocarinas tuned a fifth apart from each other. The effect of this succession of tunings is of the music moving from one dimension to another, and yet the basic material is always related to the simple, folk-like melodic fragment, so the listener is never disorientated.

John Adams's Violin Concerto of 1993 shows the composer of

Nixon in China moving towards a far richer style of musical lyricism. In the first movement, the soloist spins an increasingly fantastic skein of notes above ever-ascending figures in the orchestra that recall the drowning scene in Berg's *Wozzeck*. Other comparisons come to mind: in its sense of forward motion and illusion of acceleration, Adams's movement resembles the journey from *molto moderato* to *presto* in Sibelius's fifth symphony, while the modal harmony (in this same context) suggests the third symphony of the mid-century American composer, Roy Harris. Yet it is the hyperactive solo part that most clearly demonstrates the development in Adams's music, not only in its leaping agility, but in its mercurial nature: this violin is a raconteur and wit, prone to bouts of melancholy and easily distracted; it is a character that might have escaped from one of Elliott Carter's string quartets.

In Kaija Saariaho's *Graal-théâtre* ('Grail-theatre'; 1994), the solo instrument is as ever present as in Adams's first movement, but its role is rather different. Where Adams's soloist is ornate and often high-spirited, Saariaho's seems to be conducting a serious and intense investigation of its environment, as though waking up out of a coma, or suddenly being able to see following a period of blindness.

Finally, the Danish composer Bent Sørensen's violin concerto belongs to a continuing series of works concerned with the imagery of gardens. These gardens are as formal as Laura's garden in Meale's *Voss*, but Sørensen's have been neglected, the vegetation left to run wild. In *Sterbende Gärten* ('Decaying Gardens'; 1992–93), the listener can just make out familiar structures beneath the dense orchestral undergrowth: at the outset of the piece, the violin has simple, step-wise figures suggestive of some germinal, long forgotten tonal plan, but as the music progresses the solo line becomes entangled in a forest of other figures, occasionally emerging (like Saariaho's soloist) to look around and brush itself down.

What unites the violin concertos of Ligeti, Adams, Saariaho and Sørensen is partly their willingness to engage with common musical materials and recognisable themes and fragments of themes. But equally there is a simultaneous refusal to do this in a fashion that reinforces the familiarity. In other words, these four late 20th-century composers trust the sophistication of their audiences, and listeners who are prepared to trust these composers will be rewarded with musical experiences that are rich and strange. In a tabloid age that insists on the simplicity of the world and its events, this is refreshing. In Seferis's terms, this is music that is 'strong enough to help'. It may even bring us closer to Sontag's version of 'reality', since it says no to the cheap imitations and clichés with which tabloidism attempts to palm us off.

In 1995, the Australian chamber music entrepreneur Musica Viva marked its 50th anniversary with the first performance of a specially commissioned chamber symphony entitled *Celebration*. The composer was Brenton Broadstock, and in his program note he wrote of his search for 'a new simplicity of style' which he equated with an attempt to 'create in musical terms an art-form with a social conscience'. Composers have the right to create music in any style that takes their fancy, be it extremely simple or extremely complex, but Broadstock's implication here was that a 'social conscience' would necessarily lead a composer to produce pieces 'that exhibit a simpler and more direct musical expression'.

I couldn't agree less. If music is to be strong enough to help it will not be because composers have tried to make things easy for their audiences, but because they have offered new experiences and new visions. Strong music can help its audiences ask questions, confront lies, discover truths. But it can only do this if composers first make those demands of themselves, and then write music that is as bold and lucid as possible. A composer's social conscience begins and ends at the work desk. The best way for music to serve a public — the best way for it to help — is for it to be the most personal utterance possible, for it to plumb its composer's imaginative depths, and for it to be well made. In living up to these standards, it will be as simple or as complex as it needs to be, and its composers will be enriching a tradition. It is a tradition to which we all belong, composers and non-composers: a tradition of the imagination.

Michael Tippett wrote on this subject more than once. Tippett was born in 1905 and died in 1998, so his life spanned the century. In a talk for BBC radio in 1954, he spoke about the existence of an imaginative tradition of art and referred to W. B. Yeats's concept of the 'Great Memory', which Tippett elucidated as 'that immense reservoir of the human psyche where images age-old and new boil together in some demoniac cauldron'.

Tippett's opera, *The Knot Garden* (1970), is partly about that cauldron, and its title is evocative. Consider the following: Bent Sørensen's *Decaying Gardens* and *The Echoing Garden*; Takemitsu's *In an Autumn Garden*; David Lumsdaine's *A Garden of Earthly Delights*; Liza Lim's *Garden of Earthly Desires*; Sofia Gubaidulina's *Gardens of Joy and Sadness*; Kaija Saariaho's *Jardin secret* ('Secret Garden') *I, II* and *III*; the 'secret world' of Nono's *Fragmente-Stille*; Birtwistle's *Secret Theatre*; Tan Dun's *Orchestral Theatre I, II* and *III*; Saariaho's *Grail-Theatre*; John Buller's *Theatre of Memory*; the 'memory theatre' of Lim and Kosky's *Oresteia*. Of course, these correspondences do not begin to add up to a theory, but neither am I merely free associating. Memory, theatre, secrets, gardens: these are potent images for music, and for art in general. They speak of worlds that are simultaneously private and universal: a secret that is also a garden; memory that is a theatre; private thoughts shared. Back to Tippett. Some years after his radio talk he made a television film, 'Poets in a Barren Age', in which he became more expansive on this topic of a common stock of images:

> I have been writing music for forty years . . . Whether society has felt music valuable or needful, I have gone on writing because I must. And I know that my true function within a society which embraces all of us, is to continue an age-old tradition, fundamental to our civilization, which goes back into pre-history and will go forward into the unknown future. This tradition is to create images from the depths of the imagination and to give them form whether visual, intellectual or musical. For it is only through images that the inner world communicates at all. Images of the past, shapes of the future. Images of vigour for a decadent period, images of calm for one too violent. Images of reconciliation for worlds torn by division.
>
> And in an age of mediocrity and shattered dreams, images of abounding, generous, exuberant beauty.

I find Tippett's words moving, if perhaps a little sentimental. I also find them an accurate description of a composer's concerns, although Tippett himself, in a footnote to the printed text, did query the meaning of 'beauty'.

John Cage said the word had no meaning, at least no specific meaning. There was nothing, he said, that was incapable of being found beautiful: recognising beauty was an attitude of mind. This is the obverse of Tippett's remarks about the role of the composer, but it is not necessarily at odds with them. Cage's claim about beauty has little to do with composers, but everything to do with audiences; it is the individual members of an audience who decide whether music is beautiful or meaningful. And when it comes to the ever-presence of music in the last years of the 20th century and into the 21st — in lifts and supermarkets, from passing cars, through neighbours' walls — Cage's attitude seems more relevant than ever. By listening to these sounds, we transform them into illegal harmonies. Just by listening. We might like to bring our imaginations to bear on them as well, although Cage himself would have thought that unnecessary. Listening and accepting were enough.

Well, it may be a good, positive way of dealing with intrusive noise, but for most people, listening and accepting are not enough when it comes to music. We also need to engage with the music to some degree or other: with minimalist music, hardly at all; with a composer like Schoenberg, rather a lot (Boulez once said you don't shave to Schoenberg). But however good our powers of concentration, however acute our critical faculties, if we want music to be strong enough to help, we must begin by listening, and listening hard.

So, listen.

What do you hear?

EPILOGUE

n 2001 the singer, songwriter and 'piano man', Billy Joel released a new CD, the most surprising aspects of which were on the cover. First, Joel was not himself the performer, merely the composer. Second, the music was for solo piano. Third, the CD's design resembled the cover of a volume from Schirmer's Library of Musical Classics, a series that includes keyboard works by Bach, Beethoven, Chopin and Schubert. So what was that all about? Just another pop singer getting above himself?

And how do we explain Paul McCartney's *Liverpool Oratorio* or his symphonic poem *Standing Stone*? Or Elvis Costello's song cycle *The Juliet Letters*? Why in an interview has Joni Mitchell compared herself to Mozart? Why, following on from *Einstein on the Beach* with Philip Glass, did Robert Wilson choose to collaborate with both Tom Waits and Lou Reed? And when Bruce Springsteen insisted in 2002 that he was composing an opera, what an earth was he thinking of?

The world may indeed have gone mad — we see evidence for this all the time — but the desire on the part of pop musicians to identify themselves with a classical tradition, with oratorios and symphonic poems, song cycles and operas, is not a phenomenon unique to our times. It has been with us at least since the 1920s. George Gershwin felt it; Duke Ellington felt it. It is a need to feel somehow respectable, proper, 'legit'.

And what about the opposite side of this coin? I am thinking now of those frequently embarrassing attempts by so-called serious composers to woo large audiences back to the concert hall. Notice that it's always 'back to the concert hall', as though before those horrible, prickly modernists came along the concert halls of the world were full to the rafters, punters without tickets trying to break down the doors so as not to miss that Beethoven concerto.

In fact you don't have to look very far in the history books to discover that often enough even Beethoven's works were premiered to a handful of the faithful. But such inconvenient facts are not going to stop those concert promoters who are convinced that the only way to 'save' classical music is to give it the common touch—as though that's what audiences were paying for. Accordingly orchestras perform pieces employing the outward trappings of film music, string quartets play hip-hop rhythms and everyone plays arrangements of Jimi Hendrix. The results are seldom edifying.

Classical composers wanting to look trendy is no more recent a phenomenon than popular composers wanting to appear serious; actually, it's been going on rather longer. Throughout history composers have attempted to predict their audiences' tastes and achieve a popular success. Even Stravinsky, the twentieth century's most famous composer, craved a hit along the lines of *Valse triste* and he was bitterly jealous of Sibelius because of the popularity of that piece. You might have thought that the composer of *The Rite of Spring* would be pretty sanguine about the level of his fame.

Some of the least successful music of the last hundred years has resulted from composers trying to be something they weren't. And yet beneath these apparent attempts to be more (or less) popular was a genuine tension as 'serious' music positioned and repositioned itself in an increasingly commercial world. Since the invention of sound recordings, the barriers between musical styles—indeed, between musical types—have been sometimes impregnable, sometimes indistinct, but always persistent and never particularly helpful except to those trying to write about music.

In the late 1960s these barriers were perhaps at their haziest. Jazz musicians discovered rock; rock musicians discovered the avant-garde music of the concert hall; avant-garde composers discovered improvisation. Some of the ensuing meetings of musical minds resulted in little more than the sixties equivalent of those jazz-tinged classical pieces of the 1920s: Ravel's Violin Sonata, Stravinsky's *Ragtime*, Milhaud's *La création du monde*: musical dress-up. But there were also some genuinely interesting if short-lived outcomes from these encounters.

In 1967, the year of his guest appearance on the cover of *Sgt Pepper's Lonely Hearts Club Band*, Karlheinz Stockhausen was a visiting composer at the University of California where he attended a Jefferson Airplane concert and welcomed members of the Grateful Dead to his lectures. Just what the Dead took away from these lectures is rather hard to say, though Tom Constanten, the keyboard player on *Anthem of the Sun and Aoxomoxoa*, claims to have had composition lessons from Stockhausen. For rock musicians of this era to be drawn to Stockhausen's electronic experiments was perhaps not so remarkable as Stockhausen's seeming attraction to the rock music of San Francisco and its attendant hippie lifestyle (though in retrospect this doesn't seem terribly strange either).

Some of the works from the years that followed the German composer's West Coast sojourn seem to reflect this experience, and perhaps none more so than the group of 'intuitive' pieces for which he wrote inspirational texts the following year. *Aus den sieben Tagen* (From the Seven Days) was conceived and written in May 1968. For the seven days in question, Stockhausen was on a hunger strike— not, as one might guess from the date, out of an attack of political conscience, but in an attempt to persuade his estranged wife to return to him. But what was musically significant about this particular week was Stockhausen's realisation that music might grow spontaneously out of improvisations responding to the short verbal statements he had penned.

Working with the same musicians who were already playing his notated music, Stockhausen indeed drew from them some exceptionally intense music, and Deutsche Grammophon recorded the lot on seven LPs. To what extent these initial performances of *Aus den sieben Tagen* were the result of Stockhausen's texts which among many less controversial directives advised his players to 'Think NOTHING' (politically most unsound for 1968), it is hard to say. The fact that the players were already familiar with the composer's lexicon of musical sounds and gestures must surely have helped. Certainly later attempts to play these pieces by musicians outside Stockhausen's circle have not always gone well. But the composer and trombonist Vinko Globokar, a participant in some of the early performances, had a point when he demanded of Stockhausen just whose music they were playing. After all, the musicians were making up the sounds; all Stockhausen had done was to provide a few lines of words by way of inspiration. (Stockhausen thought the music was by him.)

Authorship in jazz has always been a moot point. When Miles Davis played 'Love for Sale', the estate of George Gershwin got the royalties, and yet the music was surely more Davis's than it was Gershwin's. By the late 1960s, however, Miles Davis had left the jazz standard far behind him. Some feared he was also abandoning jazz. Davis's discovery of rock music in 1969, tentative on *In a Silent Way* and then with no holds barred on *Bitches Brew*, was in some senses a break with tradition similar to Stockhausen's suspension of the use of musical notation. The school of bebop in which Davis had received his training had been scarcely less hardline than the Darmstadt summer schools of the early 1950s, the serialist hothouse that had produced the young Stockhausen. With *Aus den sieben Tagen*, Stockhausen was criticised by other musicians, including members of his own performing group, for having taken the easy way out. Equally, Davis's move into the world of 'fusion' was bitterly resented by fans who, for two decades, had considered him the epitome of progressive jazz, the very future of the genre.

And yet while the sound of Davis's new music was drastically different from recent albums such as *Nefertiti*, *Circle in the Round* and *Miles in the Sky*, and while the musical structures were, on the face of it, comparatively meandering and harmonically fuzzy, the real Miles Davis was becoming more apparent all the time. From the late 1950s, when his record label Columbia first took him on, Davis had tested his musical personality and the sound of his trumpet in a range of different circumstances. Collaborating with John Coltrane in the context of a quintet, for example, was an experience far removed from working with Gil Evans and his orchestra. Looked at like this, *In a Silent Way* (1969) was merely another step on the journey: what will happen when the trumpet enters a world dominated by glistening electronic keyboards, electric guitar and bass; how slowly can a theme be developed over a funky riff and a gently persistent hi-hat? On *Bitches Brew* (1970), with a much bigger band, the experiment continued, adorned with lashings of exotic percussion.

Perhaps as significant as this change of musical accent in Miles Davis's music were the techniques by which it was all put together. At the sessions for both albums, there was a good deal of freedom, a sense of the players simply seeing what might happen. The subsequent mixing and editing of the recorded music, then, were acts of composition, the final structure of the tracks decided by Davis and his producer Teo Macero after the musicians had gone home. So not only were *In a Silent Way* and *Bitches Brew* among the first attempts to fuse jazz and rock, they were also, in a sense, *musique concrète*.

Of course, Miles Davis never actually abandoned jazz for rock, any more than Karlheinz Stockhausen became bogged down in intuitive music. It is also true that neither musician was quite the same again and the legacy of their 1960s experiments can still be felt, as today's creative musicians attempt to discover in which camp they belong. The other important development of the 1960s, though it was hardly news at the time, now seems to have been the return of *musique concrète*, and in a purer form than Miles Davis and Teo Macero used it.

Pioneered in the 1940s by composers working with their new-fangled tape recorders, *musique concrète* (concrete music) involved recording sounds (generally not 'musical' sounds) that were then assembled in the studio by a process of editing the tapes and reordering, layering and mixing their contents. It was this basic approach that Steve Reich adopted in his tape pieces *It's Gonna Rain* (1965) and *Come Out* (1966), except that Reich recorded speech (and urban speech at that), turned his tapes into loops and then allowed them to get out of phase with each other, thereby distorting the words and ultimately the voices. At the time these pieces seemed modest enough: interesting experiments and provocative, certainly, but hardly a bold step into the future of music. Reich himself left the technique to one side for the next two decades (though he retained his fondness for phasing processes), but in the meantime it was taken up by musicians in another area.

Besides being urban, the voices heard in *It's Gonna Rain* and *Come Out* were African-American, and it was urban African-American musicians who now made use of the voice-sampling (for that is what it was) that Steve Reich had developed. The hip-hop artists of the 1980s and 1990s might not have been directly inspired by Reich (though some of them were), but he quickly became a touchstone of their cause, his 1960s tape pieces suddenly held up as classics and—the hip-hopper's ultimate mark of respect—sampled.

And it wasn't just Reich's samples and loops that were taken up by the musicians providing music for the dance clubs springing up across the Western world in the last two decades of the twentieth century. The purely instrumental music of Reich and his colleagues was an important exemplar in other areas of popular electronic music. Interestingly, the rather unforgiving early minimalism of the 1960s proved the greatest inspiration. But rather than merely apeing the mannerisms of minimal music—as, for instance, Mike Oldfield had done in *Tubular Bells*—techno composers appropriated the techniques and often-austere aesthetic of early minimalism. Naturally, there are important differences between the two types of music—dancing, for instance, was never high on the agendas of La Monte Young, Terry Riley and Steve Reich—but minimalism and techno share a certain implacability.

Again, Reich was sampled. The group of British techno artists known as the Orb, among the first to develop techno to listen to (as opposed to techno to dance to), used Reich's *Electric Counterpoint* in their 'Little Fluffy Clouds' (1991), and by 1999 an entire album of Reich's 'greatest hits' had appeared remixed by the likes of Howie B, Andrea Parker, Coldcut, D J Spooky and Ken Ishii (who chose to work with *Come Out*). In every case the new versions lacked the direct impact of Reich's originals, but it was a rare and overdue tribute by a group of musicians in the field of popular music to an important figure associated with the concert hall.

In the mid 1990s, when I was writing *Illegal Harmonies*, I began it by inquiring: 'What's modern?' Thinking about that first decade of the twentieth century, with its emphasis on progress and its boundless optimism about the century ahead, this seemed perhaps the most pertinent question to ask. But by the century's final decade, the question itself had lost all currency. It no longer seems even especially interesting. What might be interesting, in the light of the way music has changed over the last hundred years, is to ask the question: 'What's serious?'

Having elected to concentrate on the music of the concert hall and the opera house, I was obliged to give it a name. 'Classical' seemed quite wrong for pieces of music composed within living memory and ultimately I plumped for 'art music', though not without misgivings. Another early contender for the label was 'serious' music. In the first decade of the century, I feel it is safe to assert, Debussy and Schoenberg were more serious both in intent and in effect than the other music being created in the Western world: ragtime, say, or operetta or music-hall songs. In the next decade, Stravinsky was without a doubt more serious than Irving Berlin. As early as the 1920s, however, the issue had become a little more clouded: was Erik Satie's Relâche more or less serious than Kurt Weill's *Threepenny Opera*? By the 1930s, of course, George Gershwin and Arnold Schoenberg were playing tennis together and the world was becoming as confused musically as it was in most other areas. The confusion has continued. There were some desperate attempts to clarify matters in the 1950s—integral serialism and early rock and roll polarising things nicely—but the distinctions quickly blurred again and by the late 1960s, as we've seen, the barriers were tumbling down.

Today, it is possible to turn the whole serious/popular equation on its head. A fully notated, intricately scored orchestral work by Michael Daugherty is less serious than an album by Radiohead. Indeed, Daugherty's Superman symphony, *Metropolis*, is positively *frivolous* alongside Radiohead's *Kid A* and *Amnesiac* (2001). Not only are these two albums related, sharing riffs, themes and chord progressions in addition to lyrical concerns, they also share a solemnity that was unknown in popular music until quite recently. (I'm deliberately ignoring those rather pretentious bands of the 1970s, such as Emerson, Lake and Palmer, who were solemn to the point of risibility.)

The names we once allocated to different types of music have become less and less relevant to the way in which people actually listen. Increasingly, they have also come to mean very little to those who create music. Ultimately, then, the legacy of twentieth-century music seems to be this: serious music can be found anywhere, and so can junk. More than ever, whether as audiences or as composers, we need our ears to guide us. When it comes to music we can no longer believe what people tell us in books.

PERMISSIONS

INDEX

be-bop 140–1
Beckett, Samuel 170, 216
  Unnamable, The 170
Beethoven, Ludwig van 4, 5,
  15, 27, 43, 67, 104, 143,
  170, 237
  premieres of works 238
  Missa solemnis 203
  Symphony No.3 (*Eroica*) 96
  Symphony No.6 (*Pastoral*)
    173
Beiderbecke, Bix 60
Bel édifice et les présentiments
  (Char) 128
Berberian, Cathy 146–47, 167
Berg, Alban 49, 61, 67, 91, 94,
  100, 170, 220
  influence of 77, 91–2, 160
  use of atonality 28, 30
  Four Pieces for Clarinet and
    Piano 28
  Lulu 20, 84–91, 93, 100
  Violin Concerto 67, 84, 91
  Wozzeck 49, 85, 88, 92,
    115–16, 120
Berio, Luciano 146–51, 155,
  160, 166, 167, 177, 218
  arrangement of Beatles' songs
    224
  attitude to music 160
  influence of 182, 223
  use of voice 146–51
  Coro 148
  Epiphanies (*Epifanie*) 147–48
  Folk Songs 148
  Sinfonia 148, 170–01, 218,
    219
  Visage 147

Berlin, Irving
  on Gershwin 93
  popular songs 58–9
  Stravinsky compared with
    243
  'Alexander's Ragtime Band'
    59
  'Everybody's Doing It' 39–40
  'God Bless America' 150
  'White Christmas' 59
Berlin Philharmonic 97
Berlioz, Hector 27, 31, 170
  Damnation de Faust, La 73
Bernstein, Leonard
  as conductor 110, 112, 170
  Mass 219
  On The Town 110
  West Side Story 144, 225
Berry, Chuck 142, 151, 174
  'Roll Over Beethoven' 143
Billy Budd (Melville) 137
birdsong 106, 109, 226–28
Birtwistle, Harrison
  his music compared to folk
    music 221
  and musical landscapes
    186–88
  An Imaginary Landscape 187
  Secret Theatre 188, 235
  The Triumph of Time 187–88
Bishop, Elizabeth 189, 190
  'Sandpiper' 190
Bizet, Georges
  Carmen 93
Blackboard Jungle, The (film)
  142–43, 144
Blake, Peter 156
blues 110, 142, 157, 173, 225

ILLEGAL HARMONIES: THE 20TH CENTURY PIANO

Features solo piano pieces specially recorded for the original radio series and additional piano music by important twentieth-century composers whose work is discussed in *Illegal Harmonies* by Andrew Ford.

Stephanie McCallum, piano
ABC Classics CD 456 668-2

Featuring the following works:

Satie: Gnossienne No.1
Ravel: Menuet antique
Joplin: Original Rags
Grainger: 'Mo nighean dubh' from *Songs of the North*
Debussy: 'Doctor Gradus ad Parnassum' from *Children's Corner*
Schoenberg: 'Walzer' from *Five Piano Pieces, Op. 23*
Stravinsky: Rondoletto from *Serenade in A*
Gershwin: 'I Got Rhythm' from *George Gershwin's Song Book*
Messiaen: 'Mode de valuers et d'intensités' from *Quatre études de rythme*
Cage: Music of Changes (extract)
Stockhausen: Klavierstück V
Young: Composition 1960 #7
Berio: Erdenklavier
Copland: Night Thoughts ('Homage to Ives')
Boyd: Angklung
Ligeti: 'Arc-en-ciel' from *Etude, Book I*
Pärt: Für Alina
Takemitsu: Rain Tree Sketch II
Kats-Chernin: The Schubert Blues

UNDUE NOISE BY ANDREW FORD

On a stretch of highway I travel is a sign that reads UNDUE NOISE. There is no obvious reason for its existence and it irritates me—perhaps because it questions the very basis of what I do. I am a composer of Western Art Music and by definition most of this has been undue noise for around 200 years.

In this selection of articles, reviews, lectures and essays, some new, some originally published in a variety of newspapers and magazines, Andrew Ford shares his thoughts on music of all kinds—from Bach to Cole Porter to John Lennon, from Peter Sculthorpe to Joni Mitchell to Eminem.

'One can't imagine very many Australian composers who could sustain the volume or quality of Ford's critical commentaries and radio broadcasts . . .' Martin Buzacott, *24 Hours*